Be Not Afraid!

Building Your Church on Faith and Knowledge

Be Not Afraid!

Building Your Church on Faith and Knowledge

Fredric M. Roberts

THE ALBAN INSTITUTE

Herndon, Virginia
www.alban.org

The Alban Institute, 2121 Cooperative Way, Suite 100, Herndon, VA 20171

Cover design: Adele Robey, Phoenix Graphics

Library of Congress Cataloging-in-Publication Data

Roberts, Fredric M.
  Be not afraid! : building your church on faith and knowledge / by Fredric M. Roberts.
      p. cm.
  Includes bibliographical references.
  ISBN 1-56699-315-6
  1. Theology, Practical—United States. 2. Protestant churches—United States.
I. Title.

BV3.R63 2005
280'.4'0973090511—dc22
                    2004026932

09 08 07 06 05   VG   1 2 3 4 5

To Caralee—of course
Anyone closely connected with this project knows that it could never have been completed without Caralee. On this, as on so many other journeys, her patience, wisdom, professional expertise, and love have made it all possible. She has been God's instrument of grace in my life.

and

E. Ray Hinshaw, D.V.M., Crackers, Nick, Rocky, Spike, Cheddar, and all the critters of the Hiline Ranch, who helped me keep this book in perspective, but cautioned me not to quit my "day job."

"Without knowledge of self there is no knowledge of God: Nearly all the wisdom we possess, that is to say, true and sound wisdom, consists of two parts: the knowledge of God and of ourselves."

—John Calvin

Contents

Acknowledgments   ix

1   Introduction: Be Not Afraid!   1

2   Knowing Who We Are: Our Eight Congregations   15

3   Congregational Organization: What is Good for
    General Motors May Not Be Good for Your Church   43

4   Denominations: Are They Dinosaurs?   59

5   Pastors: What Should We Expect from Pastors?
    What Should Pastors Expect from Themselves?   79

6   Worship: What Does Worship Really Mean to
    People in the Pews?   109

7   Evangelism: Is Mainline Evangelism an Oxymoron?   123

8   Nurturing: What is Your Church's Nurturing Style?   143

9   Conclusion: Moving Beyond Fear: Embracing
    Faith and Knowledge   179

    Appendix A   Discovering and Analyzing Your Core   187

    Appendix B   A Sample of Survey Questions   191

    Appendix C   A Brief Spiritual Life History Interview
                                                                          195

    Appendix D   Some Pastor Interview Questions   203

    Notes   207

    References   211

Acknowledgments

The research on which this book is based was supported by a grant from Lilly Endowment. I am further indebted to Lilly Endowment for the wise advice and counsel of its staff, especially Dr. Chris Coble. The Department of Anthropology at Michigan State University and its chair, Dr. Lynne Goldstein, provided generous institutional assistance and personal support in innumerable ways.

Project research began in August 1997, and since then an extraordinarily large and diverse set of people and institutions have contributed their time, talents, and resources to bringing it to a successful conclusion. The project was blessed with a gifted and dedicated team of field researchers*: Angela Martin, Ph.D., Michael McCallion, Ph.D., and Randal Hepner, Ph.D. Angela's methodological acuity and her insights into congregational dynamics and the complexities of individual faith remained invaluable. Angela and I jointly developed a project Web site, which was great preparation for writing this book. She also played a major role in creating the initial outline of *Be Not Afraid!* It was a joy to work with Angela, an ideal colleague and dear friend. Mike was at the heart of this research from its inception, when we shared early morning breakfasts and social science shop talk at an assortment of professional meetings and workshops. His input was essential to the original research proposal for this project. Mike's ability to successfully juggle a demanding job with

---

*Researchers at the Mainline Protestant Field Sites. Bethel Baptist: Angela Martin (primary researcher), Randal Hepner, Michael McCallion, and Fred Roberts; Bethlehem Lutheran: Fred Roberts; Central Methodist: Randal Hepner; First Presbyterian: Fred Roberts; Holy Trinity Lutheran: Fred Roberts (primary researcher) and Michael McCallion; St. Paul United Church of Christ: Angela Martin (primary researcher) and Fred Roberts; St. Timothy Presbyterian: Angela Martin; Second Baptist: Randal Hepner (primary researcher) and Fred Roberts.

the Roman Catholic Archdiocese of Detroit, intensive field work for this study, and the duties of a doting father to a young son always amazed, as well as exhausted, me. Randy brought an encyclopedic knowledge of the history of American religion to the research team. He was often the loyal intellectual opposition during this study, forcing me to re-think key issues and become ever more critical and truly countercultural in my perspective. Our invaluable and indefatigable research support staff included Caralee Roberts, Ph.D., Raju Tamot, Kristina Derhammer, Hannah Kliewer, Chris Fraga, Pat Whittier, Ph.D., and Richard Reuther. I owe an especially big debt to James Bielo, who almost from the day he entered the graduate program in Anthropology at Michigan State University was deeply engaged in this study (usually as an unpaid volunteer).

Barbara Beasley, Sally Behrenwald, James Bielo, Dennis Bux, Christopher Coble, Roger Dahlen, Budge Gere, Jim Lichtenberger, Michael McCallion, Jack and Sandy Midgley, David Noble, Ben Roberts, Caralee Roberts, Jim and Joni Schalkhauser read through an earlier draft of this book and provided numerous helpful suggestions and corrections. Richard Bass, the publications director of the Alban Institute, has been wonderfully supportive. Among the many ways he helped me was by selecting Stacia Brown to be my editor. If you find that this book flows smoothly, much of the credit goes to Stacia, whose editorial suggestions were inevitably right on target. It was also my good fortune to have Aaron McCarroll Gallegos begin work as the Alban Institute's managing editor just as this book went into production.

For years, breakfasts with Bob Mareck on Wednesdays and Jack Midgley on Fridays have helped keep me spiritually centered when it would have been easy to get lost in the details of research and writing. My two brothers in Christ have patiently listened and generously commented on most of the major ideas in this book, even when they would rather have been concentrating on their oatmeal.

Although I am solely responsible for the writing of this book, I am grateful to all of you who made this project possible. Above all, I am deeply indebted to the people of our project churches who were so patient, hospitable, and supportive during our long sojourns in their congregations. I hope that they find this book will in some small way repay their generosity to us.

1 Introduction

Be Not Afraid!

THIS BOOK WAS WRITTEN WITH A SPECIAL SET OF READERS IN MIND. I HOPE YOU'RE one of them: lay and ordained leaders of mainline Protestant congregations where from 100 to 500 members gather in the pews to worship each Sunday.[1] These leaders love their faith communities, but they're not complacent. On the contrary, they spend much time considering how to deal with what they see as a myriad of challenges and threats to the life of their churches.

Like many other mainline Protestants, these leaders are suffering from a collective anxiety attack. They fear for the future of their individual congregations, their denominations, and even American Christianity. More specifically, they worry about generation gaps in their pews, about their congregations "dying if they're not growing," about cultural irrelevance, and about the rise of non-denominational megachurches. They continually voiced these anxieties during the over two years in which our research team (two cultural anthropologists and two sociologists) interviewed denomination officials and church pastors; sat in on congregational session, council, commission, committee, and circle meetings; and participated in worship services, Bible studies and social events.

This high anxiety level was striking because we studied eight "healthy" mainline congregations. Members of these churches participated in a wide variety of church activities; pastoral leadership was stable, and there was no debilitating rift among members. These churches were healthy; *however*, they were not extraordinary. They were not flagship churches for their denominations, and their pastors were not clerical superstars. In other words, they may well be like your congregation and its staff.

Were these "ordinary" churches healthy precisely because their leaders worried about the right types of challenges and then adopted successful programs to deal with them? No! On the contrary, we discovered that these churches were healthy *despite* the amount of time, effort, emotion, and resources they expended on those fears. Why? Because those fears were often unfounded, unhelpful, or both.

Fears distracted these church leaders from creatively addressing the real challenges facing them today. And above all, these fears—often unfounded and usually generic—led congregations to ignore the uniqueness of each of their churches. In this book I argue that for mainline congregations to survive and flourish, they must begin to honor their own uniqueness—their "countercultural" status—rather than trying to blend in or be like everyone else (including fearing what everyone else does). Honoring the uniqueness of your congregation means at least three things. It means knowing who you are, both as a present-day congregation and an historical denomination; it means knowing what you believe and why you believe it; and it means integrating your shared history and beliefs into all dimensions of your collective life together: organizational, liturgical, pastoral, and outreach.

WHY ARE WE SO AFRAID? WHAT DO WE FEAR?

Fear is a pervasive and potent motivating force in our society. In his acclaimed study of contemporary American life, *The Culture of Fear*, sociologist Barry Glassner asks: "Why are so many fears [e.g., "crime, drugs, minorities, teen moms, killer kids, mutant microbes, plane crashes, road rage, and so much more"] in the air, and so many of them unfounded?" Glassner wonders, for example, "Why, as crime rates plunged throughout the 1990s, did two-thirds of Americans believe they were soaring?" (1999:xi). Glassner's primary concern is that the false fears pervading American society are often fostered by the mass media and by those who make massive profits selling products to allay them. Such unjustified fears blind us to the more important issues that Americans should be worried about.

While Glassner wasn't specifically addressing the leaders of mainline Protestant congregations, his book can help explain and remedy the mainline's collective anxiety attack. Like so many Americans and American institutions, the congregations we studied viewed themselves as endangered and beleaguered minorities. From the pulpits, pastors repeatedly portrayed Christian values as radically countercultural and thus under siege in an increasingly secularized society. Mainline worries such as these are often so deep-rooted that they are seldom questioned, much less critically evaluated. The first goal of this book, then, is to make explicit the nature of our anxiety—to name the purported "facts" and "common sense" assumptions that trigger our collective anxiety attack.

Although I'll be talking about a myriad of false fears throughout the book, it seems useful from the outset to identify one particular anxiety that permeates or influences many of our other concerns. This is the fear of a generation gap in our pews.

An initial look at the statistics might suggest that this fear is well founded. After all, age imbalance is endemic among mainline Protestant congregations. Only 15 percent of the adults in our eight Protestant congregations were under 40 years of age while 46 percent were 60 or older.

When talk turns to the "graying" of our mainline pews and what should be done about it, someone is bound to bring up the generation gap. The phrase itself instantly raises the emotional temperature. Few people are neutral when it comes to the topic of the generation gap and the church. For some, the generation gap is a source of despair about the future of Christianity in America, prompting nostalgic recollections of the good old days. For others, the gap is a prophetic warning that mainline churches no longer reside at the cutting edge of society where things are happening. For virtually everyone, though, the generation gap is "real," and church leaders feel compelled to do something (and fast) if their mainline congregations are not to become irrelevant or moribund.

But is the generation gap real, at least when it comes to the challenge of keeping your congregation a vibrant faith community? Is the generation gap a helpful way to think about your church and its future?

WHY OUR FEARS ARE UNHELPFUL, UNFOUNDED, OR BOTH

It's true that age imbalance is widespread among mainline Protestant congregations. But mainline pastors too quickly move from recognizing this imbalance to concluding that their congregations' survival depends on learning to think and act in terms of generations and generation gaps. To me, this assumption has at least two problems. First, it is unhelpful. By this I mean that it is a prime example of mainline churches not taking seriously their commitment to be counterculturally Christian, and it reflects a failure to think carefully about the difference between a Christian congregation and secular institutions. Second (and related), it is also unfounded. It ignores the data—and the lived experiences—that suggest the gap between older and younger generations is not so broad as people fear and not so difficult to bridge.

Our Fears Are Unhelpful

To explain what I mean by our fears being unhelpful, let me introduce the phrase "Lived Christianity." The concept of Lived Christianity guided much of our research and helps explain why so many leaders worry about generational issues and generation gaps in their congregations. Lived Christianity encompasses "the types of knowledge, beliefs, practices, experiences, and feelings that members of Christian congregations bring to their religious lives." This definition emphasizes the "varied sources and resources different individuals *bring* to religious life, because an individual's knowledge, beliefs, practices, experiences, and feelings can originate both in the realm of religion and outside it" (Roberts 2000:39).

Put simply, when you come to church, you don't leave behind the rest of your experiences. That's pretty obvious. But the ramifications of this "obvious" fact for the life of your congregation may not be. Throughout this book, I emphasize that you must critically examine the assumptions, knowledge, and skills that members routinely bring to congregational life from their work lives.

Where the generation gap is concerned, "Lived Christianity" suggests that we bring our professional and cultural views of age and generations into the congregation—often unconsciously. More than 48 percent of the people in our congregations are or have been managers or professionals. It's not surprising, then, that they often bring to congregational life a view of generations based on their job experiences.

And what do these job experiences teach? If you search Amazon.com for books on generations, you will find an abundance of works offering advice on how to deal with the generation gap as it manifests in the corporate arena or as it affects the marketing of consumer goods. For example, *Generations at Work: Managing the Clash of Veterans, Boomers, Xers and Nexters in Your Work Place* and *Rocking the Ages: The Yankelovich Report on Generational Marketing.*

But the authors' generalizations about generations and generation gaps usually refer to national trends. For large corporations operating or marketing on a national or even international scale, such generalizations can be profitable bases for action. As sociologist R. Stephen Warner (1994:54) has pointed out, however, the "bedrock" of American religion (whether Christian, Jewish, Hindu, or Buddhist) has been and continues to be the congregation—the local, voluntary faith community. Because your congregation is local, voluntary, and a faith community, the younger people already in your pews and the younger people most likely to walk in your church doors are unlikely to be typical of their generation as described by a national survey.

Even more striking, contrary to what national surveys on generations may find and to what the national media dramatically report, our research discovered that:

- Your young people are often very much like your middle-aged and older members in their religious and spiritual attitudes, beliefs, values, and behaviors.
- Since the under-40s do differ significantly from the rest of the congregation in terms of a number of demographic dimensions, this similarity in religious and spiritual attitudes, beliefs, values, and behaviors is particularly striking.
- It is this intergenerational religious cohesion that may well make these churches such vibrant places. How many other institutions in America invite and encourage people from nine days old to ninety years old to meet regularly and share their lives?

Our Fears Are Unfounded

When we recognize that our fears about generation gaps may be un-helpful—that is, when we notice that we've transplanted professional and secular anxieties about age differences into the church—we also see that our fears are partly unfounded. This is not to say there is no age imbalance in our churches. Nor is it to concede defeat by following a Shaker-like approach to the future. The Shakers' religious practices—particularly universal celibacy—logically and inevitably led to the group's extinction. It is true that many mainline Protestant congregations have been forced to close their doors. But I hope to demonstrate empirically that there is cause to be optimistic about the future of many others. We can be optimistic, in a nutshell, because the young and old in our pews are not so different from each other as we tend to assume.

To arrive at this more hopeful outlook, we need to look at the "under-40" members in our pews. Who are they, anyway? Though small in numbers, these younger folks often make crucial contributions to the organizational life and unique identity of your congregation. If you don't know who they are, especially what they believe as Christians, your plans for the future (even your programs to make the church more youthful) may do more to alienate your younger members than to deepen their commitment to the congregation.

Under-40 members are demographically different from the older members in our congregations; however, this difference does not mean that they display a totally different profile. Indeed, younger people possess many of the same characteristics as older members, but the under-40 members express these characteristics to a different degree.

For example, one of the most distinct realities of our congregations is the numerical predominance of women, and *the proportion of women is even higher among the under-40s than in the older age groups.* This seems counterintuitive. After all, it's logical to assume that, given the average shorter life spans of American males, the proportion of women would be highest among the oldest group, where there are many widows. Furthermore, the higher proportion of women among the under-40s does not reflect an abundance of single women. The under-40 women are almost all married, usually married with children. Again, all of us are exposed through the media and work to numerous generalizations about gender as well as age in American society. But these statistics suggest that your congregation is not a microcosm of the larger society. It is something very different, and that difference needs to be recognized and respected to plan fruitfully for its future.

The religious backgrounds of your under-40 members who did not grow up in your denomination may also startle you. Sure, you know that at one time or another, many of the people in your pews have switched denominations. In fact, nearly half of your members have belonged to another denomination. This is not a new or unique trend but a long-term feature of American religious history. Until recently, however, *your members switched within a rather narrow band of religious groups.* The older and middle-aged denomination switchers in your pews came primarily from other mainline Protestant denominations (cf. Bibby 1999).

But in their strikingly high proportion of ex-Catholics, the under-40 denomination switchers in your pews differ radically from older members. Of the under-40s who have switched denominations, 47 percent are ex-Catholics! This is a new pattern. Only 25 percent of denomination switchers over 40 are ex-Catholics. And only 10 percent of denomination switchers 60 years or older are ex-Catholics.[2]

At first glance, these ex-Catholics in mainline pews might appear to be only a statistical curiosity or a source of anecdotes. We found, however, that this trend had major ramifications for mainline Protestant congregations. For example, all too often high profile efforts to attract younger members through changes in worship had their basis in stereotypical ideas about generational style. In practice, this meant some congregations began experimenting with special contemporary services.

Given what we have already said about "generation gaps," it should come as no surprise that these contemporary services did not necessarily attract a younger crowd. In fact, at Holy Trinity, one of the field sites studied, the younger members were strikingly absent from the Saturday night contemporary services, which were much more popular with the middle-aged and older people. Those who regularly attended comprised a small number of active core members who would also participate in the more traditional services the next morning.[3]

In light of the high proportion of denomination switchers (young, middle-aged, and older) we discovered in the pews of mainline Protestant congregations, you might assume, as well, that they would not exhibit strong individual commitments to their denominations. Happily, you would be wrong.

While a statistically significant difference does exist between the under-40s and their older fellow congregation members in their devotion to their current denomination, what remains truly striking is not this difference but the considerable value *younger* members still assign to their current affiliation. A majority of the under-40s (55 %) assigned denominational loyalty an 8 or more on a 10-point scale (where 1 = not at all important and 10 = very important). Only *11 percent* rated denomination less than 5 in importance. Simply put, although the under-40s may differ demographically from others in the pews, when it comes to denominational loyalty your young people are often very much like your middle-aged and older members.

When we turn to core religious beliefs, this similarity becomes even more noticeable, and generational differences become even less noticeable. We asked the people in the pews to indicate how strongly they agreed or disagreed with a series of nine statements about God, heaven and hell, and the nature of evil. These statements ranged from "I feel that God controls the details of my daily life" to "I believe that only Christians have the potential to enter into heaven" to "I do not believe that Satan (or the devil) exists." The under-40s' responses only differed significantly from the rest in one of nine statements—"I feel that God controls the details of my daily life." Even then, the magnitude of difference was not particularly large.

As for how frequently they read the Bible, there were also no signs of a generation gap. And the generations also displayed very similar patterns in their approach to the Bible. We asked the people to indicate how strongly they agreed or disagreed with a series of 17 statements about their understanding of and approach to the Bible. These statements ranged from "When I have a problem in my life, I often turn to the Bible" to "I sometimes don't believe what I read in the Bible." The under-40s differed significantly from the rest in their responses to just four of the 17 statements, and, once again, the magnitude of differences between the two age groups was not large.

But we did discover one superficially surprising difference between the generations when it came to the Bible—where they go to seek assistance when they don't understand or want to better understand something in the Bible. The under-40 members differed significantly from the rest of the congregation in how likely they were to make use of six of

12 possible sources for a better understanding of the Bible. While they remain the best educated of the age groups, the under-40s are less likely to take an "academic" or "scholarly" approach to seeking additional information about the Bible. They were less likely to use study aids (such as a concordance or Bible dictionary), look at the footnotes in their annotated Bibles, or go to the library. While the under-40s were more likely to go to the Internet, it remains a rarely used Bible study resource for them, as well as for the rest of the congregation. I don't think this "less academic" approach to the Bible signifies some major generational gap between younger and older members' religious beliefs or values. Instead, I suspect it reflects a reality with which we are all familiar: under-40 members are simply at a very busy stage of their family and career cycles.

When we move to the question of what members do with and for their congregations, once again the generation gap appears largely illusory. There are no significant differences between the under-40s and the rest of the congregation concerning the number of times per week they attend church for reasons other than worship. More notable is the large percentage of *all* age groups that participate in congregational activities. For example, 63 percent of the younger group is in church one to two times a week for reasons other than worship. And fewer than 25 percent of the under-40s say that their *only* activity at church is Sunday worship. This figure is almost the same for the other age groups.

With one exception, the eight congregations we researched successfully dealt with what frequently serves as a major source of conflict between generations, the establishment of what anthropologists colorfully label a "gerontocracy"—rule by the elderly—which often excludes the young from positions of official power and responsibility. As a whole, there are no significant differences between the under-40s and the others concerning service as a church officer. Over 18 percent of the under-40s are currently church officers. What is striking is not the dominance of one generation but the high percentage of all age groups who hold positions of trust in their churches. In fact, in some churches a major problem is not that the elderly hold onto power but that young people may find themselves thrust into leadership positions for which they don't yet have the experience or the time.

In the midst of all these commonalities, a glaring generation gap persists in one vital (but often overlooked) area. Participation in *nurturing activities* reveals a striking contrast between the under-40s and those 60 and over. Persons over 60 were far more likely to visit nursing homes, hospitals, shut-ins, or others facing difficulties and to write cards or notes to the same. A similar gap also exists between the 40 to 59 year old age group and those 60 and over.[4]

Although those 60 and over are more likely to be suffering from serious illnesses and other difficulties accompanying the aging process, their ethos of caring can have a profound impact on a congregation. One of the youngest churches in our study, with a strikingly low percentage of members 60 and over, had very low levels of nurturing. It also lagged behind in the degree to which its members participated in a variety of other key congregational activities.

A lack of gray power in a church can be just as problematic for the congregation as a lack of young people in the pews. It's vital that your congregation recognize that the older population is an often overlooked and undervalued source of potential new members.

So what do all these statistics tell us? Typically, statements about generations tend to highlight differences between the groups. Our research findings suggest, however, that where religious beliefs and actions are concerned, the most distinctive characteristic in the congregations is the huge amount of overlap between the younger and the older members. That is, within each age group a wide range of beliefs and values exists, and many members of each age group have values and activity patterns that overlap those of many members of the other groups. This may not be sexy or dramatic; it just happens to be true. The great danger of worrying about the differences between groups is that you may end up alienating the many people in your pews who don't fit the stereotypes. You may also be turning generation gaps into self-fulfilling prophecies—producing gaps where none previously existed.

Honoring Our Uniqueness

Earlier I said that the first goal of this book is to make explicit the deep-seated anxieties and fears that underlie much of mainline congregational life. Once we've seen, first, what it is that we fear, then we can see, second, why so many of our fears are either unhelpful, unfounded, or some combination of both. Our worries about a generation gap in the pews are unhelpful because they emerge from professional or working-world understandings of generational differences and tensions; they are unfounded because they overlook the distinctive identity of the under-40s in our pews, many of whom are more like the older members than not. The third goal of this book follows on the heels of the first two: the best way to respond to the challenges facing us in the 21st century is to honor our uniqueness, that is, to remember that mainline congregations aren't like everyone else, nor should they try to be. Being "countercultural" is something we should cultivate, not try to hide or dissolve away.

Where generation gaps are concerned, honoring our uniqueness means moving beyond cultural stereotypes about "old" and "young." And it means recognizing that just as many of the young are like the old in a variety of religious ways, many of the old are like the young. At one of the congregations we studied, for instance, a group of members returned excited and overflowing with new ideas from a conference on changing their church. One of the principles they had learned was: when you implement change in your congregation, be sure that "you bring grandma and grandpa along." But a clear lesson of our research is that grandma and grandpa may not *have* to be brought along with change! Many of the over 60s are, in fact, as open or more open to change than those 40 and under, and there are a significant number of under-40s who may be less open than their elders.

There are vital reasons, then, for your congregation to stop worrying and start celebrating its uniqueness. But celebrating includes careful self-reflection. I urge your congregation to (a) carefully and prayerfully consider greater programmatic emphasis on the practical and spiritual challenges confronting your elderly members, and (b) decide whether you need to dedicate more of your energy and resources to recruiting and evangelizing new members from among the older population. I also urge you to think carefully about the younger adults (18-39 years of age) already in your congregation. In their anxiety to recruit new, younger (preferably previously unchurched) adults, mainline Protestant congregations typically pay scant, if any, attention to a series of crucial questions, including: (a) what types of younger people already belong to your church? and (b) why did they choose a mainline congregation rather than select a more "youthful" type of church?

I hope by now you see that this is not going to be a doom and gloom book, full of dire predictions of what will happen to your church if you ignore my recipes for change. Instead, this book will debunk many of the mainline's "common sense" assumptions about what should be feared and what needs to be fixed. I will also provide an alternative diagnosis of the true challenges facing you and advise you on how to deal with those challenges. We have begun this debunking process already by looking at one central worry—generation gaps—and suggesting that the graying of your members might be helpfully seen not as a disaster in the making but as a potentially fruitful source of practical and spiritual blessing.

The graying of our congregations is a blessing, among other reasons, because it reminds us that mainline churches are profoundly countercultural in their open, frank, and compassionate responses to the realities of disease and death. Indeed, the congregations we studied revere elderly members who face physical weakness and chronic illness with wisdom and courage rooted in faith. When members of any age approach disease and death with serenity based in their faith, those witnesses rivet a congregation's attention. Each time I hear St. Paul's triumphant quotation from Hosea read at a funeral—"Where, O death, is your sting?"—I am reminded that the Christian perspective is radically distinctive and countercultural (1 Cor. 15:55).

HEEDING THE BIBLICAL INJUNCTION

Up to this point, I've explained the reasons for this book from my perspective as a social scientific researcher and analyst. However, I confess to a spiritual motive for writing as well. I find the pervasive fear and anxiety both counterproductive on a practical level and spiritually disturbing.

God and his messengers frequently bear seemingly impossible, even ludicrous, messages or promises to believers. Recall how God promised fertility to Sarah, who was barren and had no reason to expect that she could be pregnant with new life and growth. The son born to her in her old age was named Isaac because Sarah laughed when hearing the visitors (angels in disguise) at Mamre promise her elderly husband Abraham that she, his aged and barren wife, would soon bear a child (Genesis 18:1-15). Recall when an angel tells the elderly Zechariah that his barren wife Elizabeth will give birth and when the Virgin Mary is told that she will conceive through the power of the Holy Spirit (Luke 1:5-38).

Facing a relative decline in denomination membership and the graying, aging nature of the people in their pews, it is not surprising that mainline Protestants fear their congregations will be barren and infertile. But if we believe that we are doing God's work and are called to be faithful people of God, it is crucial that we also heed the counsel given to Zechariah and Mary and a multitude of Old Testament prophets: Be not afraid!

Heeding the biblical injunction to "Be not afraid" is vital. Ironically, the congregations we studied were not paralyzed into inaction by fear and anxiety. Rather, fear and anxiety about the future frequently spurred them to an almost obsessive search for change. They experimented with a series of programs whose failures left leaders frustrated and discouraged. All too often, those frequent changes were based on ideas borrowed from institutions whose values (especially their measures of "success") were radically opposed to Christian commitments and were not rooted in serious reflection on biblical principles.

This book argues that it is far better to respond to the challenges facing American Christianity in the 21st century with faith, not with fear. Essential to that faith is knowledge of who you are as a *unique* congregation—knowledge of what you believe and a commitment to have what you believe reflected in how you live as a community of faith.

Before a church commits itself to a major program for change, it needs to know what it's changing. History counts! Visioning the future, a popular exercise in many congregations, is important. There is a great deal of truth in the oft-repeated stricture from a well-known church consultant: "If you don't know where you're going, any road will get you there." But such a focus on change, on the future, can lead to a dangerous neglect of a more basic principle: *If you don't know who you are, you can't know what you can become.*

Writing for Busy People

Lay and ordained leaders of mainline Protestant churches are busy people, with packed schedules and myriad responsibilities. Even the most dedicated church volunteer or conscientious pastor struggles to find time for reading, and the books that influence the leaders of our congregations are generally brief and lively. However, many employ scare tactics. They are long on anecdotes and generalizations but seldom based on in-depth or systematic research. By contrast, a wealth of sophisticated academic research on American religion is available as a potentially valuable resource for church leaders. But such literature often goes unread by practitioners because it is too dry, too technical, or too long.

In *Be Not Afraid!* I've tried to combine the virtues (and avoid the vices) of the two types of books I've just described. Academic colleagues who read this book may be disappointed by the scarcity of footnotes and references, not to mention the absence (I hope) of scholarly jargon and theoretical meanderings. I offer my regrets to my colleagues, but this book was not written for them. The documentation that would satisfy academics would be a distraction (and quite possibly a major obstacle or irritation) for my intended readers. This is an applied study, and its goal is to offer concrete and practical assistance to the leaders of mainline Protestant churches.[5]

At the same time, however, I believe that this book remains scholarly in the very best sense of the word. In carrying out our observations and in developing questions for our pastoral staff interviews, spiritual life history interviews, and surveys, we adhered to rigorous methodological standards. In analyzing the data and drawing conclusions, we were equally exacting.

For every generalization or conclusion presented in this book, there are literally hundreds of hypotheses that never made it into the text. That's because when we systematically read through our interview transcripts and field notes or ran rigorous tests on the responses from our surveys, we found that many of our initial ideas and numerous widely shared common sense assumptions were simply wrong or statistically meaningless in the real world.

On the one hand, that was disappointing. We could not make many thundering, prophetic (or apocalyptic) pronouncements. We could not market a 20-step program for building a more dynamic congregation. On the other hand, our findings did confirm our most basic and fundamental impression after two years of research: congregations are very complex places that stand out, in many ways, as radically different from other American institutions. Each congregation can only be understood in the context of its particular and specific history. And mainline churches enjoy many strengths that are frequently taken for granted and under-valued.

In this book I encourage churches to harness these strengths to meet the challenges actually facing today's congregations. I challenge mainline congregations to be countercultural and fearless in how they evaluate the challenges they face and in how they choose to deal with them. I see immense merit in what these churches do and am confident that they are not doomed to extinction in the 21st century.

So the message of this book is to take your faith seriously and to recognize that both your congregation and its members are exceptionally complex.

Acknowledging this complexity means learning to think clearly and deeply about the unique nature of the religious lives of the people in the pews and behind the pulpit. It also means learning to think clearly and deeply about the unique and multifaceted nature of your congregations. This is what our book can empower you to do. The skills and analytic approaches that we will teach in the book are not rocket science. Your most formidable challenge will be to move beyond fear and be willing to question (and we hope abandon) some pervasive but inaccurate or misleading assumptions about congregational life and the spiritual lives of your members.

Finally, I must confess that for me congregations and their members still remain in part a mystery and in part a miracle. I need to remind

myself to fearlessly abandon the arrogant pretence that human knowledge is by itself adequate to understand fully what God has in mind for
his people and how God works through individuals and congregations.

2

Knowing Who We Are

Our Eight Congregations

AS I DEBUNKED THE MYTHS ABOUT A GENERATION GAP IN CONGREGATIONS, I HOPE you also noticed who the people in the pews of our mainline Protestant congregations are. I highlighted key facts about their gender, income, and occupations. Chapter 1 also described the denominational background and some central religious beliefs and practices of the under-40 and the 60 and older age groups in our large sample of mainline Protestants. In this chapter, you'll receive additional information about "who we are" that will help complete the profile of our mainline Protestants.

But this chapter has a larger purpose as well. In the pages that follow, I'm going to introduce you to the congregational study that our research team undertook. First, I'll explain why we chose the project churches we studied and how we studied them. Second, I'll provide you with information about common characteristics among the congregations we studied. Third, I'll discuss specific variations in the churches we studied. Although common characteristics are important to note, equally important are the ways in which our churches differed from one another. I'll conclude with a brief case study of one church.

Why do you need to know all these details? First, you should decide whether any of the study churches are at all like yours (i.e., whether the lessons we learned from them are relevant to you and your church). You also might find it useful to know how we learned about those churches. How else can you decide whether to trust our findings and suggestions, especially when they contradict so much of what you hear from other sources? Second, if understanding your church's unique character is fundamental to planning for its future, then you need a realistic picture of mainline Protestants as a whole, as well as of individual congregations, in order to discover what makes your own church unique. Finally, looking at our profile churches, hearing their stories, and learning from the struggles they shared can both inform and empower you as you face your own challenges. Knowing who we are helps us know who we can become and how we can face the future. This chapter begins suggesting "who we are" by painting an introductory sketch of the eight churches we studied.

I also hope that by the time you finish this chapter, you'll have learned a great deal about the process of comparative analysis through which you can discover your church's unique qualities. You should be ready to think creatively about your own church's uniqueness by comparing what you know about it with what you have learned so far about our sample and each of the project churches. Your skill at analysis should improve throughout the book as we go through similar processes in relation to a variety of congregational features.

A Methodological Caveat

In the previous chapter, I emphasized that mainline congregations often operate on the basis of flawed assumptions about younger people. These are typically based on generalizations from surveys where the samples do not fairly represent the types of younger people already in mainline Protestant pews or likely to become members of such churches in the future.

I hope that by now you are asking yourself some crucial analytic questions about our sample. Are the findings from our project churches pertinent to your congregation? Do the eight project churches where we carried out year-long participant observation, the 1,170 mainline Protestants from those churches who responded to the survey, and the 84 core members with whom we conducted spiritual life history interviews represent congregations and people whose dynamics, values, and beliefs are relevant to your own church? In other words, is it meaningful for you to compare your church with our data?

Ideally, we would have randomly chosen our sample of healthy congregations from an extensive list of mainline Protestant churches with a variety of sizes, locations, and socio-economic status. Practically speaking, that was impossible and probably foolish. Even compiling an exhaustive list of such churches would have taken an immense amount of time. Given how quickly churches can change, a randomly chosen congregation might no longer be "healthy" by the time we began our research, or its leadership might not invite our intimate involvement in the faith community. In fact, a major factor in the selection of our sample was the receptivity of the pastors and lay leaders of the churches to opening up their congregations for comprehensive study.

In addition, we did not begin our research with the expectation that a survey would be a major source of data, and thus a random sample was not a high priority in choosing our project sites. In my first annual report to the project's funding source, Lilly Endowment, I wrote, "We will administer a brief questionnaire." In my wildest dreams at that time, I didn't anticipate creating an instrument with 22 pages of closed and open-ended questions covering everything from basic demographic data to responses to life crises.

Even if you're not concerned about methodological details, you need to understand our most fundamental methodological assumption. From the beginning, our primary objective was in-depth, intimate knowledge of congregational daily life, and that could only be obtained through long-term participant observation and the development of trusting relationships with ordained and lay leadership. Those essential prerequisites are not necessarily compatible with a random selection of churches. As you progress through this book, I am confident that the detailed case studies will prove most useful for you, as opposed to the statistical data by themselves. The case studies provide an on-the-ground perspective of myriad elements that affect the dynamics of the congregational faith community. Understanding the nature of these dynamics—these processes—is most likely to help you make your good church better.

Why, then, did we eventually put so much effort into our survey? And how useful will the survey results be to you? The need for this kind of survey emerged from our experiences in the initial months of our study. The people whom we got to know best, the most active participants in the congregations, repeatedly asked themselves and us: Why is it always the same small group of people who do most of the work in a church? How can the other church members be transformed into active participants in congregational life? Obviously, collecting data on the lived religion of the worshiping community (all who attended Sunday services at least twice a month) would be of enormous interest to the leadership of these churches. (Roberts 2000:59-60).

And the survey did, in fact, demonstrate that the commonly quoted figure—"20 percent of the people in the church do 80 percent of the work"—can be seriously misleading. It is also too crude a way to think constructively and creatively about the leadership and volunteer dynamics in your church.

Another major reason we conducted a comprehensive survey of the worshiping communities was to examine how the religious beliefs, values, and attitudes of the most influential and active members of the congregations related to those of less engaged church members, whom we had far less opportunity to observe. In comparing "core" with "non-core" church members, we found very similar relationships in all our quite varied churches. This suggests that these relationships are relatively stable, and the information we gathered can provide insights about key dynamics between core and non-core members in your own church.

Our results are likely to be directly relevant to your church because we often discerned a consistent pattern across all of our mainline Protestant churches, despite their differences. When we compared beliefs or activities between age groups or between men and women or between core and non-core members, the relationship between these groups remained similar across the various congregations.

At the same time, when we took a congregation and systematically compared its results on a range of issues with the other project churches, a unique profile for each congregation emerged. That profile meshed well with all we knew about the church from our other research (participant observations, staff interviews, and spiritual life history interviews). Indeed, the profile often shed light on dynamics that we had observed but couldn't quite understand. In short, I am confident that my suggestions and conclusions about these congregational dynamics are relevant to your mainline church, for our findings are based on comparisons among our project churches and derived from an analysis of a wide variety of data types (qualitative and quantitative) on the same issues. Congregations and church members are very complex; consequently, only a comprehensive and multifaceted approach to examining them can succeed.

PORTRAITS OF OUR CONGREGATIONS[6]

Before we move any further, let's take a brief look at the individual congregations we studied. These portraits are not exhaustive. You'll get to know the congregations in more detail in the chapters that follow when we look at specific concerns and fears that different congregations faced. But for now, I want to give you a basic overview of each church so you are somewhat familiar with them when we move into other parts of the study.[7]

It's important to note, of course, that in each of the churches we studied significant change has taken place since our fieldwork ended. For example, we know that Rev. Jim Schalkhauser of Bethlehem Lutheran has retired and was succeeded as Senior Pastor by his long-time partner in ministry, Rev. Jim Lichtenberger. Pastor Dennis Bux of Holy Trinity Lutheran resigned his position there and has subsequently taken up a call at another, smaller congregation. Central Methodist's financial situation has altered radically, as its proximity to the newly built Comerica

Park (home of the Detroit Tigers) has transformed the church's parking lot into a significant source of revenue and the office spaces in its six-story building into a potentially valuable source of rental income.

I have not attempted to update the material in these portraits or in subsequent chapters. The congregations are portrayed as they appeared to the research team when they were actively involved in the life of those churches.

Bethel Baptist in Southgate

Bethel Baptist is a largely blue-collar church. With a worshiping community of 71, the congregation is fairly balanced in terms of age structure. It has a good mixture of young families with children and older, long-time or even lifetime members. Founded in 1917 as a Sunday school class, the congregation soon became the Ford Baptist Church of Wyandotte, a working class, Downriver community. In 1954 the congregation made the difficult and crucial decision to move out of the neighborhood where many members lived, relocating to Southgate, another blue-collar Downriver community. Today, many congregation members still live outside of Southgate. Pastor Roger Dahlen began preaching at Bethel in 1981 and was installed as its full-time pastor in 1983. His wife is a child of the church, and her family still attends. The congregation is very close-knit, and several family groups play a major role. Despite the closeness of its members, Bethel Baptist is extraordinarily open and welcoming to strangers.

Bethlehem Evangelical Lutheran Church of Lansing

Bethlehem Evangelical Lutheran Church is an urban church with a worshiping community of 231. The congregation celebrated its 75th anniversary during the study. Although the church is located in a low-income neighborhood, the vast majority of Bethlehem's members are middle class, driving to the church from more affluent Lansing neighborhoods or suburban communities. In the early 1990s, the congregation had to decide whether to renovate and expand its facilities or relocate closer to the residences of its members. Deciding for the former, Bethlehem committed itself to a program of outreach to the surrounding neighborhood. The program includes one of the Lansing area's largest food closets, open gym nights for children, a summer lunch program for kids, and a summer day camp in which half the children come from the surrounding neighborhood.

Senior pastor Rev. James Schalkhauser has been in his position for over 25 years, and the associate pastor, Rev. James Lichtenberger, for over 10. In recommending this congregation to the project, a synod official commented that the senior and associate pastors at Bethlehem had as close to perfect relationship as he had seen. The church is a very tight-knit community. It is not unusual to see families with two adult generations worshiping together. Many long-time members have close friendships that have endured for decades. Nevertheless, the congregation is also welcoming to newcomers—and newcomers are able to move quickly into positions of responsibility.

Central United Methodist Church of Detroit

Situated in the heart of Detroit's historic district, Central United Methodist Church sits in the shadows of Comerica Park, the new home of the Detroit Tigers. Founded in 1822, the church claims to be the oldest incorporated Protestant church in Michigan and enjoys a reputation as "the conscience of the city" for its long history of local (and global) peace and justice work. Over the years, Central's pulpit has attracted a lineup of notable preachers and national leaders, including Martin Luther King, Jr.

Although Central's rich and illustrious past is frequently invoked, the racially mixed congregation's worshiping community of 162 does not begin to fill the church's cathedral-like sanctuary. In some ways, the church is only a shell of its former "glorious" past. But it does remain deeply involved in city politics and local community activism.

Under the leadership of senior pastor Rev. Edwin Rowe, who joined Central in 1994, the congregation has engaged in local and national labor solidarity work. "Centralites" actively participate in anti-death penalty efforts in the state of Michigan, environmental conservation projects in Detroit and its environs, and community development efforts that respect the city's poor and working families. Central also helps sponsor the "Reconciling Congregation" movement—an attempt to create ministries that respond to the needs of gay, lesbian, bisexual, and transgender people and to change United Methodist policies prohibiting same-sex marital rites and the ordination of openly gay or lesbian persons. This sponsorship has caused some tension.

In addition to its involvement in numerous peace and justice arenas, Central also lets community and service groups use its six-story office building and spacious sanctuary. Although its numerical decline and fiscal problems are not likely to go away anytime soon, the church has attracted some new members in the last years. And the revitalization of downtown Detroit could mean rising fortunes for the church's real estate holdings.

First Presbyterian of Farmington

First Presbyterian was formally organized in 1954. It is a solidly middle-class, almost exclusively white, family-oriented, suburban congregation with a worshiping community of 301. For a complicated set of reasons, membership declined dramatically in the mid-1980s, and the church offered relatively few organized activities during that period. In the late 1980s, the congregation called a new senior pastor, Rev. Dr. "Budge" Gere, and an associate pastor and music director, Rev. David Noble. This very intentional leadership team played a major role in fostering the completion of a large building project, a higher level of participation in worship, and a dramatic increase in programming. The expansion of programs took place without a significant growth in church membership, and the congregation is graying. During our study, the senior pastor left First Presbyterian to accept a call at a larger church. It is a clear sign of the congregation's health that the loss of a successful and admired senior pastor did not cause panic but was met with a sense of quiet confidence in the future.

Holy Trinity Lutheran Church of Livonia

Holy Trinity Lutheran was founded in 1961 as part of the Missouri Synod but eventually joined the Evangelical Lutheran Church in America. It is a solidly middle-class, almost exclusively white, family-oriented suburban church with 458 people in its worshiping community, many of whom are acutely aware of their German and Scandinavian backgrounds. Its long-time, low-key, and beloved pastor, Rev. Robert Seltz, retired in November 1997 after the completion of a major building addition. There appears to have been a very smooth transition in pastoral leadership. His successor, Rev. Dennis Bux, served for two years as senior associate pastor before being installed as senior pastor during Rev. Seltz's last year of service. Rev. Bux is extremely dynamic and emphasizes empowerment of the laity, ministry in daily life, spirituality, and Lutheran identity. Holy Trinity has a highly successful children's program, including a nursery school, which attracts young families to the congregation.

St. Paul United Church of Christ in Taylor

St. Paul has a worshiping community of 219. It is on the evangelical side of the UCC, and its worship is conservative. The highly educated and relatively young senior pastor, Rev. Dr. Geoff Drutchas, has been at St. Paul for over ten years. He previously served as a college chaplain and a Unitarian Universalist minister. The congregation is primarily working-class with blue-collar backgrounds, older, and conservative. The church is 113 years old and had its beginnings as an evangelical Lutheran church with a mixed Reformed-Lutheran tradition. Taylor was originally an agricultural area, and farmers founded the church. Southerners migrated to Taylor in the 1940s and 1950s, giving Taylor its nickname of "Taylor-tucky." Today it is a working-class suburb in the Downriver area, where traditionally the auto industry has employed many people.

St. Timothy Presbyterian Church in Livonia

St. Timothy is a middle-class congregation with a worshiping community of 141. It is located in the middle- to upper-middle class northwestern suburb of Livonia. "Seed people" from St. Paul, another Presbyterian church in Livonia, founded the church in 1965. Since then, St. Timothy has only had three pastors and one interim pastor. Under their second pastor in the late 1970s and early 1980s, the church grew strong and had its highest active membership of about 240 people. The congregation built additions to the sanctuary and a meeting room for the Session. Membership began to decline, however, when the pastor decided it was time to move but could not find a calling he wanted. Significant tension and conflict emerged between the pastor and his congregation. In 1987, the conflict came to a head, and the pastor left. The Presbytery assembled an administrative commission, and an interim pastor was appointed—a retired pastor who offered a healing presence in the church. The Presbytery wanted to close the church or appoint a part-time pastor, but the congregation insisted on a full-time appointment.

In 1989 Rev. Janet Noble-Richardson, the current senior pastor, was called to the church. She has helped the congregation heal and move on to better times. Two major changes have taken place during her tenure. The church rescheduled Sunday school so that children could attend worship, and a major building addition reached completion in the spring of 1999. Little obvious conflict is present in the congregation now. The congregation is well organized, and meetings are run efficiently, largely because of the white-collar background of most of the congregation. St. Timothy is highly active in mission outreach in their local community and beyond. The congregation is close-knit, and members see each other frequently both outside of church and at church activities.

Second Baptist Church of Detroit

Thirteen former slaves founded Second Baptist in 1836. It is the oldest historic black church in the Detroit area, possibly the Midwest, and was a stop on the "Underground Railroad." Second Baptist is located in "Greektown," whose restaurants and bakeries make the area one of Detroit's major draws for suburbanites and tourists. Only a small proportion of Second Baptist's members live near the church. The congregation has a worshiping community of 266. Second Baptist has long been viewed as an elite church. It is an older, or graying, church with a membership including many retirees and former professionals whose children have moved out of Detroit or ceased being active in the church. Many older members are strongly attached to Second Baptist's stately worship demeanor. The senior pastor, Rev. Dr. Kevin Turman, educated at Harvard and Yale, has served in his position for 10 years; he would like to see the congregation move to a more contemporary, enthusiastic, and interactive style. While Second Baptist's women fill the pews each Sunday, staff various auxiliaries, and plan many of the congregation's social events, there has been resistance to including them in some leadership roles. Recently, the senior pastor successfully led efforts to authorize the ordination of women as deacons.

COMMON CHARACTERISTICS:
THE PEOPLE IN OUR EIGHT CONGREGATIONS

Now that you've met our eight congregations, I want briefly to step back and look at the larger patterns that emerged from our survey data. I'm interested, at least at this point, in highlighting common characteristics—shared ideas, demographics, interests, and so forth—that occurred across the congregations we studied. Summarized below are some of the most important statistics about our sample as a whole as represented by our survey results. These figures will serve as a set of comparative benchmarks as we seek the unique qualities of individual congregations in the final section of this chapter. I have also provided this summary so that you may perform similar analyses of your own faith community.

What Is the Worshiping Community?

We defined the worshiping community of a congregation as the people who attend Sunday worship at least twice a month, and we mailed our survey to the entire worshiping community of each of the eight project churches. The figures in the charts are drawn from responses by the 63 percent of the worshiping communities of the eight churches who completed and returned the surveys. Considering that the survey was 22 pages long and included both open-ended questions and questions that only required checking a box, we think the overall return rate is quite remarkable.

The percent of the worshiping community that returned the survey did vary greatly by church (from 44% to 81%); however, profiles of those who responded matched quite well with the entire worshiping community in terms of the key factors of gender and age structure. In other words, the population that returned the survey in each church is probably quite representative of the entire worshiping community.

How Does the Size of the Worshiping Community Compare with Membership Rolls?

The sizes of the worshiping communities are by no means equivalent to the congregation memberships claimed by our churches. For a variety of reasons, the congregations claim a far larger membership than the people who attend services at least twice a month. The church membership is often at least twice as large as what we defined as the worshiping community. Keep this in mind when comparing the size of your church to our congregations.

Who Are the People in the Pews?

I'll quickly describe the average characteristics of the people in these congregation's pews. Keep these numbers in mind when we turn later to comparative analyses among the congregations and to analyses of key subjects like worship and nurturing.

We studied eight Protestant congregations from five mainline denominations: two from the Evangelical Lutheran Church in America, two from the Presbyterian Church (USA), two from American Baptist Churches in the USA, one from the United Church of Christ, and one from the United Methodists. Two congregations are located in downtown Detroit, five in Detroit's working-class and middle-class suburbs, and one in Lansing, a smaller city about an hour and a half drive from Detroit. The largest worshiping community is 458; the smallest is 71.

The average congregation size is 231 regular worshippers. Sixty-five percent of these Protestant church members are women. The age distribution of these members is given below in table 2.1. There are fewer very old people and fewer young adults in comparison to the other age groups.

Table 2.1
Age Distribution of Protestant Sample

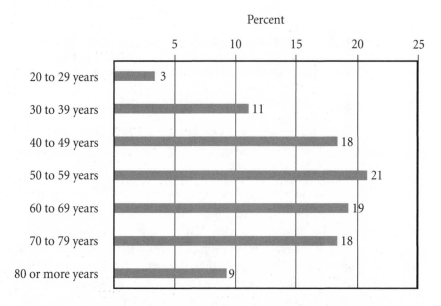

Most active church members are presently married (75%) and have young or grown children (87%). About half have completed college and almost half have managerial or professional jobs. Their average family income is widely distributed. (See table 2.2.) Since 30 percent of these members are probably retired, present household income is probably not a clear indicator of social class.

Congregation members have belonged to their church for an average of 21 years. This average, of course, is shorter for members under 40 (10 years) and longer for members over 60 (29 years). However, despite their many long-time members, 32 percent of the people in the pews have been in their present church for fewer than 10 years. Just over 40 percent of the members have changed churches for reasons other than moving to a new location.

Our survey asked several questions about Christian beliefs, more specifically about the Bible, prayer, Holy Communion, general Christian theology, and social issues. In general, 27 percent of our Protestants read the Bible more than once a week, 41 percent read it from once a month

Table 2.2
Distribution of Responders by Average Household Income

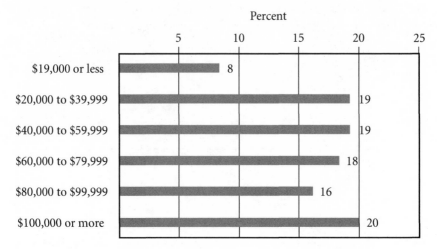

Percent

	5	10	15	20	25
$19,000 or less	8				
$20,000 to $39,999				19	
$40,000 to $59,999				19	
$60,000 to $79,999			18		
$80,000 to $99,999			16		
$100,000 or more				20	

to once a week, and 32 percent read it rarely. About 24 percent of our Protestants pray more than once each day, 59 percent pray daily, and the remaining 17 percent pray once a week or less. Women read the Bible and pray more frequently than men, but not a great deal more. There were no significant differences between age groups in the frequency with which they read the Bible or with which they pray. In terms of political preferences, 35 percent generally vote Democratic, 43 percent vote Republican, and 21 percent vote Independent or Other.

What Do People Do in Their Church?

We defined active members as those who attend worship services at least twice a month. In addition to attending Sunday worship services, most members are in the church one to two times per week for one to two hours per week. About 23 percent are presently church officers, and 50 percent have been church officers at some time. Most members (77%) participate in fellowship after church at least once a year, and about 74 percent participate in one or more church social activities. Almost 80 percent serve on committees, assist with worship, teach classes, or do other volunteer work for the church one or more times per year. Over half (58%) attend an education class or small group more than once a year. Table 2.3 shows member activities in more detail.

The activity numbers are particularly crucial: among the most impressive characteristics of mainline Protestant churches is the surprising extent to which members of the worshiping community are actively in-

Table 2.3
What Active Members Do in Church

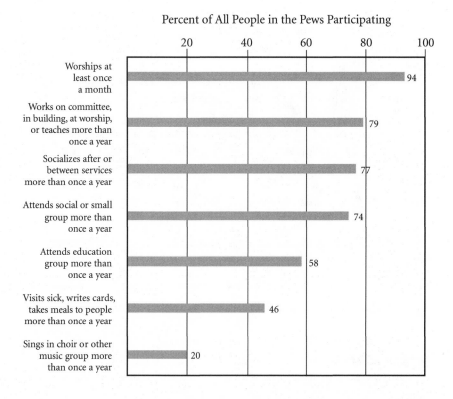

Percent of All People in the Pews Participating

volved, in a wide variety of ways, in the life of their faith community. Of course, the statistics recorded are self-reports, and it is almost a social scientific truism that people don't necessarily do what they say they do. Once again, however, in this study we were able to check self-reports against our own observations. And while probably somewhat exaggerated, the self-reports are relatively accurate in my estimation.

Core Members

One of the most powerful confirmations of the validity of the self-reported survey results comes from a comparison between the rates of activity of two categories of members I have mentioned several times—core and non-core members of the church. We expected core members to be more active than non-core members in church activities on the basis of our own observations as well as those of the pastoral staff. And, indeed, they were consistently and statistically significantly so in their self-reports (see table 2.4 on page 30).

But what do I mean by core members? Up to this point I've employed the term without an explicit definition, expecting that the name itself would be sufficient—implying people at the heart of your faith community's life. And I'm sure that almost anyone deeply engaged in a church has some idea about who are core members of his or her congregation.

At the same time, however, we found that an exact but workable definition, which allowed us to produce an actual list of core members and then carefully analyze it, remained crucial to our understanding of the dynamics of the project churches. Knowing the characteristics of core members within our sample as a whole and within individual churches was essential for our understanding of the uniqueness of each congregation. Developing such a list for your church and comparing it with what is presented here should be equally helpful to you and your congregation.

How Do You Define and Compile a Core List?

How did we define the core? How did we develop lists of core members for each church? And what did we learn through a careful analysis of the core members?

As we carried out our fieldwork in each church, many faces became familiar at Sunday worship. But we also discovered a smaller number of people with whom we became much better acquainted. These were the folks most likely to be at the round of committee and circle meetings, Bible studies, prayer breakfasts, and potlucks we regularly attended.

These are also the people who give the unique flavor or tone to each church. They remain crucial to the congregation in terms of church growth (measured either by total number of members or by level of involvement of members).

These are the people that prospective members are most likely to meet. And when peripheral members find themselves becoming interested in heavier involvement (e.g., because of a life crisis), these are the people (aside from the staff) to whom the peripheral folks are most likely to turn. They are also those with whom the pastoral staff spends most of its time.

Finally, and perhaps most importantly, knowing something about these people remains pivotal for understanding how your church responds to those proposals for change that comprise a significant part of mainline Protestant church life.

During our research period, we saw many interesting new programs discussed at great length. But only a small proportion ever progressed beyond discussion. Even fewer had a meaningful effect on the congregations. Difficulty in implementing change proved a major source of irritation, frustration, and burnout among pastoral staff members and dedicated volunteers.

The criteria we used for core members specifically addressed this issue of implementing change: "If a significant change were to be proposed for the church, would the individual play a role for or against it, and would the person have any significant impact?"

After conducting intensive research at a congregation for six to eight months, we began putting together a core list for the church. By that time we had conducted in-depth interviews with the pastoral staff and had attended numerous church activities, from Sunday worship to Bible studies, from council, committee, and commission meetings to women's and men's groups.

On the basis of those experiences, we wrote out a list of individuals whom we felt were core members of the church. We then took our preliminary list to one or more members of the congregation's pastoral staff. We asked these staff to review the preliminary list, feeling free to add or subtract from it on the basis of the above criterion.

We also emphasized that "in making this decision, we're not asking you to evaluate whether an individual is a good or bad core person," since we wanted to avoid compiling a list limited to people who were both influential *and* allies of the pastoral staff.

Notice, as well, that we deliberately avoided elitist wording in our criteria. From our observations, it was clear that successful implementation did not rest solely on "movers and shakers," those who held elected positions or made most proposals for change. Success or failure also depended on the broader group of congregation members, the core, whose voices would be effectively raised in response to new ideas. Beyond that it depended on how representative the core was of the rest of the people in the pews. In appendix A are instructions to help you construct and analyze a core list for your church.

Who Are the Core Members?

Averaging over all eight congregations, about 21 percent of the churches' active members were core members. As you might expect, core members were more likely to be middle aged (40-59 years old), had been members of the church longer, and were more active in church activities than non-core members (See table 2.4). They were also a little more likely to read the Bible, participate in Bible study, and interpret the Bible literally.

Table 2.4

Comparing the Activities of Core and Non-Core Members

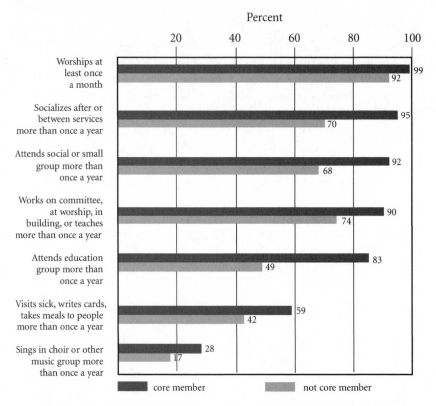

Knowing what types of people are likely to be in the core and what they do for their churches is key to understanding mainline congregations. When it comes to understanding an individual church, however, another question led to helpful—and surprising—answers: "What percentage of a church's worshiping community is part of its core?"

From Averages to Ranges: What Makes a Congregation (And Its Core) Unique?

Up to this point, I've provided you with data about the average findings on a wide variety of characteristics of our mainline Protestant congregations. As I emphasized earlier, these averages are primarily useful as benchmarks against which the figures from particular churches can be compared. It's vital to know not only the average but also the range of figures from which the average was calculated. Particularly when that range is wide, the average can be dangerously misleading. For example, an average score of 100 on some facet of a church should be evaluated and interpreted differently when it comes from three scores of 50, 20, and 230 as opposed to 90, 100, and 110. The importance of this simple principle can be illustrated by some of our most fascinating findings on cores.

Given the wide range of sizes of worshiping communities in our sample (from 71 to 458), the *percent* of people from the worshiping community in the core is a better comparative measure than the actual number of people in the core. The average percent is 21. This average, however, masks a surprisingly wide range of individual figures. Before compiling the core lists, we had the distinct impression that church cores varied from one another. Nevertheless, even we were surprised at how dramatic these differences could be: in these good mainline Protestant congregations, that figure ranged from around 8 percent to around 45 percent. There was no clear and simple relationship between size of worshiping community and percent of core members.

For example, St. Paul, with a worshiping community of approximately 220, had just about 12 percent in its core, while Bethlehem Lutheran, with a similar size of worshiping community, had a core percentage of almost 45 percent. It's not surprising that these two congregations responded to proposed changes in very different ways.

Churches also varied in the extent to which their cores were representative. Your core doesn't have to be totally representative of your congregation. There may even be good reasons for it not to be. You may be hoping to change the direction or orientation of the church. If so, you need to be sure that the nature of the core will help and not hinder those proposed changes.

For example, one church desperately needed to increase its membership. Unfortunately, its core was composed almost exclusively of long-time members. It was clearly going to be difficult to recruit newcomers of any age when even the current members who had been at the church for 10 or 15 years seemed to have little or no influence on decision making in this church.

There is no magic formula for what size a core should be. However, before you spend time and effort on ambitious proposals for change, you should have a clear and accurate view of the size and makeup of your core. Part of being intentional church leaders is to know who you are as a congregation. And an essential element in your congregation's identity is the size and composition of its core.

Table 2.5
Percent of Core Members in Each Congregation

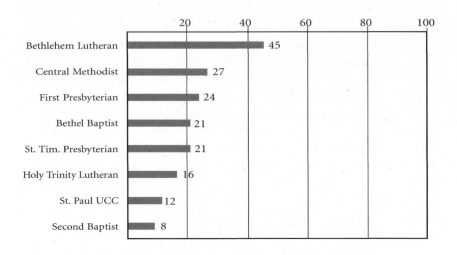

From Core Demographics to Core Beliefs

The statistics presented in tables 2.4 and 2.5 demonstrate that the core members reside at the heart of a congregation's activity. These statistics also illustrate the wide range in the percentage of core members in each church. But when it comes to issues of change, an equally (if not more) important concern is the relationship between core and non-core beliefs. Do proposals for change fail or elicit little enthusiasm from a church as a whole because core members tend to have religious values and beliefs at odds with the non-core?

An analysis of data from the sample as a whole suggests a lukewarm, "maybe yes, maybe no." Out of 54 questions related to beliefs, the Bible, and prayer, 21 questions showed significant differences between core and non-core members in the percent of time they agreed or disagreed with the different statements. On the other hand, none of the differences is particularly large (generally a difference of 8 to 17 percent between the number of core and non-core members agreeing or disagreeing with a statement).

When we looked more closely at these differences, at least a third of them reflect not a variance in beliefs but a variance in activity level, one of the core's central characteristics. The core members were more likely, for example, to say that they use a Bible study guide or commentary or that they often pray for intercessions mentioned on Sunday. In a large number of other cases, the difference between core and non-core over a given statement turned on the core members' disinclination to give "no opinion" as an answer to a question. For example, although 8 percent more core than non-core members *disagreed* with the statement that "sinners go to hell," the exact same percent of core and non-core members *agreed* with the same statement. The real difference, then, was that 8 percent more of the non-core members gave "no opinion" on that statement. Core members were simply more likely to have opinions and to express them. In another part of the survey, we found that core members were also more likely to give opinions and suggest changes in their sanctuary or their worship services.

This finding may suggest that when differences in beliefs and values occur between core and non-core members, these disagreements are minor and based almost exclusively in the core members' more active engagement in church life and greater confidence in their opinions. These two characteristics—engagement and confidence—appear connected, since the greater involvement of core members in activities like Bible studies and other adult education events may explain that group's greater degree of confidence in their beliefs.

Another related and, I suspect, more valid and significant difference between the core and the non-core may be level of boredom. Core members, who are actively involved in church activities and events from worship to committee meetings, might just feel a need to vary what they're doing, call it something new, or try another fashion. Of course, this isn't surprising since there's nothing more mainstream American than a passion for change. It's one of the driving forces behind conspicuous consumption. But I suggest that core members and pastoral staff ask themselves some critical and countercultural questions when they're contemplating a change (e.g., in worship or in worship space): Is this a change for change's sake (to keep up with the congregational Joneses), or do the proposed changes actually have a basis in the spiritual and religious ethos of your congregation? Does this change build on and enhance the uniqueness of your church, or does it make it more generic?

Before moving on from the core and non-core distinctions in churches, I hope you've asked yourself a question about what I've said so far: how does range play into the statistics we've seen? That is, are the above generalizations about the similarity between core and non-core beliefs, which are based on average figures, misleading when applied to individual churches? In this case, as opposed to when we discussed the percent of the worshiping community in the core, the answer is no. This similarity in beliefs is true for all the congregations in our sample and is very likely to be just as true for your church.

In our discussion of core size, we began to consider how individual congregations in the sample might differ both from the numerical average and from one another. In this section that approach takes center stage as I emphasize the unique character of each of the churches. My goal is to help you discover where your congregation fits within the significant variations we discovered in our project churches: how does your congregation realistically compare with those in our sample? Remember, many unfounded congregational fears and failed programs for change arise from inappropriate and misleading comparisons. More importantly, such a comparison allows you to realistically identify your church's unique strengths and challenges. And that is the indispensable first step in building on who you really are as a congregation.

Demographics

Like many of the leaders with whom we spoke, we assumed that size would be a crucial factor defining a church's dynamics. We ran innumerable statistical tests to check whether size correlated with other important aspects of church life. The most striking finding was that seldom, if ever, did size alone have any significant and meaningful relationship with other facets of congregational life.

Why would that be? Perhaps our sample of congregations was simply too small. I strongly suspect, however, that there are two far more convincing explanations. First, congregations are so complex and multidimensional that one factor alone seems unlikely to wield an overwhelming influence. Second, many vital factors can give a congregation its character, and these do not necessarily vary with size.

For example, people 60 and over comprise nearly 50 percent of the population in six of the eight congregations. The two exceptions are Holy Trinity Lutheran and St. Timothy Presbyterian, where the figures for the oldest age group are approximately 30 percent. This is not surprising. Holy Trinity and St. Timothy are located in the same prosperous suburb, where you would expect a more youthful population. Yet Holy Trinity is the largest congregation in the sample, and St. Timothy is the second smallest—one-third the size of Holy Trinity.

First Presbyterian, the sample's second largest congregation, is also located in an affluent suburb. But over 60 percent of its members are 60 or older, and its middle-aged group is strikingly small, especially when compared to St. Timothy and Holy Trinity. Indeed, the sparseness of middle-aged members is one of the key dynamics of life at First Presbyterian. And it is not related to the church's size. Rather, it stems from an intense conflict that swirled around one of the congregation's former pastors more than a decade ago.

Earlier we saw two demographic features as hallmarks of our mainline Protestants: (1) They are predominantly women, and (2) their members are generally married. Yet when we look at the variation in those two hallmarks across our congregations, very different patterns appear. The predominance of women in congregations is consistent across all eight churches, ranging narrowly between 60 and 73 percent. In sharp contrast, the range for percentage of married people in the pews is wide, from 47 to 87 percent, with the average 76 percent.

The lower end of the married range is represented by two churches: Central Methodist and Second Baptist (with 47 percent and 50 percent of the people in the pews now married). These two also have the highest percent by far of divorced members (26 percent and 17 percent, as compared to a sample average of 7 percent). They are also unique in their location, history, and racial composition. Both congregations are proud of their long, rich histories of active involvement with the social and political life of the city of Detroit, and both are located in the downtown area. While our other congregations are almost exclusively white, Central Methodist is integrated, and Second Baptist is a black church.

As might be expected, the average number of years that members have been in a congregation also varied widely. Although our churches typically are blessed with many long-term members, the average ranges from 35 years in the pews for Second Baptist (also the oldest aged congregation) to 11 years for St. Timothy Presbyterian (also the youngest). But average age is only one variable that determines the number of years in a congregation. The percent of people who had switched churches— especially for reasons other than change of residence—can also alter the average longevity of membership in a church. This percentage varied from Second Baptist at 18 percent to Holy Trinity at 54 percent. Despite this wide gap in average longevity, both Second Baptist and Holy Trinity had at one time suffered from major rifts within the church, which resulted in considerable numbers from the dissident faction leaving for other congregations.

Activity Levels

Another defining feature of our mainline Protestants is their typically high level of involvement in congregational activities other than worship. Again, there is variation here that gives each church its unique flavor. For example, 87 percent of Central Methodist respondents reported attending at least one activity per week at church other than worship, and 53 percent reported attending three or more. On the other hand, only 64 percent at Holy Trinity reported attending at least one activity per week at church other than worship, and only 20 percent reported attending three or more.

There is no simple pattern of activity in our congregations based on church size, average age of members, or denomination. Bethel Baptist members, for instance, participate in Bible education to a much greater extent than other small churches or the other Baptist congregation. Holy Trinity, the largest church, has less participation in social, educational, and nurturing activities but is about average when it comes to participation in work for the church itself (on committees, at worship, in education, or around the church building). The next largest church, First Presbyterian, is about average on all these measures of church activity. St. Paul stands below average on all activities except the social ones. Central Methodist has a very active membership generally, especially in internal church activities.

What about participation as church officers? Only 35 percent of the people at St. Paul UCC have ever been officers, while the corresponding figure for Bethel Baptist is 69 percent. The size of the congregation, the average age of its members, the average number of years members have been in a congregation, and the number of officers required by the church's organization all contribute to variations in this type of participation in church life. In addition, church history, pastoral styles, the presence of power cliques, and individual personalities can increase or decrease the likelihood that a high percentage of members are elected or serve as officers. It's easy to see why these figures vary greatly even among active, healthy churches.

Beliefs

Although mainline Protestants see themselves as theologically quite similar, there are significant differences in belief among individual mainline Protestants and among congregations of Protestants. Some of this variation is denominationally based, and we will discuss that factor in more detail later. Other differences simply reflect a significant range of beliefs within denominations and within congregations. In both Baptist congregations we studied, for example, over half the of members reported reading their Bible more than once a week. At the other extreme, only 11 percent of St. Paul UCC members read the Bible that frequently, and over 57 percent reported reading it rarely. Members of the remaining congregations also varied widely in how frequently they read their Bible.

When we look at variation in opinions of the Bible, at least some people in every congregation disagreed—while others agreed—with each of the statements that we asked them to evaluate. Differences in agreement among congregations also emerged. For example, members of Central Methodist were less likely than other congregations to agree that the Bible's creation story was accurate or that the book of Revelation was an accurate guide to the end times, and they were more likely to agree that sometimes they did not believe what they read in the Bible.

When we asked people to agree or disagree with statements such as "All good people go to heaven," "Only Christians have the potential to go to heaven," "God controls the details of my daily life," and "I do not believe that Satan or the devil exists," some members from all congregations agreed, and some members from all congregations disagreed. Central Methodist and First Presbyterian members were more likely to disagree that "Only Christians go to heaven." Members of Bethel Baptist, Second Baptist and Bethlehem Lutheran were more likely to agree that "God controls the details of my life." Some of these differences are based in denominational identity, but others reflect variations in the age structure of congregations and, quite possibly, disparities in the average educational and occupational levels of members in various congregations.

An Important Caution: It is easy to misinterpret the meaning of responses to survey questions, especially surveys of religious belief, since respondents may understand the questions in radically different ways. For example, compared with other churches, the people at Central Methodist were less likely to agree with the statement, "All good people go to heaven." At first glance, that was startling. It seemed at odds with that congregation's pattern of responses to other related questions, as well as with our researcher's in-depth experiences with the congregation. I checked to see if errors had occurred in data processing. No errors could be found. When I presented our findings to Central Methodist, I openly admitted that I was baffled by their answers to that question. The Central Methodist people, however, had no problem explaining the results and showing why their answer made perfect sense to them. When they read the question, they focused on the concept of "good people." They weren't sure anyone could define what that meant, and they also didn't necessarily believe in heaven; so they disagreed with the statement.

This brief example from Central Method highlights why, when studying something as complex as congregations, survey results need to be supplemented by extensive participant observation, in-depth interviews, and dialogue with people. So let me conclude this chapter on "who we are" by providing one case study that illustrates how comparative analysis of survey results can be included with other forms of information about your congregation to define and explain its uniqueness. Above all, read the case study with this point in mind: your church and its history are no less complicated than Bethlehem's. And even your long time and dedicated members may assume, like the excellent leaders at Bethlehem, that they know more about their church, its identity, and how it runs than they actually do. To know yourself as a congregation is almost as difficult as to know yourself as a person. As a church, you may not be exactly what you thought you were. It's easy to fool ourselves—as individuals *and* as a church—and fear the wrong things while serious problems are left to fester.

A CASE STUDY

When I sat down to analyze the survey data from Bethlehem Lutheran, I didn't expect to be surprised. Instead of the hour and a half commute to the other churches in the sample, Bethlehem was located quite close to my home, about 15 minutes by car, and I was able to dedicate more time to participant observation there than at any other church. I joined its choir, a crucial group in a congregation where singing played a powerful role in worship. I also spent a week as a counselor for Bethlehem's Summer Day Camp program. That program served both the congregation's children and kids from the surrounding neighborhood. As mentioned earlier in the congregational portraits, very few of Bethlehem's members live in the church neighborhood, which has a history of poverty and drug- and crime-related problems.

Bethlehem members repeatedly emphasized their church's mission and outreach orientation. They were proud that in 1995 the congregation had decided to remodel the church building, expanding facilities for outreach-oriented activities, rather than relocate to a more suburban neighborhood. And they were proud of the congregation's Food Bank, its neighborhood kids' night, the Family Growth Center located in the basement, the church's previous participation in a rotating homeless shelter, and its sponsorship of a refugee family from Southeast Asia.

I was initially quite startled to discover that, according to survey data, no significant difference existed between Bethlehem people and the other Protestants in their levels of involvement in mission work (including local, national, or international outreach). I reviewed my observations on outreach at Bethlehem. While Bethlehem's outreach activities were extraordinary, they actually resulted from the efforts of a relatively small number of individuals, and there was much overlap in the people who were involved in the various activities. Many Bethlehem people generously gave financial support to outreach activities but seemed less prepared to give their own time. Later interviews with the pastoral staff revealed that while deeply committed to outreach to the neighborhood, even the pastors only knew a small number of neighborhood people. The pastors primarily received their information from these neighborhood "gatekeepers," and they channeled their support to the neighborhood by way of this small number of people. In addition, there was virtually no communication with other neighborhood churches in order to coordinate local outreach efforts.

These findings had practical implications. They suggested that efforts to expand Bethlehem's local outreach activities were not likely to be successful. The cadre of members willing to dedicate time and effort to local outreach was already stretched thin, heavily committed to other church programs. Quite possibly, new outreach activities could only succeed if already-existing programs faded out. These findings may also explain why the Outreach Board stood among the congregation's least active committees and had trouble attracting new members. It seemed to function primarily as a place in the church organization where groups responsible for existing outreach activities could give official reports about activities and funnel budget requests to the church council.

Another area of comparative survey responses also surprised both the Bethlehem congregation and me. In the previous chapter I emphasized the need for congregations to reevaluate their ideas about generation gaps. Particularly in terms of religious values and beliefs, younger members already in the pews of our mainline congregations were very similar to the older members, and the younger members were surprisingly active in their church's activities. At Bethlehem, the survey analysis not only uncovered an unexpected generation gap, but one that was both quite different than the popular images that pervade the media and unique among the congregations in our sample.

What is that gap? The oldest group has been less involved in the church's organizational life than the younger members. Along with Second Baptist, Bethlehem is a church distinguished by its extraordinarily high percentage of long-time members, who are, naturally enough, older. Of those 60 and older, 48 percent have been at Bethlehem for 40 or more years (compared with the 33 percent of the other Protestants). Even more striking is the proportional size of Bethlehem's core, which includes a whopping 45 percent of the church's worshiping community. Yet the older group, with its high proportion of very long-time members, is greatly underrepresented in that core. While those 60 and over comprise over 58 percent of the non-core population, they are only 36 percent of the core. This is reflected in the age structure of those currently serving as church officers. Among other Protestants, 22 percent of the oldest group serves the congregation in an official capacity. The corresponding figure for Bethlehem is only 11 percent, and at Bethlehem that oldest group has the lowest frequency of participation in church committee meetings. This lack of involvement in the organizational life of the church by the oldest age group is not a recent phenomenon. When asked whether they had ever been elected an officer at their current church, again the pattern at Bethlehem differed from our other Protestants, with the percent of the oldest group at Bethlehem significantly lower.

What explains this odd pattern? There are probably two key factors: the church's historical governance structure and the educational, occupational, and income gaps between the younger and older members of the congregation. Bethlehem's current governing structure is extremely inclusive, with a large number of committees and a church council that consists of two representatives from each standing committee. These representatives are expected to report back to their committees on the council's important discussions and decisions. They also provide the council with feedback from their fellow committee members.

This quite open and democratic system contrasts dramatically with how Bethlehem functioned until the early 1970s. Until that point, the Church Council was a small, all-male, elite group ruling the church with a heavy hand. The system changed with the arrival of Pastor Jim Schalkhauser and the passage of a new church constitution. I suspect that this democratization of church organization took place at many congregations during that time period. What is distinctive at Bethlehem, however, is that many of the then middle-aged members did not take advantage of these opportunities.

Why did Bethlehem's current older generation react in that way to organizational change when they were middle-aged? It's difficult to say; however, the survey suggests one possible explanation. Compared with the other Protestants, Bethlehem has a significantly wider gap between the oldest group and the rest of the worshiping community. In particular, there is a significantly greater social class difference between the older members and the rest of the church at Bethlehem than at the other congregations. This is evident in the unusually wide household income gap at Bethlehem between those over 60 and the younger groups. This is not an entirely new phenomenon, of course: among the eight congregations we surveyed, those with lower household incomes ($39,999 and below) are overwhelmingly from the oldest age group who are far more likely to be retired, on fixed income, and widowed. But at Bethlehem the percentage of the oldest age group in this income category is strikingly large: 63 percent as compared to 44 percent for the older age group in the other congregations.

For Bethlehem, there are some important implications of these surprising generation gaps. The oldest group remains vital to Bethlehem's church life, particularly its nurturing activities. While they may be less involved in the organizational facets of the church, older members are most likely to make visits to the ill, send get-well cards, and pray on behalf of those requesting it. Because of their strikingly lower incomes, however, the current oldest generation of members may soon be in need of some serious nurturing themselves. And because they have an unusually low level of involvement in the day-to-day organizational activities of the church, older members may find it difficult to inform the pastoral staff and the younger members when personal problems arise. Thus while Bethlehem, like virtually all other churches, spends much of its time and energy worrying about attracting new, younger members, it seems fair to ask if this worry bypasses a more pressing concern: Bethlehem needs new programs to minister to those elderly "nurturers" whose increasing age and decreasing income levels render them vulnerable.

CONCLUSION

This chapter has introduced the eight congregations that comprised our research sites. It has discussed some of the common characteristics of these churches but has also shown how each of the project congregations (and your own church) may differ in a wide variety of significant ways (e.g., in size, activity levels, history, and beliefs) from other mainline churches with which they otherwise have much in common. For the remainder of this book, each of the chapters will focus on one particular facet of a church's life and mission. These facets (such as worship and evangelization) comprised major areas of concern and anxiety for our churches, and probably for yours as well. The following chapters reevaluate the widespread but misguided fears attached to these facets of church life, and they suggest a more realistic appraisal of the true challenges you may face. I also try to show how your congregation can use its own unique identity as a tool or foundation for tackling these challenges. I will continue to employ a comparative method, generally beginning with an overview of sample averages related to the topic at hand and then providing in-depth comparative case studies. I hope that as you read you will compare our findings with what you know of your own congregation. I also hope that in reading these chapters your appreciation of the unique complexity of your church will grow, as will the number of new questions you ask yourself about your congregation as you plan for its future.

3

Congregational Organization

What Is Good for General Motors May Not Be Good for Your Church

THIS CHAPTER FEATURES THREE MAJOR THEMES: (1) THE ORGANIZATIONAL CHARacteristics of mainline congregations that uniquely distinguish them from businesses and most other institutions, (2) the consequences of lay leaders relying primarily on their work experiences and professional skills to deal with fundamentally spiritual and religious issues, and (3) encouragements for churches to celebrate their distinctly "noncorporate" values, or ways in which mainline congregations are—and should be—uniquely different from businesses and most other organizations:

- They routinely deal with the major joys and sorrows of life, from birth to death.
- They are truly multigenerational and kinship-based.
- They are truly full-service organizations.
- They require both professionals and volunteers to survive and flourish.

When it comes to the organizational issues they face, once again mainline Protestant congregations often ignore serious religious and spiritual challenges. Instead, they articulate fears, define problems, and adopt "solutions" that reflect the "common sense" or "bottom line" assumptions of the surrounding secular society. These diagnoses or fears (e.g., "if you're not growing, you're dying") frequently ignore essential elements of our Christian faith and lessons from Christian history, as well as encourage congregational leaders to avoid asking themselves vital (but potentially scary) questions about their beliefs. These are questions that could lead to profound changes in how church leaders live their individual and community lives: Does my Christian faith or my professional expertise form the core of my identity? What would happen to our congregation's organizational life if we consciously and consistently acted as people of God (e.g., asking "How would Jesus have made this decision or conducted this meeting?"), even if it that meant being truly countercultural?

CONGREGATIONS VS. CORPORATIONS

A post-communion prayer:

> O Lord, you have invested so much in us…
>> your flesh and blood, your love and forgiveness.
> Make us profitable, O Lord,
> that we might provide healthy returns on your investment.
> Then we shall truly praise you.
>> Then our thanks will return to your throne!
> We bless you now and evermore.
>> Amen.

From the pulpit, pastors often emphasize that their members should live out their faith not only on Sunday morning but also in the working world. This same world is frequently characterized as hostile to Christianity. Important as that message may be, in this chapter we suggest instead that pastors (and church leaders in general) seldom give serious consideration to another major challenge that we observed in many of our congregations: members bring their work experiences, skills, and values to congregational life in ways that subtly but seriously hinder, even undermine, the spiritual growth that comes when members participate in the church's organizational life.

The post-communion prayer quoted at the beginning of this section was offered during Sunday worship at one of our congregations. It powerfully underlines just how easy it is, even for pastors, to inappropriately confuse the conflicting values and practices of the church and business worlds, particularly in a society that idolizes those who know how to "profitably" invest their capital. In my opinion, the image of God as an "investor" in humanity contradicts a conception of God as full of grace, a Supreme Being who freely and abundantly loves humans regardless of their merit, despite the disturbing frequency with which we fail to respond "profitably" to the grace we have been offered.

If God is an investor, he is a foolish, even insane one, and would have long ago gone bankrupt waiting for "healthy returns" on his investments. By corporate (and prevailing American) standards, God is a supremely incompetent C.E.O. In a world in which "being a real professional" is one of the highest compliments you can pay someone, God is almost criminally amateurish as an investor. During the Christmas season, we may root for George Bailey's bank management style to triumph in *It's a Wonderful Life*, but for most of the year it's the Mr. Potters of the world who are lionized by the American media, appear on the cover of *Time*, and write best-selling how-to-be-successful books.

This liturgical example of the complex and often unnoticed importing of corporate values into congregational life is even more striking because the pastor who offered the prayer is one of the most spiritually serious and thoughtful church leaders I know. Moreover, his sermons regularly emphasize—and his daily actions embody—a lifestyle that directly counters what the prayer implicitly expressed.

Congregation Members Know Corporation Methods

As our research took place in and around major metropolitan areas in Michigan, it's not surprising that a good number of the people in the pews had been or still were connected in some way with one of the big automakers. Historically, one of the great drawing points of Second Baptist Church in downtown Detroit had been the close connection between Ford and one of its long-time pastors. A personal recommendation from the pastor went a long way toward getting members a job at Ford. For decades, the fortunes of our eight congregations have been closely tied to the health of the American auto industry. Hard times for the auto industry often bring hard times (emotionally and financially) for the people in the pews, and boom times frequently have the opposite impact.

The people in our congregations have filled roles in the auto industry from janitor to line worker, from foreman to middle management to top executive. At the time of our study, however, most of our churches remained solidly middle-class in education and professional background, especially the members under 60 years of age. For that reason, I'm going to focus on a particularly striking phenomenon—the way in which church members brought their professional experience to church life. When it came to the organizational life of the church, these members unwittingly wasted much time in their attempts to force their churches into the more familiar mold of their professional lives.

This is not to suggest, however, that your congregation's professional experiences are entirely unhelpful. On the contrary, members' professional talents can be immensely useful to their churches. One congregation had committed to a large building expansion, and a member with much experience in construction contracts reviewed the church's building contract. He noticed that the out-of-state architect had based his estimates on practices prevailing in Ohio rather than in Michigan. As a result, they were significantly too low. Warned in advance by the member, the church and contractor were able to avoid a potential disaster. The outreach program at one church benefited from the professional connections and expertise of its social workers, and its health ministries flourished with the aid of members who worked in the health professions. It certainly helped our congregations as well to have treasurers familiar with bookkeeping procedures and computer experts volunteering their time to put up church Web sites.

Congregations Not Consciously Viewed as a Business

Relatively few professionals consciously believe that a church is like a business. The pastor who offered the post-communion prayer was surprised and dismayed when I later pointed out what it implied about God. He had not given the prayer's content much thought but simply plucked it off a Web site when putting together the Sunday morning worship program.

In our survey, we specifically asked people in the pews to rate how similar or how different pairs of items were to each other at their current church. Among the items we paired with "congregation" was "business," and only 30 percent agreed that there was a similarity between the two. In fact, the only descriptors for "congregation" that survey-takers disliked even more than "business" were "a crowd of strangers" and "a dysfunctional family." In contrast, the images that people saw as like a congregation included "people of God," "friends," "a community," "a support network," and "the body of Christ." When we used wording to emphasize the organizational or functional nature of the congregation (i.e. pairings with "making a church work"), issues of scale predominated. The only image that received less than 50 percent agreement was "A large corporation." Approximately 70 percent or more agreed that the other small-scale alternatives—making a "family," "marriage," "small group," and "small business" work—were like "making a church work."

Congregations Unconsciously Treated as a Business

Despite these consciously held attitudes, in committee, board, and council meetings members frequently lapsed into forms of behavior rooted in their work life. These behaviors often seemed at cross-purposes with the mission and actual organizational needs of their congregations. This is not surprising. If members have no positive and detailed models of how a church meeting (a meeting of the people of God, the body of Christ) should operate (including what are the appropriate sources of knowledge and values to be drawn upon), it's certainly natural that they would fall back onto what they do know, their wide experience of meetings in the work world.

This may explain why church meetings are so irritating and frustrating to many people in the pews, especially the core members who spend so much time attending them. Aside from the opening devotions (if they occur), church meetings usually are not very different from what people experience in their work life. If anything, the meetings are less efficient: participants have little time to prepare and are already weary from a day on the job.

That lack of distinct differences between church meetings and non-religious ones is clear from the careful notes I took at meetings. I virtually *never* observed religious or spiritual principles or sources explicitly playing a role in the style or content of the discussions or in the decision-making process. I was struck by how seldom the Bible and God were even mentioned in these meetings. Although "W.W.J.D." bracelets were popular during our study, I rarely heard someone ask at a meeting, "what would Jesus do?" Sermons repeatedly emphasized the importance of bringing religious values to the work place; however, it was rare for congregation members (and pastors) to bring explicitly religious values to the daily organizational life of the church.

By contrast, a number of our congregations did spend much time and effort writing mission statements or visioning and developing lists of congregational goals. I applaud those efforts, particularly when they aimed to provide overall guidance for deciding whether the congregation should support a given activity. However, the low number of times that I saw those mission statements actually and explicitly applied in practice, in committee and council decision-making, for example, suggests that these statements do not begin to meet the range of organizational challenges congregations face.

One reason those mission statements are rarely used is that they are almost always generic and vague. That characteristic would become even more exaggerated if congregations followed the advice of one influential church growth conference and shortened their mission statements so that members could easily memorize them. This is one case where it is almost true that "when you've seen one [mission statement], you've seen them all." And, in practice, the vagueness means that someone can "spin" virtually any activity to fit somehow into at least one element of a mission statement.

It is true, of course, that developing a mission statement may provide a form of community building for those involved in the brainstorming process. But the high turnover in membership in many middle-class congregations means that currently active leaders may not have participated in the mission statement process, and so the generic end product may have little significance to them. This is also true of vision statements and master planning. Finally, mission and vision statements are very much a part of members' experience in the work world where they are presently almost *de rigueur*, and the contrast between those vague noble statements and the realities of daily corporate life can be startling.

What Are Your Congregation's Spiritual Goals?

Shouldn't a congregation's actions and decisions be rooted in its beliefs and spiritual goals? But what specifically are these beliefs and goals? These are difficult questions for mainline congregations, which generally pride themselves on being open and inclusive. As a result, congregations formulate mission statements that are the theological equivalent of support for Mom and apple pie. Frequently, statements in worship folders (or brief announcements by the pastor) that delineate who is welcome to take communion constitute a congregation's clearest public effort to define explicitly its beliefs—as well as its openness to variety in belief. Even these statements, however, are still typically vague and open to broad interpretation. I virtually never heard a pastor at a mainline Protestant church talk at length in a sermon about what he or she felt was the specific significance of communion, much less the meaning of the Apostles' or Nicene Creed, whose group recitation was frequently a regular part of Sunday worship. Our survey and spiritual life history interviews suggest that the apparent congregational unity expressed by all members participating in communion and reciting together the Creed or the Lord's Prayer does not necessarily reflect any real, explicit, and conscious consensus among members about the exact meanings of these activities or even about the range of meanings that could be attributed to them.

If this is the case in worship, it is even more so in organizational life where few attempts are made to relate the church's activities to its creeds or other religious principles. In each congregation there are, however, implicit, unwritten, often unspoken and even unconscious rules that delineate the type of religious and spiritual diversity allowable in congregational life. The rules are often negative, such as "Don't ask, don't tell" (Davie 1995:25). They powerfully influence what members feel they cannot say in church life or express publicly. They limit the types of knowledge, beliefs, and experiences people feel they can bring to the organizational (as well as worship) life of the church. For example, churches differ immensely over how much personal, spiritual experiences were voiced at meetings (even at Bible studies). In some churches, speaking from experience was commonplace; in others it was extremely rare or nonexistent. I knew from our spiritual life histories that even in the latter congregations, core members had had deep spiritual experiences, but perhaps they sensed it wasn't appropriate to express them in church.

Yet the conflicts that emerge in organizational life often reflect not only divergent professional experiences (e.g., social workers' vs. accountants' approaches to finances) and individual personalities but also underlying or deep-seated differences in religious beliefs, backgrounds, and experiences. As noted earlier, these were seldom if ever explicitly articulated in the meetings. Most of the time they were left unsaid. In some rare congregations with many long-term members, people might have felt they knew about each other's religious backgrounds, so it became unnecessary to restate them publicly. But our congregations' rates of turnover in membership generally precluded people in the pews from making such an assumption. In fact, one reason we conducted spiritual life history interviews was because we needed to learn more about our congregational participants and their unexpressed beliefs in order to understand better what was going on in meetings—especially tension-filled ones.

In sum: in meetings members usually don't express their own religious views openly, and the congregation seldom if ever articulates any set of group beliefs that can be directly connected to the decision-making process. Nor does the congregation generally express what beliefs should provide the appropriate foundation or basis for decision-making. It's not surprising, then, that meetings don't strike most participants as religious experiences or opportunities for spiritual growth. Rather, most of us see them as simply business that has to be done. Why do we avoid or ignore these opportunities to witness to our Christian beliefs when we participate in our congregation's organizational life? Why do we accept or even welcome what amounts to a taboo? Whatever the reasons may be, this pervasive taboo raises a series of troubling questions.

- Can you really claim to be a seriously inclusive congregation when "don't ask, don't tell" is the basis of your diversity? Doesn't that make the line between mutual tolerance and mutual ignorance a very thin one, and one that is clearly not based on mutual understanding (let alone agreement)?

- If the spiritual and religious principles on which your church's daily life are actually based remain unstated (beyond vague mission statements), can you consciously, as a group, reflect on them, making them a matter of ongoing, serious discussion and prayer?
- If these principles and practices are left unstated, how can you expect new members to learn them, except through a long process of osmosis?
- Given the typically high membership turnover in mainline congregations, can you expect your church to develop any sense of continuity if you don't articulate your faith community's basic principles and practices (which may include the sanctity of keeping religious beliefs private)?
- As should be clear by now, a real challenge facing many congregations is not fear of change or lack of interest in change but an obsession with change for the sake of change. Without any serious and explicit basis of conscious religious and spiritual principles and practices on which to decide about appropriate changes for your church, congregations move like ships without rudders, lurching from one short-term set of fashionable changes to another rather than following a serious, well-mapped, and long-term course of change.
- Given the rapid turnover of pastoral staff, isn't the lack of a well-articulated set of religious and spiritual principles guiding congregational life a real danger to serious lay leadership and the priesthood of all believers? Put differently, doesn't this suggest that an incoming (and often transitory) pastor can feel free to mold the church to fit his or her own principles and practices? And isn't it less likely that even the most well-intentioned pastoral candidate will be able to decipher how and *why* you operate on a daily basis as a faith community? The short-term nature of most self-studies (and the natural desire of congregations not to remain long without a pastor) rarely provides the opportunity to produce a document that can express these truly important dimensions of your church's life.
- If your congregation is first and foremost a religious and spiritual community, do you want people to join it when they can't know what they're joining? For this is what's happening when people join a church that doesn't really know what it believes and that can't articulate the relation of its daily organizational practices to religious beliefs and principles.

FUNDAMENTAL DIFFERENCES
BETWEEN CONGREGATIONS AND CORPORATIONS

So far in this chapter, we've seen that a variety of fears (e.g., our anxiety about moving beyond our professional- or career-based definitions of who we are as people) contribute to the mainline Protestant tendency to unconsciously adopt corporate models for our communal life together. We've also seen how problematic it can be to transplant a corporate worldview onto a congregation. Indeed, doing so can actually *keep* us from being relevant and productive because it prevents us from thinking carefully about our core values: what we believe, how our spiritual values shape our congregational activities, and so on. Having provided these critical observations about the differences between the organizational and spiritual lives of congregations, what practices do I suggest as wiser alternatives?

I return to a main premise of this book: each congregation is truly unique in how it lives as a faith community. Instead of trying to be corporations, churches should be trying to be themselves: Who are we as a body of believers? What do we value, and why do we value it? If mission statements don't reflect the uniqueness of your congregation, then they are probably not a very effective means of spiritually enriching your organizational life.

Means and Ends are Both Important

There are at least two ways to encourage your congregation to honor its uniqueness. First, in the church (and in spiritual life generally) we should be concerned as much with means as with goals. Or, to put it more bluntly, we need to make sure that how we do things (the daily organizational life of our congregations) clearly reflects why we do things (our most deeply held religious and spiritual values). If the how doesn't match the why, then either we are not very clear on the meaning of our values, or we are not really committed to them.

After I made this point at a meeting of local clergy, one pastor commented that his denomination gave very little guidance for dealing with these issues. He looked instead to corporations for models for community building. I suggested to him that this was another example of people confusing two very different types of organizations. While it's true that the current trend is for corporations to adopt more humane forms of management or personnel administration (i.e., means), their goal stays

constant: increasing the financial bottom line. The latest research conducted by prestigious business schools may (for the moment) indicate
that humane techniques are more profitable. But remember the rise and
fall of Japanese corporate policies as positive models for American business, and realize that the next wave of business gurus (influenced by the
contemporary economic/political climate) may very well proclaim a new
paradigm for increasing the ongoing and constant goal of maximizing
profits. Then the more humane "means" could lose their rationale and
relevance for the corporate world.

Also, essential to this difference in goals and means is the way that
churches diverge from businesses in their time perspectives. The
congregation's ultimate concern should be its members' eternal salvation, but the corporation's is with annual profits. Henry Ford, that great
apostle of American business, fervently declared that "History is bunk!"
Older employees in highly competitive work environments soon discover
that what really matters is not past achievements, but "What have you
done for us lately?" Much of a church's life revolves around the study of
how God has worked in history, which should include the history of
your church as well as the events recorded in the Bible. In Bible studies
it's common for teachers to point out that St. Paul's letters often deal
with congregational problems as relevant to contemporary churches as
they were to ancient Philippi or Corinth. Thinking about the congregations with whom Paul corresponded can also help you view your own
church in a spiritually relevant perspective. Even those congregations
that Paul praised most highly in his letters no longer exist. Yet the demise
of that particular congregation as an organization (a means) does not in
any way diminish its contribution to making disciples, spreading the
gospel, and building the body of Christ (the end).

This confusion about the relationship between means and ends is
also seen in the newspaper and magazine stories that pastors love to quote:
scientific research has found that people who belong to a congregation
or pray regularly or sing in a church choir are physically healthier. Are
Christian practices just another way of reaching a mainstream cultural
goal—a narcissistic worship of one's own body? Is Christianity a new
spiritual diet fad? No. Christian practice should be judged by its ability
to reach a long-term result—spiritual growth.

Celebrating Your Congregation's "Noncorporate" Outlook

In addition to making sure both our means and our ends are in line with
our spiritual commitments, there is a second way we can honor our

uniqueness as congregations. We can first identify and then cultivate or celebrate those ways in which our churches, by their very nature, are not only different from corporations but actually better suited than corporations for meeting human needs in at least four central areas.

From Birth to Death

Joyful or tragic events viewed in most other organizations as interruptions of "business as usual" are central to the ultimate purposes of congregational life. To take just one example, think about the unique significance of illness and death for congregational life.

From the bottom line perspective of a business, employee illness and death are expensive and inconvenient. When a member is sick or dies, a mainline congregation also has practical concerns: a women's circle needs to arrange for meals to be delivered to a family with a loved one in the hospital, or the altar guild must prepare the sanctuary for a funeral. For a church, however, serious illness and death are also riveting spiritual dramas, and active participation in a congregation virtually guarantees that a member will be regularly absorbed in them. This is such an important characteristic of church life that I will devote an entire chapter to a series of vital but seldom asked questions: When bad things happen to the good people in your pews, how does your congregation respond? How does your congregation nurture its members? We shall see that your congregation's unique nurturing style is integrally connected with virtually every other facet of your church's life as a faith community.

Multigenerational and Kinship Based

In America, where can you find people of every age regularly gathered together? In church, on a Sunday morning. Outside the home, where can a whole family be actively involved and kinship ties play a major role? In church, throughout the week. In their concern over relatively small numbers of younger members, churches often forget that, in comparison to virtually any other organization, mainline congregations are truly multigenerational.

The multigenerational character of a congregation should not be judged solely or even primarily on the proportion of its members from various age groups. The crucial measure is the degree of serious involvement people of different generations in the congregation have in each others' lives. Some quick ways to assess this involvement: Observe who socializes with whom during fellowship or who shares a table during a Lenten meal. Visit the Sunday school or vacation Bible school and take note of the teachers' ages. Look at the members of a church circle or the composition of a church committee. More difficult to observe but worth pondering: who telephones whom to inquire about their health?

Closely related to the multigenerational nature of a congregation is its kinship character. While churches often *metaphorically* describe themselves as a family, they are also, quite literally, composed of actual families. The vast majority of members are married with children. Members have to be understood not only as individuals but also as husbands, wives, mothers, fathers, and children, not to mention in-laws, grandparents, grandchildren, uncles, aunts, and cousins of other members.

Long-time members are reminded of kinship's vital role in church life each week at Sunday worship. Glancing around the sanctuary, they see the same pews regularly occupied by groups of relatives. They notice when an upcoming marriage between younger members of the congregation prompts a rearrangement of seating as families soon to be united as in-laws move closer to each other in the sanctuary.

Family ties can make a church feel like a small rural village. The same warning I received in a tiny Finnish community was offered as advice in one of the congregations, "Don't say anything bad about anyone in the congregation because the person you're talking with could be a relative of the individual you just criticized."

As in a village, kinship ties can divide as well as unify a church community. If one person is offended by a decision made by the church council or the pastor, other family members may find themselves drawn into the dispute. A change in kinship relationships can have serious repercussions for the church, as when a bitter divorce has an immediate impact on the youth and music programs in which both ex-spouses had been deeply involved.

Pastors, like the rest of the congregation, are usually married. The roles their spouses choose to play in the church can add further complexities to the faith community. In some cases, spouses actively engage in a whole array of church activities; in others, they are only marginally involved. In either case, they can become targets for sharp criticism. And when a pastor gets divorced, the event can split a church, especially when the spouse is also deeply involved in the congregation.

Full Service Organizations

Even the most diversified corporations cannot offer the wide range of services our churches provide. Congregations are centers for spirituality, prayer, and worship, but also for education, music, sports, fellowship, counseling, health, hobbies, and outreach. At one officers' retreat, the discussions seemed sharply self-critical, focused on what the church wasn't doing. The pastor, however, suggested a different tack: list all the activities we already offer. Even these deeply committed volunteers were surprised at the range and variety of existing programs in their congregation.

Most of our churches offer a wide range of programs, and very seldom are they unique to that congregation. However, each church is unique in the activities it emphasizes or views as central to its identity. All the congregations, for example, had music programs, but there is something special about the identity of a church where the associate pastor is also director of music, the congregation stages musicals, and weekly Bible studies discuss the history of the denomination's hymnal. Most of our churches had an active outreach program, but members of one congregation viewed theirs as the church's hallmark. In its oral history, this congregation's defining moment became the decision to expand on the current site (with increased facilities for neighborhood groups) rather than rebuild in suburban areas where the majority of its members now live.

Both Professional and Volunteer

In terms of volunteerism, today's mainline Protestant churches are probably better off per capita than in the "good old days." Our survey found that members are typically more involved in their church than their most religious parents had been. This is welcome news; however, some complex organizational challenges arise as a direct consequence of our congregations' success in recruiting deeply committed volunteers.

Congregations rely on a sometimes bewildering combination of volunteers and professionals to operate their programs. Professionals run the gamut from full-time to part-time, from the highly credentialed to the noncredentialed. Volunteers range from the very occasional to the absolutely dedicated. Considering the salaries some part-time staff receive, the borderline between paid professional and dedicated volunteer may be difficult to establish.

Our churches significantly differed in the degree to which active leadership in key areas was exercised by volunteers as opposed to paid staff. Most of our churches, for example, offer a variety of Bible study opportunities, with some classes led by pastoral staff and others by volunteers. These same churches part ways, however, over how much expertise and effort the volunteer leaders bring to their teaching responsibilities. Leadership for lay-led Bible studies rotates regularly in some churches, and responsibilities are minimal. The leader for a particular session generally looks over the study guide in advance and tries to stimulate discussion.

But in other congregations, adult Bible studies are led by volunteers who have taught the class for decades and carefully prepare each lesson.

In one congregation, few, if any, volunteers appear when a call goes out for help in cleaning up the church grounds; in another, retired men regularly mow the church's lawn and weed its flowerbeds. They also set up tables for funeral luncheons, install new towel dispensers, and repair broken railings—chores normally assigned to a paid janitorial staff.

At one congregation, the associate pastor and two part-time, paid employees are responsible for the bulk of administrative and leadership duties for the children's education program. At another church with an even larger children's program, the associate pastor relies on several long-time volunteers to cover many of those same responsibilities.

No particular mix of volunteer and professional leadership is inherently better than another. But reliance on a mix of volunteer and paid staff presents some difficult organizational challenges. These seldom get the attention they deserve, especially considering how often they cause serious problems.

Volunteers must be handled quite differently than paid staff since they are motivated by something other than money. A church will wither if its volunteers don't enjoy what they do and feel appreciated. That's obvious, but it is easy to overlook the consequences for your congregation.

No matter how much a pastor or church council supports an activity, if it doesn't attract committed volunteers, it will fail. One pastor felt that his church's outreach and evangelization efforts would be strengthened if the congregation had its own van (to transport neighborhood children to church programs). Although firmly committed to community outreach, the church council raised a bevy of practical objections whenever the van issue arose: what about insurance liability, maintenance costs, and storage space? The major roadblock was more fundamental; no well-known, well-connected, and highly respected congregation member was willing to put in the effort necessary to find satisfactory answers to these questions raised and to take responsibility for guiding a van-purchase proposal through the church governance system.

Why a well-known, well-connected, and highly respected volunteer? That type of volunteer is as necessary a prerequisite for a new program to be successfully adopted as the support of a pastor. For example, parish nurse programs became increasingly popular during the period of our study. In two congregations where the program had been successfully implemented, the parish nurses were well-known, well-connected, and highly respected long-term members of the parish. This proved particularly crucial in one church, where the parish nurse eventually became a paid, part-time member of the staff.

Although many practical questions could have been raised about the position, it passed with virtually no public opposition because members knew who the parish nurse would be. The congregation trusted her judgment and commitment. They had faith in the program because they had faith in her. This same issue, however, can be viewed from another perspective. If many serious objections had been raised, or if the program had been rejected by the church council, it would have produced a major crisis: failure to support the program would have infuriated the woman's many close friends in the church.

As a paid staff member, this parish nurse became the kind of hybrid church professional on whom churches increasingly depend and who pose greater organizational challenges to the congregation than do pure volunteers and pure professionals. She is a "homegrown" church professional. She was a long-time congregation member who only became interested in the parish nurse concept (and began training in that specialization) after a long and successful nursing career with local hospitals and the county government. She insisted that the parish nurse be a paid member of the pastoral staff not because she needed the money but in order to affirm for herself and her eventual successor that it stood as a professional position.

A variation of this pattern emerged when two other individuals became key paid staff members at one of our churches. They did not continue their previous professional career in a church context. Instead, as a result of the aptitude and the skills they displayed in their extensive volunteer experiences in the church (as well as their spiritual gifts and faithfulness), they eventually became part-time employees of their own congregation. In one case, the person went on for extensive professional training in her chosen church vocation; in the other, the individual depended on her immense natural abilities and occasional workshop experiences. Salary was not an important consideration for either of them, and both were zealous workers, putting in far more hours than they were actually paid for. They were great assets to their congregation. But each in her own way eventually presented the pastor and the church council with an organizational challenge. Budget and personnel decisions involving their areas of work could become highly personalized, drawing into the conflict family members and friends who were also committed volunteers. When budget and personnel decisions placed these two at odds with each other, the result was nearly catastrophic: bitter divisions erupted among the core members, and in a congregational meeting a major proposal advocated by the pastor and supported by the church council was defeated.

I strongly support these new hybrid church professionals and greatly admire the three people I have just described. However, congregations and church leaders spend too little time carefully and creatively thinking about the additional organizational complexities and challenges these hybrid professionals present and the broader issues that churches face because of their necessary reliance on volunteers for organizational and spiritual health.

CONCLUSION

I hope that this chapter has given you a keener appreciation of the complexity of congregations and sensitized you to the radical differences between a congregation and a business or corporation. I have tried to describe some basic features of the organizational structure of congregations. These features make congregations unique as organizations, and much of a particular congregation's uniqueness flows from its own peculiar mix of these features. Although such organizational features may appear obvious to you, congregations expend large amounts of time on counterproductive (often bitterly divisive) efforts because they routinely ignore them. Congregations are unique not only because of their complexity but also because they have a unique goal: the spiritual growth of their members. This goal should be reflected in their daily behavior.

Of course, few churches operate just like businesses. Some do make decisions based on long-term spiritual goals. Yet congregations lose a major opportunity for fostering spiritual growth among their members (and the faith community as a whole) when conscious attention is not given to basing the church's decision-making process and decisions exclusively on their religious principles. Aren't you more likely to apply religious principles in your secular business life if you see how these principles are applied in the business-like aspects of your church?

4

Denominations

Are They Dinosaurs?

DOES DENOMINATION MATTER TO YOUR CONGREGATION?

With nondenominational megachurches enjoying tremendous growth, very few issues facing mainline congregations today are more complex than their own denominational identity. Virtually all the denominations to which our eight congregations belong (and the mainline as a whole) have been undergoing long-term losses of membership, particularly compared to more conservative denominations and nondenominational churches. This trend has dismayed mainline denominational officials and led many prominent commentators to view denominations (particularly mainline ones) as organizational dinosaurs in the postmodern world. Once again, however, national or regional trends may be at odds with your own church's realities.

James Bielo, my research assistant, made the following astute observations after reading the responses of pastoral staff members to a series of questions about how they viewed their denominations:

> There seemed to be one giant paradox looming over the data as a whole. There was a general sense, throughout most of the interviews, that denominational identity was declining and that there was a struggle to maintain any such identity ("I think it's a challenge just to have an identity as a church...."). However, most of the interviewees (including many of the same people) professed that they had a strong denominational identity themselves. In other words, there appeared to be a common idea along the lines of, "Everyone is experiencing a decline in denominational identity, except for me and my church."

Unfortunately, local leaders are inclined to approach their congregation's denominational identity on the advice of national "experts" rather than on their own faith community's experience. This can become a self-fulfilling prophecy: the congregation neglects (or even consciously downplays) its faith community's denominational heritage, identity, and theology. This minimization, in turn, leads to the loss of something quite important, even precious, to many of the people already in the pews.

This chapter addresses a seldom-asked question: how much does denomination really matter to you? You may be surprised by the responses we received when we asked this question. I hope that by the time you've finished this chapter, you'll recognize, first, that the common mainline fear that denominational identity is outmoded and irrelevant (if not worse) is unfounded. In fact, you'll discover that the people in the pews hold very distinct ideas about the most important features of their denomination and feel a strong commitment and loyalty to their denomination. Second, I hope that you'll see that a mainline congregation's particular vision of denominational identity is a crucial component of its uniqueness and one of the most valuable assets it can build on in the future.

Denominational Loyalty

A decrease in the number of members of a denomination doesn't necessarily mean a decline in denominational loyalty and identity among remaining members. For example, Greeley's (1990:21-25) research suggests that the sharp decline in the percentage of Catholics attending Mass and participating in other church-related activities in the period a few years after Vatican II (particularly following Pope Paul VI's birth control encyclical) was primarily an exodus of those who were only marginally loyal to the Church. Our own more recent survey of four Catholic parishes found high levels of denominational loyalty. Catholics were asked to respond on a scale of 1 (not at all important) to 10 (very important) to the question: "How important is it to you to be in your present denomination, as opposed to any other?" The average response was 9. This degree of loyalty emerged even at a very liberal parish where harsh critiques of the hierarchy and the official church were commonplace.

In some ways, however, it's unfair to compare Catholics and Protestants in terms of denominational identity. Only 18 percent of the Catholics in our sample had ever belonged to a church of another denomination, while the corresponding figure for the mainline Protestants was 53 percent. So it's startling that the overwhelming majority of these Protestants say they place considerable importance on being members of their present denomination: their average response was approximately 8. About 66 percent placed a value of 8 to 10 on the importance of their current denominational affiliation (with 32 percent indicating the maximum value of 10). Only 7 percent of Protestants indicated a value between 1 and 3 (table 4.1).

Table 4.1

Importance of Denomination by Congregation

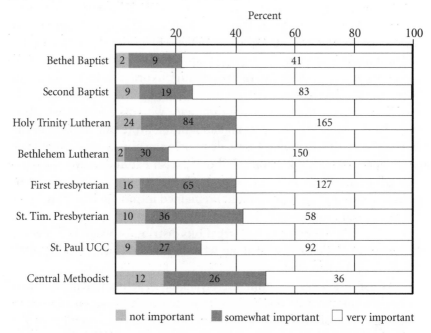

It is only fair to point out that the youngest group of Protestants places considerably less emphasis on denomination than does the oldest age group. The same pattern prevails among Catholics. This may be a function of the present stage of life for young people and not a reflection of how they will feel as they grow older.

Another Paradox: Loyal Switchers

So, here's another paradox: mainline Protestants routinely switch denominations, yet they are surprisingly loyal to their present one. An important clue is that the lively "circulation of the saints" (changing of denominations) primarily occurs within one family of denominations, the mainline itself (Bibby 1999). Very few of your present or future members have evangelical, Pentecostal, or fundamentalist backgrounds.

Does this pattern reflect an attachment to the mainline in general, in addition to an attraction to a particular denomination? If so, what do people find attractive about being members of mainline denominations? If you neglect or downplay your denominational or mainline identity, could you be alienating a significant number of your present members as well as eliminating a major attraction for the people most likely to join your church in the future?

In the previous chapter, I emphasized the serious consequences of mainline churches routinely taking a "don't ask, don't tell" approach to key issues of religious and spiritual belief. How does this relate to denominational identity? Are there spiritually significant costs to downplaying your denominational identity in order to be an open and welcoming congregation?

Take, for example, a striking difference we noticed when we compared a Roman Catholic Mass and a mainline Protestant service; in the former, virtually no attempt is made to help the non-Catholic follow or participate in worship. At one Catholic parish I studied, several people attending the RCIA training (Rite of Christian Initiation, required of adults wishing to become Catholic) remained intimidated by how to act in Mass even months into the intensive training program. By contrast, all our mainline Protestant congregations distributed worship folders at the services that clearly spelled out what to say and when to say it, when to stand and when to sit.

Worship folders are immensely valuable. Each congregation worships in a unique way, and many vary their worship style from week to week. Even a visitor from the same denomination (or a member of the congregation who rarely attends services) may appreciate the worship aid. But in their commendable zeal to attract new members by making visitors feel at home, mainline Protestants have a tendency to approach planning for worship as "liturgy for dummies" (i.e., assuming that the people in the pews are total newcomers not only to the church but to Christianity). One casualty of this approach is that you lose the opportunity to explore your denomination's rich historical and contemporary heritage of music, theology, and biblical interpretation with the regulars in your pews.

If your congregation does attract believers—or hires staff—from very different Christian traditions (outside the Protestant mainline), potential drawbacks can arise. One of the most destructive conflicts I observed during our study occurred when a congregation hired a music/choir director with excellent technical credentials but from a radically different religious tradition. The problems that quickly emerged resulted partly from her style of leadership. But her religious background also influenced her choice of music for worship, as well as her approach to the choir. In a short time, a music program that had been a source of great pride to the church became a center of bitter controversy.

Debate and discomfort are not necessarily bad for a church. You can learn a great deal from people with radically different religious and spiritual perspectives. Having firsthand experience with people who differ religiously but don't fit the caricatures that so many mainliners hold about fundamentalists or charismatics can help you notice some of your own spiritual limitations—such as a neglect of the role of the Holy Spirit. Members from different denominations may also publicly raise questions and doubts secretly shared by longtime members. But what's the best way to welcome such new ideas and new people? More to the point, how does your congregation's commitment to becoming welcoming interact with its commitment to its denominational heritage?

What's Our Denomination's Identity? We Can Tell You What We're Not.

Whether discussing forms of worship, interpretations of the Bible, or approaches to social issues, members often define their denomination's key features by contrasting them with their perceptions of how *other* denominations, religions, or ethnic groups believe and act. If "Who are we?" is the question, the response is often, "We're not like _____ [fill in the blank with the name of another denomination]." For example, when a number of our churches tried to establish or revive their healing or wholeness services, they felt compelled to reassure members that the services were not going to be like "what happens in those other denominations; you won't see people throwing away their crutches here!"

Catholics were the group with whom mainliners most frequently contrasted themselves. Catholicism remained a popular topic of discussion at Bible studies, retreats, and men's or women's groups. These discussions were often enlivened by critical comments made by ex-Catholics, of whom there are many in mainline Protestant pews. Earlier I said that 47 percent of the youngest denomination switchers were ex-Catholics, and 26 percent of the denomination switchers in all age groups combined were ex-Catholics. It was common for these ex-Catholics to play leadership roles in our Protestant congregations.

The other two groups with whom the white mainliners frequently contrasted themselves were evangelicals and African Americans. As we'll discuss in more detail in the chapter on evangelism, mainliners often compared their own reluctant and tentative approaches with the aggressive, hard-line proselytizing of evangelicals. Mainliners faced a troubling dilemma: how do you evangelize without imposing upon or embarrassing people, and without being stigmatized as a fundamentalist or evangelical?

White mainliners often contrasted their own staid worship with what they believed to be the more outwardly expressive forms of praising the

Lord in African-American churches. As with mainline attitudes about evangelicals, these contrasts could be made in the spirit of self-congratulation or self-criticism, with attitudes ranging from "thank goodness we don't do that here" to "I sure wish we did that in our church." I observed a particularly striking example of "worship envy" at one of the most liturgically conservative of our churches. The congregation held a workshop on worship and for inspiration they watched scenes from *Sister Act*. In the movie, Whoopi Goldberg plays a Las Vegas nightclub singer on the run from her murderous mobster boyfriend. For her own protection, the police hide her in a convent, where she teaches the nuns in the choir to sing with rhythm and soul.

Important Features of Mainline Denominations

In practice, many members of our churches describe their denomination indirectly or negatively, emphasizing how different it is from other groups. Do they also have more direct and positive ways to define their denomination? Are there significant differences in mainline churches' positive definitions of their denominations? Do the people of our two Lutheran churches, for example, describe their denomination in a different manner than do the members of the two Baptist or two Presbyterian churches? If they do, how much uniformity exists within a group; do almost all Lutherans, for example, agree on the most important features of their denomination, or does considerable variety persist within the group?

To find out, we included in our survey an open-ended question: what do you consider to be the three most important features of your denomination? A quarter of those responding to the survey did not complete this question. Perhaps too much effort was required to fill in an open-ended question. However, a surprising number of core members also had difficulty answering a similar question in the spiritual life history interviews. I believe it's safe to assume that a substantial proportion of the 25 percent of survey respondents who failed to answer this question either couldn't articulate their view of the denomination or (an alternative we will shortly consider) did not think of their church in terms of its denominational affiliation or identity.

At the same time, 75 percent of the survey respondents did provide answers, even in an open-ended format. What did they have to say? Table 4.2 demonstrates that Baptists, Lutherans, and Presbyterians do display distinct patterns in what they consider the most important features of each of their denominations. Baptists more frequently mentioned bap-

Table 4.2

People's Perception of Their Denomination's Most Important Features

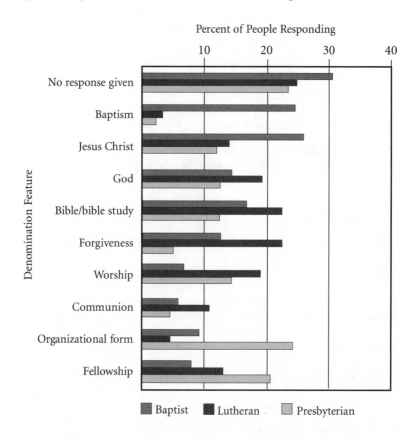

tism as an important feature, along with Jesus Christ and the Bible. Lutherans were more likely to mention forgiveness, the Bible, worship, God, and communion. Presbyterians tended to mention organizational form, fellowship, and worship. The quotations below are drawn from responses to similar questions on our spiritual life history interviews. They spell out what survey respondents probably meant in their necessarily more limited answers.

What is Distinctive about your Denomination?

From interviews with Baptists:

> "Following Jesus and baptism are commitments that go beyond salvation. [There's a responsibility to] membership in the church."

"We believe the Bible is the word of God, and we want to follow it as our main guideline. And we then we believe in…baptism by immersion."

"You have your own free will in speaking what you want to speak. You're not obligated by anyone, you have that free will. That makes me want to be a Baptist."

From interviews with Lutherans:

"When I think of Lutherans, I think of singing and I think of deep tradition. And the way that we go through the service."

"Justification by faith is important to me."

"I know that my parish emphasizes God's grace, over, and over, and over again."

"There's open communion. In the Missouri Synod the churches don't have open communion, only confirmed [Missouri Synod] Lutherans can go. But here anybody who feels the need can go to communion."

From interviews with Methodists:

"What I've known about the Methodist church is that it has a social concern, they have social principles which are adopted nationally."

From interviews with Presbyterians:

"I guess you could sum it up in *The Book of Order*. To me I always get a kick out of *The Book of Order*. Everything is very, very structured, you do it this way, or this way."

"Democratically organized and administered."

Denominational differences are also clarified by responses to other survey questions. For example, the official Lutheran position on communion diverges from those of the other denominations represented in our congregations. This showed up when we asked people to indicate their level of agreement or disagreement with statements about how they feel when taking communion. The Lutherans, in accordance with that church's official position, were significantly higher (55% vs. 28%) than any other Protestants in this study in agreeing they "feel that Jesus' actual body enters into me." Lutherans also were significantly higher in their agreement that communion "is essential to my salvation" and that when taking communion "I feel close to my family."

In their responses to survey questions about the Bible, prayer, and the existence of evil, the two American Baptist congregations differed significantly from the Lutherans and the Presbyterians. Seventy-four percent of the Baptists agreed with the statement, "When I have a problem in my life, I often turn to the Bible." The corresponding figure for other Protestants was 47 percent. Over 50 percent of the Baptists agreed that, "The Holy Spirit guides where I will read in the Bible," as compared with 28 percent of other Protestants. The Baptists were also significantly more likely to consider the Bible to be historically accurate and a reliable guide to the future. Seventy-five percent of the Baptists agreed that the book of "Genesis provides an accurate description of creation," compared with 47 percent of other Protestants.

Even more striking was the Baptists' understanding of the book of Revelation. Over 60 percent of them agreed that, "The book of Revelation is a reliable guide for recognizing the end time." The corresponding figure for other Protestants was approximately 25 percent. In fact, most of our churches normally avoided discussing the book of Revelation. I heard lots of moans and groans from circle members when the coming millennium prompted leaders to make the book a topic for their Bible studies. When, for the same reason, a number of other adult education classes dealt with the book of Revelation, the teachers emphasized that it must be understood metaphorically and symbolically—not literally. At First Presbyterian, the Bible study class viewed a series of videotapes featuring renowned biblical scholar Dr. Bruce Metzger of Princeton Theological Seminary. In *Breaking the Code*, a book that accompanies the tape, Metzger stresses that

> The book of Revelation is unique in appealing primarily to our imagination—not, however, a freewheeling imagination, but a disciplined imagination. This book contains a series of word pictures, as though a number of slides were being shown upon a great screen. As we watch we allow ourselves to be carried along by impressions created by these pictures. Many of the details are intended to contribute to the total impression, and are not to be isolated and interpreted with wooden literalism [1993:11].

At Bethlehem, the teacher of a Sunday morning adult forum deconstructed the popular *Left Behind* series, which is based on a literal interpretation of the book of Revelation.

Baptists were also significantly more likely than the other Protestants to agree with statements that emphasized the power of prayer like, "Prayer is a central part of my life," "I often get what I pray for," "Prayer is an effective way of solving problems," "I feel that I have been healed by the prayers of others," "I pray for success at work," and "I pray to obtain the items I feel I need." Nearly 80 percent of Baptists also felt that "God controls the details of my daily life," a statement with which only somewhat more than 50 percent of the other Protestants agreed.

Baptists also differed from the other Protestants about questions of heaven and hell or good and evil. Over 40 percent of Baptists agreed that "Only Christians have the potential to enter into heaven." The figure for other Protestants was approximately 15 percent. Just over 30 percent of Baptists agreed that "All good people go to heaven." For other Protestants, this figure was over 50 percent. While over 40 percent of Baptists believed that "sinners go to hell," fewer than 30 percent of the other Protestants agreed. Nearly 60 percent of Baptists felt that "People can be possessed by evil spirits," compared with just over 40 percent of other Protestants.

Recall that the two Baptist churches differ markedly from one another in almost every important sociocultural dimension. Second Baptist is an elite African-American church with many highly educated members. Bethel Baptist is a white working class congregation. That their members hold such similar views about key religious subjects, and in doing so differ markedly from the Lutherans and Presbyterians, strongly suggests that denomination remains a crucial and spiritually significant factor in their beliefs.

The patterns are complex, however. When asked about the most important characteristic of their denomination, no one feature received mention by people in a denomination more than 25 percent of the time. And numerous members did not necessarily agree with statements reflecting fundamental positions taken by their denomination. For example, although 55 percent of Lutherans agreed with a statement approximating their denomination's official position on the "real presence" in communion, almost 45 percent did not. A quarter of the other Protestants agreed with a "real presence" statement that stood at odds with their denominations' general understanding of communion.

A Tale of Two Congregations

Before considering the consequences of these findings for your faith community, let's examine denominational questions from a different and complementary perspective—the individual congregation. At that level, complexities multiply. Once more, it's crucial that each of us understand our own congregation's uniqueness.

Denomination does matter. Presbyterians clearly differ from Lutherans and Baptists in their identification of the most important features of their denomination. Yet in terms of the importance ascribed to denomination, striking differences can arise even between churches with the same affiliation. At Holy Trinity Lutheran, approximately 60 percent of the people in the pews rated the importance of their denominational affiliation to be between 8 and 10 on a 10-point scale (with 10 being most important). The corresponding figure at Bethlehem Lutheran was over 80 percent. This partially reflects demographic differences: Holy Trinity is the youngest of our congregations, while Bethlehem is one of our churches with the highest percentage of long-term members. But that only begins to explain their distinct approaches to denominational identity. During spiritual life history interviews at Holy Trinity, core members repeatedly underscored the Evangelical Lutheran Church in America's (ELCA) ecumenical approach, its openness to other denominations.

> "The thing that strikes me the most is that it's really ecumenical. It really wants to reach out to other denominations and cross bridges, build bridges. . . ."

> "The ELCA is open as opposed to some of the others. . . . And it's ecumenical."

> "The ELCA welcomes other denominations . . . to take communion with us."

> "[It is] not as restrictive in beliefs as some of the other denominations or some of the Lutheran denominations. [It is] a church that welcomes all and a church that believes in differences among members."

> "There's open communion. In the Missouri Synod the churches don't have open communion. . . . But here anybody who feels the need can go to communion."

No one interviewed at Bethlehem Lutheran cited openness and ecumenical orientation as a distinct feature of that same denomination.

These responses are rooted in the histories of the two Lutheran congregations and the backgrounds of their recent pastors. Until 1976, Holy Trinity was affiliated with the Missouri Synod. The church left the Missouri Synod after an acrimonious debate that split the congregation and led to an exodus of some members. Members and staff have relatives who belong to Missouri Synod congregations, and Holy Trinity draws new members from people dissatisfied with local Missouri Synod congregations. At Bible studies and retreat meetings, individuals voiced anger and resentment at being denied communion at a Missouri Synod church (sometimes the one where they were confirmed) when they returned as part of a family visit. It's not surprising that for many at Holy Trinity, the ELCA is defined by how open and ecumenical it is compared to their former denomination. This issue virtually never arose in conversations at Bethlehem Lutheran, which had never been affiliated with the Missouri Synod and had few former Missouri Synod members.

Holy Trinity's two most recent senior pastors grew up in the Missouri Synod and were trained in its seminaries. First, the current senior pastor, Rev. Dennis Bux, was a student during "Seminex," an open revolt against the Missouri Synod hierarchy, and this experience became crucial for his religious and spiritual formation. Seminex was the Lutheran "seminary in exile" established by faculty and students who left the Missouri Synod's Concordia Theological Seminary in St. Louis in 1974 when the denomination's national leadership purged the latter of "liberal elements." As a Seminex graduate, Dennis initially found it almost impossible to obtain a conventional position, and his first pastoral call was as a "worker priest" (employed by day in a factory while he attempted to set up a new congregation). In 1991 Dennis wrote a paper on the biblical experience of exile.

Second, Holy Trinity's much-loved, long-term pastor, who retired just before our study commenced, was deeply committed to an ecumenical approach as well. An ecumenical conference was the setting for one of his life's turning points; he broke with his upbringing and training by sharing communion with pastors from outside the Missouri Synod. For years, he played a major role (including a term as president) in a broadly ecumenical organization, Psychological Studies and Clergy Consultation, which provided a wide-range of support programs for pastors and their families.

At Bethlehem Lutheran, however, the core interviewees emphasized the Lutheran liturgical heritage, which the core from Holy Trinity barely mentioned.

"When I think of Lutherans, I think of singing and I think of deep tradition. And the way that we go through the service."

"Other than that [the close personal relationship between myself and Christ], I've always enjoyed the services, the liturgy."

"Probably their services, the liturgy, the way they run things during the service."

"They sing a lot [laughs]. And the potlucks."

"I look at the liturgical services. The calendar of the year and how it is the same every year. I think of it as a lot like Catholic, but not Catholic."

Surprisingly, in most ways the liturgical order of the services is almost the same at Bethlehem and Holy Trinity. Both congregations rely heavily on the Lutheran "Green Book" for hymns, though both also occasionally use a more contemporary songbook. Bethlehem, however, is a singing church. Its long-term senior pastor is a musician with a powerful singing voice. During Bethlehem's 75 years, little turnover has occurred among the directors of the senior choir, who have almost always been long-time members of the church. Holy Trinity's choir directors have changed regularly and were often outsiders.

DISTINGUISHING BETWEEN CONGREGATION AND DENOMINATION

Obviously, a congregation's approach to denominational identity is closely tied to its unique local, historical experience. I suspect that in their responses to denomination questions in the survey and spiritual life history interviews, some people did not differentiate between their denomination and their congregation. These folks seemed to describe their own congregation's most important characteristics when answering questions about denomination, not realizing that what attracted them to their local congregation frequently derives from its denominational heritage. In the spiritual life history interviews, one colleague observed,

> Many of the people for whom denomination was not important said that what was important was they would feel comfortable in the congregation they joined [if they needed to switch churches because of a move], or that it had a similar worship, liturgy, beliefs, or organization to the church they were presently in. These people frequently expressed a strong loyalty to their particular congregation, saying if they had to change churches, they would look for a similar congregation in any denomination.

In other words, while denying the importance of denomination, they would look for a congregation that had many of the same features as their present church—including those features rooted in their church's denominational background.

REGIONAL VS. NATIONAL DENOMINATION ISSUES

There is an additional wrinkle in the multifaceted relationship between mainliners and their denominations. Attitudes toward their denomination might vary depending on whether they were discussing regional or national organizations (e.g., the synod or presbytery) or describing a denominational ethos (a more general approach to religion and spirituality).

The Presbyterians were unique in how much they explicitly identified their denomination in organizational terms. On the survey, nearly a quarter of the Presbyterians included organizational form as one of the three most important features of their denomination. This sharply contrasts with the Baptists, who mentioned it less than 10 percent of the time, and with the Lutherans, who included organization as an important denominational feature less than 5 percent of the time. The Presbyterians' strong views on their denomination's organizational identity are spelled out in the spiritual life history interviews:

> "I guess you could sum it up in *The Book of Order.* To me I always get a kick out of *The Book of Order.* Everything is very, very structured. You do it this way, or this way. The process."

> ". . . the type of government, in that you do have some central governmental control, but yet it's a very congregational faith."

> "Democratically organized and administered."

> "That there are a lot of places, both within the hierarchy and at a local level, that they can become involved."

> "It's a very structured church, very hierarchical."

> "The self-governing portion of it."

> "The way committees are formed and the way they meet."

> "It's a democratic kind of government where no one is considered infallible and where no one is considered to be closer to God, if you will, than another person."

> "Committees [laughs]. Just kidding [laughs]."

> "One of the things that I really like is the representative form of government which distinguishes it from other reformed faiths."

Firsthand experiences with local-level denominational personnel influence a congregation's attitudes towards denomination. For example, the senior pastor at one of the Presbyterian churches was deeply involved in presbytery affairs and was closely tied to the executive presbyter, with whom he shared a deep interest in business approaches to church management. In addition, several congregation members served on presbytery committees, and one had been a staff member. Attitudes toward the local presbytery seemed to shift, however, when that senior pastor accepted a call at a much larger congregation. His former church found itself having extensive dealings with the presbytery's bureaucracy, which insisted on what many core members considered to be an unnecessarily elaborate and time-consuming process for selecting a new senior pastor. These feelings were intensified by the rocky relationship that developed between the "professionally trained" interim pastor and many core members. It's interesting that this interim pastor, who relied on the denomination to legitimize his career specialization, expressed even stronger positive feelings than the other staff about that denominational identity: "You know, I am a card-carrying, flag-waving, mainline Presbyterian. . . ."

At Bethlehem Lutheran, the attitude towards the local synod was clearly influenced by the presence of a congregation member who worked as an assistant to the bishop. Bethlehem's relationship to the denomination was also affected by the fact that a former associate pastor had come to Bethlehem after serving for a number of years on the denomination's national staff. When he took a call at Bethlehem, he brought with him and successfully implemented a number of programs and approaches (e.g., to stewardship) that had been developed by the ELCA on the national level.

Several pastors made it clear, however, that their own attitudes toward their local denomination differed from their approach to the national organization. In one case, this reflected the pastor's very critical view of the bishop. In another, the pastor had been disappointed with how little connection existed among his denomination's churches in his region. "At the regional level, they are asking themselves why they exist, what is their identity, and so they ask the churches what they can do for them and the churches say we don't know."

Moreover, hot topics on the national or regional levels—including feminist concerns over inclusive language and the ordination of practicing homosexuals—did not necessarily play a prominent role in the congregational scene. Even in churches with a significant numbers of feminists in the pews, for example, I was amazed to find God repeatedly referred to as "he" from the pulpit and in informal discussions without any public protest or even mild criticism.

There were exceptions, of course. Central Methodist was far and away the most politically active and socially conscious congregation, with members identifying the church and sometimes the denomination in terms of its stances on social justice:

> "But at least what I've known about the Methodist church is that it has had a social concern; they have social principles which are adopted nationally."

"In some studying of the history, I know that Methodists have been involved in some of the tough issues at the forefront of our society, [such as] the anti-slavery movement,[and] involved I think in some of the civil rights movement."

"I guess I don't think of Central as being typically a Methodist church, so it's hard for me to say. But what I think of being distinctive about the church I choose to attend and be part of and participate in and contribute toward is inclusiveness, both gender affiliation, I guess I would say, and race and diversity of various kinds."

At Holy Trinity, in contrast, a controversial denominational issue became divisive locally. After our study there was completed, senior pastor Dennis Bux voted at the synod assembly in favor of a resolution that would have recognized and affirmed "the blessing of...committed same gender relationships by pastors of this synod after counseling couples seeking such a blessing." Our survey had shown that the people in the pews at Holy Trinity were very conservative on this issue. It was not surprising then that some members of Holy Trinity became angry with Dennis for voting as he had. They felt that he should have consulted with the congregation prior to the synod assembly. From Dennis's perspective, however, the synod assembly was not primarily a legislative body, where he was obligated to represent the views of his congregation. Instead, the synod assembly was a worshiping deliberative body whose members were called together to vote their consciences.

Organization vs. Ethos (Theology)

Even when a denomination's organizational identity is of little interest, its ethos or distinctive approach to clearly spiritual or religious or theological issues may be vitally important to many pastors and people in the pews.

The people in the pews at Bethel Baptist gave the second highest level of importance to denominational identity, yet the pastor observed that:

There is a real lack of interest by the congregation in the denomination, too. As a denomination, the American Baptists started out to support missionaries, and we at Bethel contribute generously to American Baptist missions, to various other missions, and we pray and trust the denomination to handle that money well. And the people at Bethel don't give a hoot about the rest. We really don't do much with other congregations in our denomination.

When asked about how important his denomination was to him, senior pastor Rev. Dr. Turman at Second Baptist responded:

> To me being a Baptist is very important. Last Sunday my parents joined a non-Baptist church, but I was born and raised in a Baptist church. I have literally been Baptist all my life. *I think the doctrines are important*; unfortunately, they have been neglected by many churches. I wouldn't say that my convention is particularly important. I have more frustrations with my Progressive Baptist Convention [Second Baptist's affiliation in addition to its membership in the American Baptist Churches in the U.S.A.] than satisfaction. But as a denomination, *being a Baptist in the wider sense*, it's very important to me, being Baptist. I believe in the way Baptists do what we do. [Emphasis added]

The interviewer, Dr. Randal Hepner, then made the following comment to Rev. Turman:

> Sociologists are saying today that denominational affiliation is on the decline, that people are no longer thinking in terms of the old denominational identities that informed so much of American religious history.

Rev. Turman's reaction is worth quoting at length:

> But you see, I think though that's because pastors are not teaching well what it means to be a Baptist. And therefore if you're not concerned about what it means to be a Baptist, why would it matter whether you're Baptist or Methodist or other faith. Now for ministers who have taken the time to learn what it means to be a Baptist and think it means something distinctive, we understand and have adopted that way of life as a practice for our faith. But for our members, if we haven't taught them what it means to be a Baptist—that's why I took this time out today to talk with them [at Bible study where he talked at length about the baptismal ritual]—if Baptists can't talk about the meaning of baptism and its relationship to salvation, well who is going to talk about it? So for me that's an extremely important point. So I think, the reason it's [denominational affiliation] on the decline is because a lot of those of us who are in charge of making sure our congregations understand the distinctiveness of being a Baptist, of being a Methodist or Presbyterian, aren't doing a very good job.

Although Holy Trinity's core members emphasized the ecumenical nature of the ELCA as an organization, they simultaneously stood among those who most clearly identified what they considered to be a theologically distinctive facet of Lutheranism. Repeatedly, they underscored the concepts of grace and justification by faith.

> "I know that my parish emphasizes God's grace, over and over and over again."
>
> "I think the grace is so important in theology, and I feel very grateful to have that."
>
> "I would have to say that their belief that our God is a God of grace and that that's our saving. That the saving power of God is through grace and that this faith that we're given is a great gift and it is only through grace of God that we have this and that we are dependent on this grace from God."
>
> "A church, religion, based in grace…"
>
> "I think it's justification by faith."

These responses reflect their senior pastor's conscious and continuous emphasis on those facets of Lutheran identity. In his new members' class, he highlighted the core elements of Lutheran theology. The concepts of grace, justification by faith alone, as well as the Kingdoms of the Left and the Right were reiterated in sermons and small groups.

This pastor explicitly stressed the difference between organizational issues and identity. He was impressed by the general environment of

> … flux, shift to globalization, the restructuring that business is doing to be flexible. To learn from organizations that are downsizing, on my own I am reading leadership manuals, not necessarily church ones.
>
> I've learned in exile [his experience at Seminex] that the chief issue is how to maintain identity, which is a real challenge in our dynamic and pluralistic world of spirituality—everything Western, Eastern, New Age, etc. There is a need for an identity of a Christian who is a Lutheran that will help navigate life in work, family, and civic life. I can't anticipate what will be on the other side. The best way is to be flexible in organization but firm in identity. We are trying to firm up our identity as a Lutheran church.

By this time, I hope you've been convinced that the questions posed by the title of this chapter (Denominations: Are They Dinosaurs?) cannot and should not be ignored. Once more, I have emphasized the complexity of the issues and stressed that they need to be handled in light of the very unique historical and contemporary experiences of your own congregation and its members. However you may eventually decide to answer this question, I hope you now realize that it poses a crucial challenge to your church and that, spiritually speaking, a great deal is at stake for your faith community.

Above all, do not dismiss the importance of denomination to your congregation's future simply because some national pundits have proclaimed that denominations are dinosaurs. Such anxiety-inducing pronouncements may be completely false when it comes to your congregation's unique identity as a faith community. Furthermore, such fears ignore the quite real possibility that celebrating and exploring your denomination's theological or organizational ethos can foster spiritual growth in your current members and actually *increase* the number of people in your pews.

5 Pastors

What Should We Expect from Pastors? What Should Pastors Expect from Themselves?

THE EMPOWERMENT OF THE LAITY AND THE MINISTRY OF ALL BELIEVERS ARE BOTH ideals and realities in our eight mainline Protestant congregations. Nevertheless, pastors remain central and defining figures in the lives of these faith communities. Each of our pastors has a distinctive style of ministry and a unique, complex relationship with his or her congregation. So does yours.

Unfortunately, both pastors and their churches often ignore this uniqueness and establish foolishly unrealistic and spiritually questionable expectations of what pastors can and should do for their congregations. Pervasive fear of failure and envy of the "successes" of megachurch pastors lead too many mainline congregations to a dubious conclusion: "Our pastors must do what those megachurches are doing if we are to compete successfully for new members." Frequently the results are burned-out pastors and frustrated lay leaders.

In reality, many congregations already have fine pastors. These dedicated women and men can become even better pastors *if* their church leaders help them build on their already existing talents and interests rather than expecting them to be all-purpose "superpastors." Like their churches, pastors have long histories and multidimensional backgrounds that cannot and should not be ignored. If you don't know who your pastor really is (e.g., his or her religious upbringing, reasons for pursuing the ministry, and most firmly held faith commitments), you can't know who your pastor, together with your congregation, can become.

Finally, just as your congregation is not a corporation, so your pastor is not a CEO. Ultimately, the bottom line for pastors is not how many people are in the pews but how they help their faith communities towards spiritual growth and salvation. The pastors who are most successful in those ultimate tasks don't rely on a set of management and motivational techniques. Instead, they model what it means to be a Christian in their personal lives and in the leadership of their faith communities.

I hope you come away from this chapter with a deeper appreciation of what it means to be a pastor in a mainline Protestant congregation today. More specifically, I hope that by comparing your ministers with our pastors, you come away with a practical and *realistic* means of appraising and understanding your pastor, including his or her unique combination of strengths and weaknesses.

Surprisingly enough, realistic expectations are probably more of a challenge for pastors than for lay leaders. One of the greatest challenges for pastors is their frequent professional isolation. Their lives are usually so taken up with their own congregations that they have little firsthand knowledge of what actually goes on in other churches. And it can sometimes be difficult for them to share their professional concerns with fellow staff members in the congregations—who can be among the pastors' greatest sources of tension and anxiety.

I am therefore deeply grateful to our pastors for being so open and candid with us. I hope that they and their colleagues in many congregations will find this chapter helpful, even liberating. At the very least they will discover that they are certainly not alone in the frustrations they sometimes feel, as well as the joys they often experience, as a pastor. I also hope that lay leaders will come away from this chapter with a new sense of the complexity of their pastors' lives and the need to take this complexity into account when planning realistically for the congregation's future.

Before going further I need to emphasize that, especially in this chapter, I don't rely equally on descriptions of each of the eight senior pastors. The researchers in the project differed in terms of how well they got to know the pastors with whom they worked. In some cases, the relationships were very close. In others, there was more distance between researcher and pastor. When dealing with individual cases or case studies, I will be relying more heavily on the former situations, particularly on my own first-hand knowledge of the pastors.

How Congregations Feel about their Pastors: A Positive Consensus

All the congregations and key demographic groups within the congregations (men/women, core/non-core, and age groups) saw their senior pastors in a very positive light. Over 90 percent of those responding to the survey considered their senior pastors to be similar to prayerful persons, leaders, spiritual models, counselors, and teachers (table 5.1). Over 90 percent also agreed that their senior pastor knows the Bible, is a spiri-

Table 5.1
Protestants Agreeing that Their Pastor is similar to a(n):

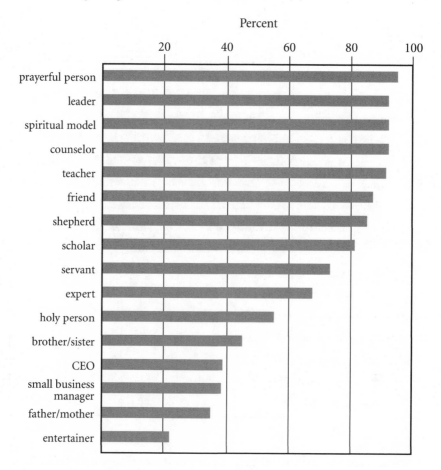

tual leader, and preaches good sermons (table 5.2). Over 80 percent agreed that their senior pastor made them feel included, was there when needed, and was like a shepherd to them. On the other hand, the people in the pews did not see their pastors as similar to CEOs, small business managers, parents, or entertainers. Less than 20 percent agreed with any of the negative descriptions of pastors included in the survey questions (e.g., pastor intrudes on members, gives no personal touch, resists changes in worship, only listens to some members).

Given the nature of our sample congregations, this result is not surprising. We purposely chose vital churches with stable leadership and numerous activities. However, even successful and well-appreciated

Table 5.2
Protestants Agreeing with Statements about Their Pastor

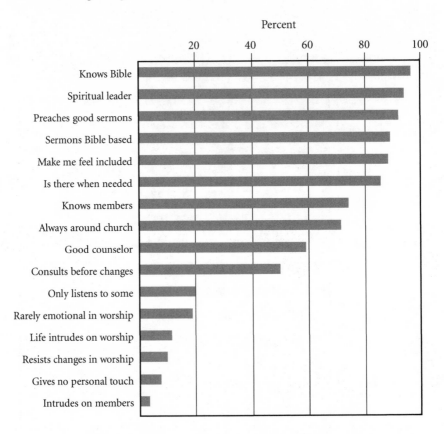

Percent

pastors face many difficult, challenging, and stressful situations in their jobs. How they handle these situations—and the positive parts of their job—is what makes each of them unique.

WHAT MAKES A PASTOR UNIQUE?

While our pastors are clearly appreciated and admired by the vast majority of the people in their pews, each remains as unique as his or her congregation. Let's look at some of the factors that make a pastor unique—the dimensions that affect how these pastors (and your pastors) deal with their congregations.

Some of these dimensions will be obvious, such as the pastor's gender or age or years serving the same congregation. Others we found equally crucial, though much less widely discussed:

- their own (sometimes changing) understanding of the role of a pastor
- their spouse's relationship to the church
- what they had experienced as pastors in their previous calls (e.g., before they arrived at their current church)
- the nature of their present church when they took up their duties
- their relationship with other staff at their congregation
- their family background (including whether they were pastors' kids)
- how and why they decided to become pastors
- their experiences at seminary
- how they were influenced by major national and international events they lived through (e.g., the sixties, the Vietnam War, the Civil Rights movement)
- their attitude toward denominational identity and organizational structure
- the crises faced at their present church

As we discuss these dimensions of pastoral identity, I will focus on several long and many short examples from the lives of the pastors at our eight congregations. My aim is to give you a deeper understanding of how pastors' backgrounds affect who they are and how they interact with their congregations.

A UNIQUE PASTORAL STYLE

A comparison of the scores for each senior pastor with the overall average evaluations found in tables 5.1 and 5.2 provided us with a quantitative profile describing who that pastor is in the eyes of the people in the pews. How well did these statistics fit with what we knew about individual pastors from spending a year interacting and observing them?

The people of Bethlehem Lutheran, for example, think very highly of Rev. James Schalkhauser, usually known as Jim S. (to distinguish him from his long-time associate pastor, Jim L.). Almost all of Jim S.'s evaluations on positive characteristics of pastors are above average. We learn what makes him a unique pastor to his church members when we focus on the characteristics where he scored well above the project average. Compared to other pastors, Jim S. is especially similar to: a friend, a shepherd, a brother/sister, and a father/mother. The people of Bethlehem Lutheran particularly agree that Jim S. preaches good and Bible-based sermons, makes them feel included, is present when needed, is always around the church, is a good counselor, and consults before making changes.

Why do the people of Bethlehem view Jim S. as a nurturing pastor with close, familial relationships to his parishioners? First and foremost, he is a long-term pastor. Bethlehem was only his second call, and he has served there for over thirty years. For most of their married life, Jim and his wife Joni have been at Bethlehem; many of their intimate friends come from the congregation. Jim and Joni's children grew up at Bethlehem, and their kids' church friends know the pastor as Ruth and Steve's dad. Jim and Joni's parents have also been active in the congregation. In fact, Jim's father, Rev. E. "Rusty" Schalkhauser, was an associate pastor at Bethlehem just prior to his retirement from the ministry.

When Jim and Joni first met, she had graduated from the Lutheran Bible Institute in Minneapolis and was a regional parish worker in Livonia, a Detroit suburb. Her job, says Joni, "was working with a pastor to establish a new congregation in a community, and I'd do a lot of door-to-door stuff and just help organize." Joni now works part-time for a Christian counseling service. She is deeply immersed in the organizational and spiritual life of the church. For years, she and Jim jointly led the confirmation retreat. Joni participates in the annual women's retreat, sings in the choir, and is active in a circle small group (both the choir and the circle are key groups at Bethlehem).

I never saw Joni assert any priority or privilege as the pastor's wife, and I never heard anyone complain about her doing so. People tended to sympathize with Joni. They understood that the downside to being their senior pastor's spouse is the amount of time Jim spends away from home. In fact, the people of Bethlehem agreed more strongly (85%) than any other congregation with the statement, "My pastor always seems to be around the church."

Although in a number of ways Jim S. is an introvert, he has also chosen to be very open about his personal and family life in a variety of settings. He regularly refers to them in sermons, and at the men's Saturday morning Bible study sessions he sets the tone for others to be candid about their own spiritual worries, concerns, and weaknesses. Many pastors refer to their family in sermons, but it often comes across as a gimmick to get a laugh, a technique. The people of Bethlehem know Jim and his family so well, including their shortcomings and weaknesses, that it would be foolish for him to try to maintain some elaborate, self-conscious facade.

Indeed, one reason the church has such a familial feeling, and Jim S. is often seen by his congregation as like a father or a son, is that when he has faced crises, the intimate and reciprocal relationships he and his wife enjoy with congregation members have allowed the congregation to feel comfortable nurturing and ministering to their pastor. Jim S. is understood to be a very strong but sensitive, vulnerable person; that is not seen as a weakness but as one of the strengths that bonds his relationship to his congregation.

Before comparing Jim S. with other pastors, I want to clear up some misconceptions that might arise from what I have just written. While open about his family and personal life, Jim's style is definitely not "confessional," lurid, or intrusive. In fact, Jim's parishioners at Bethlehem registered the lowest rate of agreement (5.1%) with the statement that the current pastor's "personal life and opinions often intrude on worship."

Pastoral Styles: A Comparative Case Study

Let's compare Jim S.'s pastoral style with that of Budge Gere of First Presbyterian, another long-term senior pastor of the same generation. Like Jim S., Budge had earned the deep respect of his congregation, having served as senior pastor for over 10 years. When Budge left First Presbyterian for another pastoral call in the middle of my fieldwork there, he made elaborate plans to ease what he assumed would be an emotionally trying transition for his congregation. However, his departure did not seem to upset the church's core members. About a week after the letter went out announcing Budge's acceptance of a new call, I discussed this phenomenon with David Noble, Budge's long-time associate pastor. David observed that no group in which he had participated had even brought the issue up. He had asked the congregation's office secretary what she had heard, and she also had said that nobody had talked to her about it.

David's own view was that Budge and he had worked hard for ten years to give the congregation the sort of self-confidence that would make such a departure easier. But David also observed that Budge "had been careful not to get emotionally hooked into the congregation." David quoted Budge: "I don't want to slime myself on them."

Clearly, Budge did not have the same type of quasi-familial bond with his congregation that Jim S. does. Where 61 percent of the people at Bethlehem agreed that Jim S. is similar to a brother and 48 percent that Jim S. is similar to a father, the corresponding figures for Budge Gere were only 34 percent and 26 percent (well below the overall averages for our eight congregations).

Budge's relationships with members of First Presbyterian were clearly influenced by the congregation's age structure; relatively few members are from his generation. While at Bethlehem Jim and Joni S. could have many friends who were their contemporaries, this was not the case for Budge and Anne Ruggles Gere at First Presbyterian.

Anne Gere's role in the congregation and in her husband's career also differed markedly from Joni's. Before I even met Budge, the local Executive Presbyter had mentioned that Budge's wife was a professor at the University of Michigan, one of the nation's leading research institutions. Budge brought this up during our first telephone conversation. Pastors often have pictures of their spouse and children in the office; Budge also had a copy of one of his wife's books sitting on his office coffee table.

Budge's choice of potential calls has been circumscribed by his wife's career. When she took her first tenure-stream position at the University of Washington in Seattle, Budge moved there without any job. He did eventually receive a call in that city, where he served for 10 years, initially as an interim pastor. The subsequent decision to move to the Detroit suburbs was clearly influenced by the job offer his wife received from the University of Michigan. When Budge accepted the call to a large congregation in St. Louis during our study, his wife continued to commute between Ann Arbor and St. Louis with no expectation that she would leave her position at the university.

Although I conducted research at First Presbyterian for several months before Budge left, I never met Anne Gere. But I learned that the congregation greatly admired her. First Presbyterian has a large contingent of loyal University of Michigan alumni who took great pride in Anne's academic position and accomplishments.

In all of his calls to be a senior pastor, Budge had arrived at churches in crisis. He describes how he approached his first call as a senior pastor:

> I tried to make that church the type of church I'd like to go to. I have my pet corn theory. You stay off my corn, and I'll stay off of yours. I listened to everyone.... E. B. White [the famous essayist from *The New Yorker*] talked about the "hen house." There is a group of nervous hens in the hen house, and one starts off and then all of them. They wanted a "non-anxious presence."

Referring to his recent exit interview at the Presbytery, when he had the opportunity to review his years at First Presbyterian, Budge again described himself as a non-anxious presence. Prior to his arrival at First Presbyterian, he said, "The way people got their way was to stamp their foot. You know, in a church, I don't need that." Budge had tried, instead, to be "as clinical as possible—honest too—but clinical."

Budge's sermons were carefully written out in advance, with copies (complete with footnotes) available in the church lobby. That wasn't possible with children's sermons, which involve dialogue with kids who are predictably unpredictable, and he was less at ease during those times.

Budge prided himself on his planning ability and his diplomatic skills; he once described his communication skills as "indirect." He liked to characterize his leadership style as "intentional." Even his conversation often seemed carefully thought out in advance, as though he were uncomfortable with too much spontaneity. In my early field notes I observed:

> It's clear that a number of the . . . things that Budge has said to me in the first two sessions were paraphrases or quotes from this dossier [entitled "My Work" that he had been circulating as part of his search for a new pastoral call], and . . . some are paraphrases or quotes from his sermons.

After Budge left First Presbyterian, it was evident from many comments by core members that they had often been aware when he had been carefully and (he thought) indirectly and subtly maneuvering them ("Budge's nudges") towards a particular goal. They just respected Budge and his judgment so much that they saw no point in challenging him. Perhaps unknown to him, Budge's motives and maneuvers were often transparent to many core members.

They knew that Budge's great strength was as an administrator. As David Noble commented, "It's amazing that he was able to administer this congregation into health. Usually if a congregation is looking for help, it turns to an inspiring preacher. But it's not [his] preaching; it was his leadership." Budge felt he had been called to First Presbyterian "to do two things primarily. One was to jump-start a program, and the second was to help the church decide how it wanted to meet its building needs." Budge made it clear to me, and undoubtedly to the congregation, that David and he felt they had already succeeded in fulfilling those goals. It was now time, he said, for "moving to the spiritual level...now we need to go deeper."

While many may have agreed that Budge correctly assessed where their church was and where it should go, they also probably knew that his strengths and interests did not really reside in those directions. Budge gave David much of the responsibility for those areas. And that is why it must not have surprised them when he accepted a call at a church not only with organizational problems but also with interest in a new building program and with a larger membership than his present congregation. In his understated way, Budge is an ambitious man, pleased to be called to a "tall steeple" church. In a typical Budge way, that same call also humbled him.

One of the most important lessons about pastors to be learned from this comparative case study is this: if you have been at your church for any extended period, the core members probably understand your character, including strengths *and* weaknesses, far better than you think or maybe want.

SENIOR AND ASSOCIATE PASTORS: A COMPLEX RELATIONSHIP

Despite their contrasting pastoral styles, Budge and Jim S. both had excellent relationships with their long-term associate pastors: Rev. David Noble at First Presbyterian and Rev. James Lichtenberger (Jim L.) at Bethlehem Lutheran. The assistant to the bishop who recommended Bethlehem as a research site described Jim S. and Jim L. as having "almost an ideal working relationship." Jim S. and Budge were the only two senior pastors who insisted that their associate pastors be included in our first meeting. Several other senior pastors did not even mention their associate pastors during our initial interview.

Nevertheless, the pastoral teams at First Presbyterian and Bethlehem operated in distinctly different ways. Clearly, Jim S. is the lead pastor at Bethlehem, but he treated Jim L. as an equal. For example, on the staff page in the Bethlehem Church Membership Directory, Jim S.'s name is listed above Jim L.'s, but neither is identified as "senior" or "associate" pastor. Jim S. and Jim L. are equally responsible for leading worship, and each preaches on alternate Sundays. In virtually all the other churches, the associate pastor plays a distinctly subordinate role in worship, seldom preaching, for example. In some cases, these were part-time associate pastors, but additional senior/associate interactions suggested that there was more to this division of labor than time commitments.

At First Presbyterian, in contrast to Bethlehem, there was never any doubt about who the senior pastor was. As the congregation's music and choir director, David was prominent in worship, but he usually preached only once a month. With overall responsibility for the youth programs, David often led the children out of the sanctuary during Budge's sermons. While Budge preached, David ran "the worship game," in which teams of children competed in answering questions on the liturgy.

Associate Pastors Jim L. and David have strikingly different skills and interests. Jim L. is a small-town boy (from Waldo, Ohio). He is also a sports junkie, in tip-top physical condition and ready at any time to shoot some hoops in the church's gym. The congregation expects that, in some way or another, he will work a sports analogy or reference into every sermon. David is a very talented musician, a graduate of the University of Cincinnati College-Conservatory of Music, as well as Princeton Theological Seminary. While a rabid sports fan, he might hesitate before meeting the youth group on a basketball court.

Jim L. and David do share one trait that probably explains their close working relationships with their senior pastors: neither is personally ambitious—except to improve his congregation. Each has a good deal of well-deserved self-esteem, but neither seems to hunger for personal power or prestige. Senior and associate pastors can become bitter rivals, each with his or her own clique of supporters. This didn't occur with Jim S. and Jim L. at Bethlehem or with Budge and David at First Presbyterian.

Jim L. had already been a senior pastor in a small congregation in rural Nebraska before moving to Bethlehem to be closer to his and his wife's families. Almost everyone in the congregation expects him to become Bethlehem's senior pastor when Jim S. retires. By then Jim L. will have served as associate for over 15 years. Similarly, when Budge accepted a new call, a good number of people at First Presbyterian wanted David to become senior pastor. When the Executive Presbyter came to talk to the congregation about the transition, he faced some hostile questions about the denomination's policy of not allowing associates to become senior pastors in their own church. David, however, had no real desire to become a senior pastor at a church as large as his present congregation. He knew that administration per se was not his strong suit:

> I have always loved to dream, and that's part of my personality. Myers-Briggs shows that is in my make-up. Detail work is not big in me. That's helped me to share with people. The other people in the congregation are good at details.

When asked how he transforms his dreams into reality, he responded:

> I have to be persistent and insistent. I'm politely insistent. I keep after them with much personal contact and one-on-one. I have to do it enough so that they know it won't go away. I have been getting braver in my old age. I put in all the classrooms a sign that said: "As an adult, are you satisfied with a child's view of God? Wouldn't you like to join an adult education class?"

A devoted father, David does not intend to look for a different call until his two children graduate from high school. When he does decide to move, it could well be to a very different type of congregation than First Presbyterian. In our first conversation, David remarked that "suburban ministry was harder than urban ministry." When I later asked him to elaborate, he commented:

> Because they are conforming, and conforming is why they've gotten to be middle class. I don't want to spank them, but open their eyes. Last Sunday I talked about divorce and other issues and what makes us different. It means that when it's lunchtime at school, you sit with the person who has no friends.... We have an evangelical message.... In [this wealthy suburb, where he could not afford to buy a home], there are many unchurched people. What are we going to say to them? How are we going to say it? Do we want to say that? How do we exist in a community? Do we go out to them or wait until they come to us? It's not polite to tell people, "I'm a Christian," but we need to do that.

In fact, when asked on our survey about their willingness to participate in evangelism activities, First Presbyterian's members are far and away the least willing to do so. David also commented that when he first arrived at First Presbyterian, the surrounding suburban community

> impressed me then and still does as a really well-to-do area where people are very comfortable, and it would be hard to be a minister if I were true to my vision of feminism and antiracism.

When David leaves for another call, it may well be to a place where he can be true to those visions.

In the congregational organization chapter (chapter 3), I emphasized the extraordinary organizational complexity of congregations. Having to deal routinely with the diverse demands of their jobs, frequently in an emotionally charged atmosphere with limited resources, can fray the nerves and try the patience of any pastoral team. It's not surprising that the smooth working relationships between pastors at Bethlehem Lutheran and First Presbyterian were unusual. Just how rare they were is underscored by the fact that earlier in their careers both Jim S. and Budge experienced rocky relationships with other associate pastors.

THE CALL TO MINISTRY

Budge, David, Jim L. and Jim S. share a characteristic with the other pastors in our study; their call to ministry did not derive from a single, overwhelmingly powerful, emotional, or mystical experience. Rather, it emerged from a pattern of undramatic but nevertheless compelling circumstances and experiences. The shapes of those patterns, however, were unique for each pastor and can be seen in their pastoral styles.

Budge describes his call:

> You're raised up from among the folk for having specific gifts and skills...and a specific call, and therefore the community recognizes that and nurtures it, and I would suggest that I was nurtured in my home church in New York, and nurtured by Christian believers, and nurtured by Princeton Seminary, nurtured by my congregation, even as I've tried to nurture people in their faith. And so, this has not ever been Damascus Road stuff. This has been a life—a person—who's tried to be faithful to what he believes and his understanding of the call of God.

During college Budge considered seminary as a possible future option ("the only questions that I really had were the God questions"). Nevertheless, he signed up to go into the Navy for four years after completing his undergraduate degree. After the Navy, he would decide whether to go to seminary or become a "Christian businessman." But an injury prevented him from entering the Navy. After a year of teaching, he entered seminary. Even while completing seminary, he continued to consider several other career options (including earning a Ph.D. in academic administration in order to become a college president) in addition to parish ministry. It was the dean of the seminary who precipitated his decision. "One night in February of 1970 I was having dinner with the dean of the seminary.... He said, 'I'd really like to see you in a parish.' I said, 'I'm okay with that.' He set up interviews for me with people coming through the seminary."

Our pastors' calls to ministry could involve pain and doubt, however, as well as moments of affirmation. Rev. Roger Dahlen of Bethel was divorced around the time of his graduation from seminary:

> I was single and so I just flew out to San Francisco, and I could just be myself. I worked at Radio Shack and got a bleeding ulcer, and this is my Prodigal [Son] story you could say. And, as I lay in my hospital bed, I said to myself that "I am going to die if I don't change." And so that is when I started writing some inquiries to different places, and one of those places was Michigan.... It was providential.... I was driving into Ann Arbor thinking, "Where am I going to stay for the night?" I looked up in the Yellow Pages the American Baptist churches, and I saw a name

of a former colleague of mine, and so I called him, and he set me up. It was good. I needed to clarify for myself what I wanted to do, and so I prayed about my call to the ministry and that is what I began to feel, called to ministry. And so my friend and others were able to hook me up with two very small communities back in Illinois.

There were at least two pastors for whom ministry was a second career, who attended seminary only after extensive experience in other professions. David Noble graduated from a major conservatory of music and applied for teaching positions. He eventually accepted his dream job, music teacher at a small, 120-year-old, denomination-supported boarding school where his uncle was the pastor of the congregation (and David became choir director). After subsequently serving as the admissions director for the school, David took a similar position at the school of music of a Midwestern university. For three years, he found himself caught between the university administration and the music school, both of whom "hated each other." He went to the pastor of his church for help in resolving a particularly stressful conflict:

> We spent a long night talking. The pastor had just had recent training in conflict management....He had an answer for me. We laid out a plan, and it worked....We talked more....I'm drawn to the pastorate. My uncle was a pastor, this other guy I'm drawn to is a pastor. I told him that I didn't want to be an administrator. I wasn't doing any music. He asked me, "What makes you happy?" I love being and working in church. I had been an elder in the church [at the boarding school]. I've always been a church person. He says, "Why not seminary?" And I'd never thought about that.

Rev. Anna Souto, the associate pastor at St. Paul United Church of Christ, has a different but not unrelated call story. She had been an accountant for 10 years, but "got tired of numbers and was exploring other careers." However, marriage and having kids slowed down the process. When she did return to college, she first considered a career as a geologist and then thought of pursuing a Ph.D. in medieval literature.

Although she had not been terribly active in church after high school, Rev. Souto had never lost her faith. Her return to church and her unexpected call to ministry began when she decided to take her kids to Sunday school.

> I didn't intend to be Sunday school superintendent. The pastor asked me. I guess he was getting to the bottom of the barrel. I decided it was

God calling. This was a growing time. It was an opening out time, though I didn't see it at that time.

It was then that she struggled with being a woman and a minister:

At this time, I was asked by the denomination to take part in the Ecumenical Decade for Women. This was a gathering of women from throughout the country. It was an eye-opener, five meetings with all these women ministers. I could see I could do it. God was calling.

The pastors described thus far were all actively involved in church while growing up. But for two pastors in particular, youthful immersion in church life went even deeper. Jim S. of Bethlehem Lutheran and Rev. Janet Noble-Richardson of St. Timothy Presbyterian were "PKs" or pastor's kids. Still, in neither case was the decision to become a pastor straightforward.

Jim S. is a third-generation pastor in his family. One of his sisters is married to a pastor who was Jim's roommate in seminary, which was also the same seminary Jim's father had attended. Jim grew up in a parsonage and, in his own words, "always had a feeling that being a pastor's son meant I had a role to play...to value the church and my spiritual life." Not being a rebel by nature, at first Jim went along with the direction he was being led. He recalls "playing church and thinking I want to be like Dad someday, but that changed. I'd say it changed during high school...I've always had just a keen interest in math and in scientific things, physics. To this day, I love computers and that technology." So although Jim went to a Lutheran college, until his last year there he actually planned to be a high school science teacher.

As I progressed through college, the last couple of years I really kind of got away from regular Sunday worship attendance....I'm not sure why. Maybe, it was just kind of a pulling back to kind of reassess, you know, things, what I really was believing and what my commitments really were. That turned around dramatically during my last year in college, and I've never been able quite to put my finger on this one either, except that I remember going to see a movie in one of the local theaters that had to do with St. Francis of Assisi, kind of his story, I think it was, and it rather profoundly touched me because I saw a deep spiritual commitment in that individual and I thought, you know, that's really where my heart is and I saw the kind of work he did and the way in which he was there to help people, to minister to people and I thought that's really what I should be doing. And so I changed my course. I decided to complete my work on the science degree because I was so close to finishing anyway, but in that last year of [college] I remember going home at Christmas time and announcing to my Dad that I was going into seminary. And of course, he was elated.

Janet Noble-Richardson is the only female senior pastor in the study. Her parents served as Presbyterian missionaries in Pakistan, and her family only returned to the United States when she was in high school. For Rev. Noble-Richardson the key question was not whether she would go into church work but in what capacity. She met her first woman pastor during her sophomore year in college. Prior to that meeting, she lacked any substantive role models. She considered doing a Master's in Christian Education at seminary, but her father told her she "might as well join the union" (i.e., become a pastor). Rev. Noble-Richardson's denomination had minimum salary requirements for pastors. But her father's main concern was that she wouldn't be able to baptize, marry, or bury the people she had taught if she didn't become their pastor. So her father became the greatest influence on her decision to become a minister. Rev. Noble-Richardson's sister has become a pastor as well.

In 1987, soon after graduating seminary, a congregation considered her as a candidate for interim pastor. Out of 21 members on that church's session or council, six abstained from voting, nine voted in favor, and six against. Presumably the opposition was based solely on gender as the members of session had not yet met her.

Rev. Anna Souto, the associate pastor at St. Paul, had a somewhat different experience:

It was a lot less painful than I thought to be a woman pastor. It seemed like there was little resistance. I'm sure there must have been some die-hards, but I never heard. Most of the women were delighted, and there were many churches in the area that had woman ministers. I never encountered any resistance because I'm a woman.

Like Rev. Noble-Richardson, however, Rev. Souto had no role models of women pastors while growing up. In her case, that absence proved to be a "big mental obstacle," and as a result, "God and [she] struggled for two years."

Obviously, coming from a family deeply involved in church had a major impact on most of our pastors' choices of profession. Yet several pastors had family backgrounds that made their eventual calling rather surprising. One associate pastor grew up in a non-religious household (his father was a "self-proclaimed humanist"). He only started going to church with a girlfriend who attended. Later he became more involved through friends who played basketball at another congregation. He was particularly impressed that what these friends

> professed about Christ was seen in their behavior....In playing basket-ball, I'm dribbling, and I foul someone. Where, if I'm on the street doing it, it's predictable there's a fistfight, they at [this church] just smile, "You'll hurt somebody. Praise the Lord!"

When I commented, "It's amazing how few of the pastors with whom I've spoken had lives that have gone in a straight line," this associate pastor responded:

> God has set it up so it's not a straight line, which is boring. I was saying to a young fellow whose father had died and all hell broke out, and he was doubting God, "It's okay. Once it's settled down, you'll see the hand of God."

One of the first times Rev. Dr. Geoff Drutchas ever considered a ministry-related vocation was when, as a five-year-old from an unchurched family, he saw the movie *The Inn of the Sixth Happiness*. The 1958 film is a "true story of an English servant who, despite her lack of credentials, realizes her dream of becoming a missionary in China" (Maltin 2002:668). According to Geoff, "The next morning I said to my mother, 'That's what I want to be.' The idea of being a missionary stayed with me, but I didn't talk about it in the family."

Not until Geoff was about 11 years old did his father became involved in a formal religious group, the Unitarians. In college, Geoff went through several "crises" over his vocation. After some senior year soul searching, he determined to proceed with plans to become a minister and began investigating seminaries.

"I wrote a letter to my father. My father [an engineer and inventor], in one of the few letters I received from him, did a cost-benefit analysis, and thought it wasn't wise." After receiving his father's cost-benefit analysis of the ministry, Geoff investigated the employment outlook for Ph.D.s in History, which turned out to be similarly bleak. Instead, he went to law school. After one and a half unhappy years there, as well as some time working in a law firm, he finally entered seminary. Harvard Divinity School had Unitarian roots, and after graduation he initially served in Unitarian Universalist Association (UUA) communities. But as a result of his increasingly strong Christian faith [which, beginning in seminary, had been much influenced by the work of Paul Tillich], Geoff found he had to "backpedal" a lot of what was important for him, his own concerns, when working in a UUA church. At one conference of UUA clergy, he was appalled at how viciously his colleagues attacked a guest speaker. "My response was [that this] was very unchristian. But many of them [his UUA colleagues] aren't Christians." He also concluded that

> The individualist emphasis [of UUA] had become obsolete. It missed the needs of our time. It was inclined to see people as victims of the environment and institutions. It was strongly anti-institutional. My feeling was we need to reconstitute institutions, not tear them down. Life of community needs to be in balance....You need to balance the individual and community. The UUA lacked any way of holding its own members really accountable. I began to believe that all of us need discipline, and so it's so important to have someone who embodies for us this discipline. This is, in part, at the heart of Christianity with the figure of Jesus.

So Geoff sought the privilege of a call with the United Church of Christ and subsequently became pastor at St. Paul.

GENERATION AND PASTORS:
THE SIXTIES AND SEVENTIES

The importance of generational differences among the people in the pews is often overexaggerated in the church world. But how significant a factor is generation among pastors? Almost all the senior pastors had been young adults during the tumultuous events of the 1960s and early 1970s. A number of them had been in seminary during the sixties, and those times had a strikingly powerful and lasting impact on their approaches to the ministry. These commonalities of experience have been filtered through the unique backgrounds and personalities of each pastor.

Pastor Ed Rowe of Central Methodist was the most directly influenced. He came from a strong union family on the east side of Detroit. He only became involved with the Methodist Church when his family "moved to a place that was a block away from a United Methodist Church, and the John Birch Society and Donald Lobsinger [a leader during the 1960s and 1970s of an avid and ultra-conservative anti-Communist group, Breakthrough, that vociferously opposed liberal groups in Detroit] were picketing the church.... And for whatever reason I thought, if Don Lobsinger and the John Birch Society were picketing the Mt. Hope United Methodist Church, there had to be something good going on there. I must have been seventeen at the time. So I started to attend Mt. Hope Church." Pastor Rowe expected to be a factory line worker, but the

pastor of Mt. Hope had other plans for him. Eventually he went to seminary in Chicago:

> [When Rev. Martin Luther King, Jr. was killed in 1968,] I was an intern
> on the west side of Chicago at Olivet United Methodist Church with
> an African-American pastor by the name of Ulysses Dobbs. And then
> the riots hit, and some brother jumped in the car with a gun intent to
> kill him [Ulysses Dobbs] because he had just married a white woman.
> And he [Dobbs] jumped out of the car while it was still moving and
> ran through a grocery store, went home, packed up his family and went
> to Iowa to teach black history at some college . . . and left these three
> white interns with this black church during the middle of this upris-
> ing. So, I think at this time I had some designs to teach, but I came out
> of that experience realizing that somehow or other that was not where
> I wanted to be; that I needed to somehow relate to the pain and the
> struggle that was going on in Chicago right then and all over the world.
> So, I think that was one not only traumatic event but life shaping event
> for me.

During the same time period Jim S. was attending seminary in Dubuque,
Iowa. But when I asked him about "any particular events that stand out
in your mind during seminary," his response similarly reflects the impact of the sixties.

> You know, what really stands out in my mind was not at the seminary
> so much as, again, what was happening in the country, civil rights
> movement...if there had been a way, I would have been probably march-
> ing in the streets, but nothing in Dubuque was calling for that [laughs.].
> Some of that took shape for me when I went on internship, which was
> in Blue Island, Illinois, the south side of Chicago. [It was] an old, old
> city...and the [parochial] school [at the church where I interned]...was
> mixed racially...and then things, of course, were happening on the civil
> rights scene in Chicago. I can remember Dr. Martin Luther King [Jr.]
> coming to town, and my wife and I going down to hear him. That was
> important.

The biggest change in Jim S.'s religious perspective during the college
and seminary years entailed recognizing "the importance of a ministry
that was not turned in on itself but was open to the world around it and
taking seriously the needs, the issues of society and community." He was
first called to a church in suburban Detroit, where, according to him,

> I think they would have been happy just being a country club, but the
> summer of '67 was the summer of the riots in Detroit and that spread

out. It leaked up into the Pontiac area even. There were problems up there. I can remember riding a school bus for a while with kids, trying to keep the peace there. So there were issues beginning to loom for us that said, we need to look at these things, we need to take a stand as Christians in the face of these things.

When Jim left for his next call, Bethlehem Lutheran, he did so because

I wanted to be in a more urban area, a more center city area than West Bloomfield, which I considered to be a suburb. I like the city, and I like the challenges and the issues that a city community presents.

When he arrived, Bethlehem also was

a very enclosed ministry. I mean they did nothing outside of the congregation. It was strictly an in-house thing. [And the church had little to do with the poor neighborhood in which it was located.] In some ways, for some people, kind of a country club thing because of the social connections. They went to Michigan State games together, and they partied together, and they did everything together, they came to church together and . . . that was it. Church was a place to be with their friends.

Jim made it clear from his first contact with Bethlehem that he wanted to move the church in a slightly different direction, "to become a congregation with a ministry with a society around it." He recalls, "I think they were at a point where they were willing to give anything a try just to get a pastor here." Initially he remained cautious. Eventually, however, the church developed a major food bank, adopted a Vietnamese family, supported the establishment of a neighborhood association, opened the doors of its gymnasium for neighborhood kids during the summer, and periodically served as a shelter for the homeless.

Budge Gere reflected on some of the dramatic changes that occurred between his college years and his time at seminary:

In the 1960s the civil rights movement was around and Vietnam, but I was a comfortable child of the '50s. My [college] class was the last one that acted like people from the '50s. We were pre-pot, pre-war, pre-women's rights. By 1968 the anti-Vietnam war movement was in gear. In 1969, I was at the Princeton Theological Seminary and visiting with the local [U.S.] Representative, lobbying about Vietnam. Though we were not in the vanguard. When our seminary class graduated in 1970, business was not as usual. I didn't wear a graduation gown but a suit. However, I was hardly a radical.

Nevertheless, during that period he and his wife ran a summer camp for disadvantaged 8-year-olds from Manhattan's Lower East Side and Bedford Stuyvesant in Brooklyn. When asked what it was like to be a white teacher of black kids during such a tense time, Budge responded:

> There was a need to minister to the hurts of the world. It was bringing kids out to the country. Kids are kids. It was like a fresh air camp. Ultimately, I was led to see the number of kids who are not wanted. We decided to adopt children by choice—minority kids. It was a broadening of a worldview to us.

One of their two adopted minority children is a Native American, a young woman who, in Budge's words, is perhaps "the most severe case of fetal alcohol syndrome ever to graduate college." She and her mother are writing a book about her experiences.

If he was hardly a radical in seminary, this pastor's first call after seminary plunged him into the midst of a radicalized situation.

> I arrived to a sit-in. The Black Economic Development League and another group had taken over the church and demanded reparations. When groups want something, they go to their friends. And [the congregation] was a dynamic leader. It had worked hard with self-discipline....The resolution was that we started an interfaith coalition of congregations that did make a pledge to meet demands. Some felt that it was being taken hostage, and others saw it as legitimate.

When asked what he learned from that experience, Budge replied:

> There was this whole area of social justice and...the church has to balance that against its other major calls. What does it mean for a church to be a church? My understanding of the gospel is that there are individual salvation and community concerns. We need both. We're not just a social justice agency but about individual salvation. "To love God, and love our neighbor." We need both.

The turmoil of the sixties and early seventies radically altered the curricula at many mainline seminaries. Pastor Ed Rowe fondly recalls that one of his favorite seminary professors "dropped his systematics textbooks and started teaching [Marshall] McCluhan, and everybody was in flux trying to figure out what was going on. And we did finally start meeting with the professors and designing classes."

Others pastors were less enthusiastic about such intellectual developments. Budge Gere recalls that

I was in [Princeton Theological] seminary in a turbulent time. The face of seminary education had changed. Major theologians, like Barth, Bonhoeffer, Niebuhr, and Tillich, were now in decline. The seminary curricula were like a smorgasbord rather than a true canon. Everything was in flux. I came out of seminary without the grounding a person 20 years before would have had, though I had a broadened worldview. At the time, President McCord of Princeton Theological Seminary had said that the church was suffering from theological amnesia. I realized [several years after graduation] that I needed to get into a Doctor of Ministry program to prepare myself for the rest of the journey. Ministers were leaving the church in droves. Many had gone to seminary for the draft deferment.

Geoff Drutchas attended Harvard Divinity School during these turbulent times. He recalls wondering how absurd it must have sounded to others that he wanted to go to seminary when the media kept issuing stories about the church disappearing and when in 1967, *Time* magazine's cover posed the question: Is God Dead? In his view, Harvard Divinity School was "dysfunctional," a "burned out" institution, "already tottering, everything coming apart." Geoff feels fortunate that he was mature enough to develop a more structured theological foundation for himself, reading theologians like Tillich and Niebuhr who were officially out of fashion.

The impact of the sixties and seventies on our senior pastors stands in stark contrast to the experiences of many core members. In our spiritual life history interviews, we explicitly asked, "Were you influenced by the events and movements associated with the 1930s, '40s, '50s, '60s, '70s, or '80s?" We had expected that those who had gone to college during the sixties and early seventies would, at a minimum, have had their beliefs challenged during that tumultuous period. We were thus surprised at how seldom these decades were mentioned as an influence. We also asked, "During this period [college years], did you have any experiences involving religion or spiritual issues that particularly stick in your mind?" Again we noticed how little the college or university experience seemed to have affected core members' religious or spiritual values, even during the sixties and seventies. Perhaps this means that the middle-aged people in our pews are not necessarily typical of their generation, or at least not similar to the people who are seen as representative of that generation. Except for Central Methodist, our congregations tended to be conservative on social issues.

These very different approaches to social justice issues seldom led to conflict between the senior pastors and the more conservative people in their pews. Maybe what was radical in the sixties and early seventies is solidly middle-of-the road today. In most cases, however, these successful pastors also understood that to move their congregations in new directions they needed to act carefully and with prior consultation for planning and implementing change. The following case study illustrates what can happen when an excellent and much respected pastor forgets that lesson.

SLOW DOWN, YOU'RE MOVING TOO FAST: A CASE STUDY

Although Rev. Dennis Bux of Holy Trinity followed a straight and seemingly unproblematic road to seminary, he and his classmates experienced firsthand the spiritual and political turmoil characteristic of the early seventies.

> The watershed for me was in seminary. There [was] a big split when I was in my second year at Concordia [a Missouri Synod seminary in St. Louis], when most of the faculty and student body went into exile and affiliated with a small denomination. This had a huge impact on me. The issue in the church was: Could a small group take power and control? We took a stand to support the faculty, who we did not believe were heretics. A small cadre of very conservative people had captured the synod's presidency and made it powerful. We wanted to take a stand. Persuasion didn't work. We tried to get the dispute adjudicated, and then took the step of setting up a seminary in exile [Seminex].
>
> The whole dynamic of being in exile is a key metaphor for me and my view of the ministry. It wasn't so clear to me then, but it became clearer in 1991 when I had a sabbatical and worked on this issue. At the time of exile in the seminary, there were major changes in how the seminary worked. There was a ruling board of faculty, students, and outsiders that worked together. The structure of the classroom was affected, where teaching was done differently. It was a good year for the professors. The students were highly motivated, for there was something more important than grades. There was a lot of anxiety about calls and where we would serve, since the small denomination didn't have many opportunities available.
>
> I've learned subsequently that, sociologically speaking, exilic communities are structured for adaptation, have changes in the leadership process, have increased importance of the role of ritual and worship, have people who become heroes, people who had more at stake. These four characteristics are with me in how I grid my theology. Exilic parts of the scriptures are the most important to me.... During my first call as a worker-priest, being in both worlds allowed me to make

connection with the exile. It's also [crucial] for the lay folk, who gather together on Sunday and during the week are scattered....

Seminary training [in Seminex] centered on the historical critical method of interpreting scriptures [to which the synod officials objected]. It forced us to deal with how to keep the gospel free, and not wrapped in legalistic [concerns].... A lot of what Luther talked about was related to that issue. It was déjà vu. My identity as a member of the Lutheran Church was set. Another thing that helped was that I learned from Luther that...the true church has to stand for what it believes. It was a time to put up or shut up. Since then I have not been afraid, since it couldn't get worse than when it was possible that I couldn't become a minister. I learned a little about oppression, being judged by a label, not being accepted, no matter how qualified, because of where you had graduated.

Those experiences from 20 years earlier explained much about how Dennis still approached ministry. His claim to having "not been afraid" since the Seminex experience was echoed by his predecessor, the former senior pastor at Holy Trinity, Rev. Bob Seltz, "That is what is neat about Dennis. He charges in where angels fear to tread." One can see the impact of this mindset in Dennis's very successful innovations in worship, such as Beanie Baby Sunday, where everyone who had a Beanie Baby was invited to bring it in. "And he had a lot of adults come up with Beanie Babies, too, with their kids. He must have had a hundred people up there. When he did it, it was a splash. I mean a splash!" Another huge "splash" was his blessing of the animals, which took place in a fellowship hall crowded with virtually every conceivable pet, in addition to the owners. Other pastors make passing references to popular culture, but Dennis preached an ongoing sermon series called "St. Paul at the Movies," where he imagined how St. Paul might have reviewed contemporary cinematic hits like *Pleasantville* and *The Apostle*. Dennis delivered one sermon, which took Spam as its topic, while wearing a baseball cap emblazoned with the product's name.

Not surprisingly, the percentage of people agreeing that their pastor was similar to an "entertainer" was far and away the highest at Holy Trinity (33.5% versus a sample-wide average of 21.9%). Dennis also received the second highest percentage of agreement with the statement that my pastor "preaches good sermons." However, the people of Holy Trinity recognized that Dennis often used his daring sense of humor as a vehicle to deliver serious spiritual messages. They registered the highest level of agreement with the statement that their pastor is similar to a "teacher," as well as to a "scholar" and an "expert."

Dennis also emphasized the need to examine the relationship between your religion and your work world. During worship, in place of the second scripture reading, lay folks delivered a series of moving "Slice of Life" messages about how their religious values had influenced their careers.[8] One of Holy Trinity's most active members told of being fired from his executive position, apparently as a result of proclaiming at a company retreat that he placed his duties to God and family before those to the corporation. Later, another senior executive of a major corporation, who had delivered a memorable talk about the relationship between his work and his faith, left his job to pursue a ministry-related career.

We've seen that Dennis's "identity as a member of the Lutheran church" was set by his Seminex experience, and his ministry reflected that commitment. Many experts have proclaimed that denominational identity has become irrelevant. Dennis's view was precisely the opposite:

> I've learned in exile that the chief issue is how to maintain identity, which is a real challenge in our dynamic and pluralistic world of spirituality—everything Western, Eastern, New Age, etc. There's a need for an identity for a Christian who is a Lutheran that will help people navigate life in work, family, and civic life. I can't anticipate what will be on the other side. The best way is to be flexible in organization but firm in identity. We are trying to firm up our identity as a Lutheran church.

Dennis was the pastor most likely to emphasize the Lutheran church's theological distinctiveness and to quote extensively from Luther's writings in sermons, Bible studies, and new member classes ("I try to get in all my sermons Luther's idea of law [diagnosis] and gospel [prognosis]").

Many Seminex-inspired characteristics of Dennis's ministry were admired and enjoyed by the people of Holy Trinity. Some characteristics, however, seriously disturbed his parishioners. Dennis felt that in church issues it was crucial to be fearless, to "put up or shut up." He dismayed many in his congregation when he followed that philosophy in his approach to the place of gays in the church. When asked about gay marriages, only four percent of survey respondents at Holy Trinity said they were happy with the idea. As mentioned earlier, Dennis infuriated a number of members when, at a synod assembly, he voted in favor of a resolution that would have recognized and affirmed the blessing of committed same gender relationships.

Dennis was also profoundly influenced by the organizational innovations at Seminex; one of his major goals was to cut administrative red tape, or as he described it elsewhere, "be flexible in organization."

Unfortunately, sometimes others perceived him as a sloppy administrator, not paying enough attention to details or showing poor judgment on personnel issues. For example, when he delayed taking decisive action in one crucial area of church ministry, a conflict was allowed to fester disastrously. He also pushed too fast to add a new ministerial position, leading to a congregational meeting that decisively overruled him and the church council.

PRIVACY AND THE PASTOR

Dennis's unexpected announcement that he was asking for a divorce from his wife hurt his relationship with the congregation. Dennis eventually decided to resign his call at Holy Trinity because his preoccupation with his marital problems prevented him from focusing on leading a large congregation. I heard stories of pastors' marital problems damaging their church in virtually all of the study congregations. Marital difficulties that would be considered strictly private in other work situations became matters for public discussion and could even lead to congregational rifts when they involved pastors. Pastors' children could become topics of widespread discussion among members as well. In some cases, the pastor's parenting skills earned admiration; in others, they became targets of highly critical, even scathing comments.

Above all, it is not so much what a minister says in sermons or other formal settings that influences the people in the pews but who the pastor is as a person. In all his or her actions, the pastor is a living model to the congregation of what it means to be a Christian. I don't mean that they are expected to be "plaster saints." As pointed out earlier, many pastors would be very surprised to find out how much the core members of their congregation know about their frailties and shortcomings. And it is in this way, as "mere mortals" who must struggle with the everyday frustrations of life as well as with life's major crises, that congregation members see pastors as models for how they themselves should or should not be Christians.

DEATH AND THE PASTOR

Pastors' frequent and intimate contact with death is an often stressful and counter-cultural facet of ministry. This was driven home to me at one of the first project interviews, which took place at a restaurant. In deciding how much time they had for lunch, Budge Gere and David

Noble had to take into account a visit they needed to make to the family of a congregation member who had just died.

Three ministers listed events like the first time they had to deal with the death of an active congregation member as major moments in their careers. Here is one example:

> It was a growing experience for me, being directly involved in pastoral congregational ministry. I can remember the first member of the congregation I was with as he died was quite an experience for me....Well, it was just powerful. I was very close to this man and his family, and he had cancer, and he knew he was dying. I spent a lot of time with him and felt a lot of grief when he died. It was a learning experience, too, cause I'm kind of muddling my way through this thing, you know, trying to be the pastor in that situation.

In the congregations where I conducted research, the illness and death of core members often became dramas in which not only the pastor but also other core members found themselves deeply immersed. I mentioned earlier that our pastors were like physicians who actually made house calls. But when the patient died, pastors, unlike physicians, shouldered the responsibility of helping family and friends deal with their sometimes agonized questions about why it happened.

Although as an outsider I was struck by this intimate contact with death and dying, death was not a theme that many pastors mentioned as a major challenge of their ministry. This is probably a tribute to how much they saw dealing with death and dying as an essential and highly meaningful part of their job. For long-time pastors who had developed personal relationships with congregation members, however, this involvement with death could serve as a major stress on their lives.

The same pastor quoted above, who recalled the first time he was with a congregation member as he died, says that even today, more than thirty years later, dealing with such circumstances remains a challenge. "I've been touched too many times by tragedy....And it's harder to walk into situations, knowing people so well." As a long-time pastor, he has to deal more and more often with the death of congregation members whom he has known well for many years.

Pastoral Time Wars

A topic frequently discussed in publications for pastors is how to find the time to do everything ministers need to do. When I asked my

research assistant, James Bielo, for a preliminary analysis of the staff
interviews, his observations began with the following:

> Undoubtedly, the notion of time/energy was the most recurrent con-
> cern throughout the [answers to the] series of questions. In short, there
> was a basic concern among the staff...that there was not enough time
> to do what they wanted and what was being asked of them, not enough
> energy to do all that they had to do, and/or more help was needed to
> satisfy the needs of the congregation.

Yet a comment all too familiar to pastors is: "It's certainly nice to have a
job where you only have to work on Sundays."

Our pastors reported different numbers of hours put in on the job.
One finds that 40 hours a week is about all he can work without losing
effectiveness. Others rarely seem to be off the clock. But regardless of the
number of hours each put in, the pastors shared a common stress. *Their
time is not their own.*

Pastors usually did get one day a week off, but during the rest of the
week they had to work their own schedules around the often complex
and conflicting schedules of congregation members. Typically these pastors attend meetings, adult study groups, or confirmation classes in the
evenings; and they do administrative work, hold staff meetings, prepare
sermons, and visit the sick and homebound during the day. Pastors were
often the first to arrive at the church in the morning and the last to leave
at night.

It's not surprising that 70 percent of the people in the pews agreed
with the statement: "My pastor always seems to be around the church."
As with most other facets of congregation life, however, there was great
variation among individual congregations, with the percentages of agreement ranging from 45 to 85 percent. Two of the congregations with the
lowest percentages of agreement about this statement had members who
came from throughout the metropolitan Detroit area. These were also
congregations who expected their pastors to be deeply involved in the
political, civic, and social issues of the wider community.

Almost all of the pastors passionately supported the goal of a more
lay-driven congregation. In some churches, the worship bulletin emphasized this goal every Sunday morning, describing "the people of the
church" as the congregation's ministers. This was not merely wishful
thinking. But successfully empowering the laity does not necessarily
lessen the demands on a pastor's time. Indeed, it is more likely to increase them. Empowerment often meant members became interested in
developing new areas of church ministry, resulting in more meetings for

pastors to attend and more need for pastors to coordinate sometimes overlapping activities. One of the most stressful and demanding facets of a pastor's job involves finding diplomatic ways to discourage new lay-led initiatives, which, although well intended, may well be impractical, inappropriate, or even divisive in a particular congregation.

For example, an initiative like a small, unofficial group of women deciding to create banners to decorate the church sanctuary may appear on the surface to be inoffensive or noncontroversial. Yet without effective pastoral coordination and facilitation, it can lead to serious conflicts between the *ad hoc* group and the congregation's worship commission, not to mention heated discussions at the church council over the appropriate environment for Sunday worship.

Nearly 85 percent of the people in the pews agreed with the statement, "The pastor is there when needed." And while this testifies to these pastors' dedication to their job, it also meant that they were pretty much always on call for emergencies. For example, one pastor and his wife planned to attend a late afternoon concert on Sunday. Then a member called with unexpected bad news; a hospitalized parishioner had taken a serious turn for the worse. The pastor needed to get to the hospital immediately. The pastor and his wife did attend the concert, but only after spending time with the dying parishioner.

Earlier I suggested that congregations are often too eager to embrace the prevailing values of mainstream America, even when the people in the pews see themselves as standing in opposition to these values. Embracing popular mainstream approaches without critical self-reflection means ignoring some of their serious spiritual consequences. The stress pastors experience from the many demands made on their time is, to a great extent, the result of the peculiar nature of their vocation. However, the demands also reflect our unwitting embrace of certain popular trends in American culture like the desire to have it all and, in pursuit of that goal, to live an overscheduled life.

Church youth programs, for example, often compete with a myriad of other children's programs, including organized sports programs for kids that begin at extraordinarily young ages. At the regular meetings of one group of younger men committed to deepening their spiritual lives, much of the first hour was spent describing the incredible number of organized activities to which they were taking their kids or the intensive help they gave their children on homework and school projects. I admired the great effort these men put into trying to enrich their kids' lives (and to keeping their children away from bad influences). I couldn't help but feel, however, that other motivations were at work: keeping up

with the Joneses, wanting to have it all, and trying to squeeze in everything rather than being willing to make choices.

   This is also an underlying source of tension even in healthy congregations, which sometimes seem obsessed with keeping up with
the megachurches rather than building on the unique gifts of their
own location. Pastors, in turn, often buy into this same mainstream
cultural set of values. As a result, they find themselves burned out
from the "time wars" they and their parishioners have declared upon
themselves.

CONCLUSION

Throughout this chapter I've included extensive direct quotations from
pastors, which often provide intimate details from their personal histories. I hope that, as a result, you've come to recognize the extraordinary
complexity and uniqueness of each of these pastors. If you are a core
member of your congregation and have trouble filling in this type of
background information about your pastors, then you certainly should
ask yourself why. The insight I've been trying to relay to you about your
congregation—you must know who you are before you can know what
you can become—is just as applicable to the relationship of a pastor to
his or her congregation. In their commendable zeal to improve their congregations, our church leaders often give little thought to how proposed
changes fit with the abilities, skills, inclinations, passions, and interests
of their pastoral staff. I've stressed that you need to build your congregation on the basis of its overall strengths (and take into account its weaknesses) rather than on wishful thinking. You need to follow the same
strategy with regard to your pastoral staff. Few churches can afford the
luxury of specialized staff members to deal with each of the incredibly
diverse services that they provide to members. The pastor who may spe-
cialize in youth groups often has to visit the elderly members who are
sick or dying. The pastor who has to prepare a sermon for Sunday may
also have to spend much of the week trying to handle an explosive personnel situation involving paid staff and volunteers. When it comes to
what the pastor can contribute to a congregation, you cannot have it all!
Realistic choices have to be made and priorities set. Otherwise, you are
setting up a situation that will disappoint the core members and lead
wonderful and devoted pastors to feel inadequate and burned out.

6 Worship

What Does Worship Really Mean to the People in the Pews?

Fear and Temptation in the Liturgical Marketplace

Based on what they hear about the worship styles of rapidly growing churches, our local leaders certainly fear that their congregations' liturgies are increasingly outmoded and irrelevant to the needs of people they hope to attract (especially the younger ones). Assuming that their older members will be afraid of change, local leaders typically recognize that implementing changes in worship can be tricky. Yet temptations abound. A myriad of exciting materials are available for purchase—new hymnals for the people in the pews, innovative music for the choir or a small contemporary music group, even pre-packaged sermons for the pastors, who can also pep up their presentations by learning how to operate user-friendly computer presentation software. But if there's one area where "keeping up with the Joneses" is likely to send your congregations in fruitless directions, it's in changing worship. This chapter explains why.

Worship is a vital expression of your unique congregation, inseparably linked to the inimitable way in which your local faith community strives to fulfill its mission every day of the week. That's why this chapter on worship appears late in the book, only after you've read about church organization, denomination, and pastors. In the following pages, we first ask: do congregation members really want their worship changed, and if so, what do they want changed and why? Second, we recall that worship is first and foremost about praising God together in community and not about recruiting new members. Your worship style should express your congregation's deepest spiritual commitments (its theology) and your faith community's unique way of serving God, each other, and the world. Finally, we look at the private dimension of worship: how does worship affect congregation members' spiritual well being? Examining these three areas will help us see that honoring what is unique about our worship—rather than trying to "be like the Joneses"—will actually strengthen our churches.

WHY CHANGE YOUR WORSHIP SERVICE?

In addition to recruiting new members, congregational leaders seek to change their worship service for other reasons: to try out something they enjoyed while visiting another church or attending a conference, for instance, to keep from feeling "in a rut," or to grow professionally. But these motivations could be irrelevant to the people in the pews, who may well view liturgy differently than the would-be innovators.

We asked the people in each of our congregations what they would like to see changed in their worship service (table 6.1). Surprisingly, only a little over half of respondents (57%) were able to suggest *any* change that they would like to see. Frequently people responded, instead, that they liked their services just the way they are.

Predictably, core members are more likely than non-core members to suggest changes (69% to 52%). However, there are no differences between men and women or between age groups in the level of desire for change or in the type of changes suggested.

Music garnered the most suggestions for change: just over 30 percent of the 57 percent of the people who made a recommendation, or 17 percent of all respondents. In addition, 22 percent of those who suggested changes (only 12% of all respondents) suggested alterations in what is included in or excluded from the worship service or liturgy. Other suggestions receiving more than minimal support included the length of service, the sermon, and the general atmosphere of the worship service.

If we look at the specific alterations recommended, the patterns become complex and contradictory; there is generally little agreement either within or across congregations. This is especially true for music. When people commented about music, some asked for more, some for less, some for more traditional music, some for more contemporary or lively music. A similarly confusing pattern appears in the worship comments; some people asked for more frequent communion, some for less frequent, some for more contemporary liturgy, some for more traditional liturgy, and some for more variety in the liturgy. People generally agreed on one point; services should not be more than 60-75 minutes long. But they suggested a variety of ways to shorten them: briefer sermons, fewer announcements, shorter children's sermons, and less music.

Concerns about the so-called generation gap often lead congregational leaders to advocate more contemporary-style worship, so we analyzed relevant survey responses by age group across all congregations. There was essentially no difference in the opinions of the younger age group (19-39) and the middle-age group (40-59). In music, 2 percent of these age groups expressed a desire for more traditional music and 2 percent expressed a desire for a more traditional service. In music 5-6 percent of these age groups expressed a desire for contemporary music and 2 percent expressed a desire for a more contemporary service. In addition, 3 percent expressed a desire for more variety in services. Although few respondents age 60 and older expressed any opinion on this topic, they were more likely to favor traditional music and worship. Three percent asked for more traditional and 1 percent for more contemporary music. Less than 1 percent expressed their opinion of the service, but those that did preferred either more traditional liturgy or fewer changes in the service.

All of the statistics just quoted are very small in magnitude. Our congregations' younger members are not crying out for more contemporary or lively services. Indeed, the people in our pews seem to have no strong desire for major changes in worship at all. If this is also true in your congregation yet changes are still desired by the leadership, then consider introducing them a little at a time, and perhaps the resulting services should provide a variety of options (i.e., different styles of worship at different times of day or on different Sundays of the month), since some people prefer the traditional service and music and some prefer the contemporary.

Table 6.1
Suggestions for Change to Worship Services

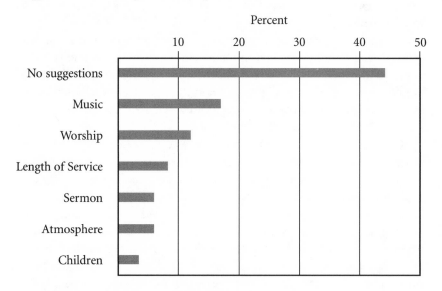

Less than 3% of survey respondents suggested changes related to announcements, details of the ritual, the Bible, the number of services, participation in service, and clothing.

It Is All About Worship

While music style and worship format remain important considerations, they are not the sum total of what worship is really about. Worship is, above all, about worship—how your faith community publicly and communally praises God. It's amazing how often congregations forget that simple spiritual truth when they start to consider changes in worship. All too often, leaders drift into seeing the main goal of worship as attracting new members. They interpret "if you're not growing, you're dying" as a statement about the number of people in your pews or as a (fear-based) motivation for following the latest "successful" fashions in worship. But we might understand this statement, instead, as a legitimate truism about the relationship between your worship and the quality of discipleship in your members.

Preoccupied with luring new people into their pews, church leaders considering changes in worship almost never ask themselves more fundamental and vital questions: Why do the people already in their congregation's pews return Sunday after Sunday to worship there? What in their current worship remains vital to their spiritual lives? A good way to begin answering those questions and return to a vision of worship as praising God in community is to reiterate the major point of this book: every congregation is unique. Obviously, a vital part of what makes your congregation unique is its way of worshiping as a community. Or better, the nature of your congregation as a community makes your form of worship unique.

From the very first Sunday, we experienced worship in each of our eight congregations as unique, and that distinctiveness became ever more apparent the longer we took part in the congregations' wider lives. No one factor or set of factors could explain the significant differences and similarities among the congregations, and we were never able to develop a simple typology of worship styles.

For example, a shared Lutheran liturgical tradition (particularly a shared view of communion) gave a distinctive flavor to our experience of worship at our two ELCA congregations despite their very different sizes and radically different types of worship spaces. However, Bethlehem Lutheran's strong sense of worship as an extended family gathering was missing at Holy Trinity Lutheran; Bethlehem's style seemed more like worship at the much smaller Bethel Baptist. This may reflect the shared working-class roots of both congregations. It might also flow from their common experience of long-term pastors whose families are deeply involved in every facet of their faith communities.

Worship Reflects the Congregation's Activities

The boundary between what transpires in your sanctuary during worship and what occurs in the rest of the church building on Sunday morning is artificial and porous. Those other Sunday morning activities often contribute much of what gives your worship its distinctive flavor. For example, do a significant number of your adult members attend Bible study on Sunday morning or, as at St. Paul, are no adult Bible studies held during that time? Certainly that can affect participants' attitudes toward worship even before they enter the pews. So can the nature of that Bible study; if you've seen one Sunday Bible study at a mainline Protestant congregation, you haven't seen them all. Long-time lay teachers at Bethel Baptist and Bethlehem Lutheran lead well-prepared and well-attended Bible studies on Sunday morning in which participants bring their own life experiences into lively discussions. At Bethlehem, the teacher offers a brief prayer at the beginning of class. At Bethel, prayer concerns of class members can take up the first 5 or 10 minutes of the session, especially when other participants offer advice or support in response. By contrast, the senior pastor usually teaches the main Sunday morning Bible study at First Presbyterian. The class remains largely academic in tone, with a surprising number of participants having diligently completed pretty stiff homework assignments.

You can probably think of examples, as well, for how your congregation's children's programs influence what occurs in your sanctuary. The pastor of one congregation has a playful side to his personality and stages a puppet show as part of the church's summer camp. During the "children's moment" in Sunday services, he is at ease with the off-the-wall ways in which the kids almost invariably respond to his questions. Another pastor is obviously uncomfortable with youngsters' spontaneity. It's not surprising that the role of children in services is a major issue in his congregation.

The how, what, when, where, and who of your church's Sunday morning fellowship activities also influence how your members approach worship. In some churches, fellowship is vital to the Sunday morning experience; in others, it remains a marginal activity. Some members find the buzz of conversation in the pews prior to the service a serious distraction as they prepare to worship; for others, sharing a "Hello" with their neighbors helps prepare them to praise God in community. Whatever you may feel about the issue, it's important to recognize that much fellowship activity (inside or outside the sanctuary) is not just socializing or gossiping but a key element in your congregation's unique style of nurturing its members. Fellowship in the pews or in the fellowship hall often provides a way to catch up on the latest news about members going through hard times. Even members not mentioned in the church's public prayers are certainly in the minds and prayers of people in the pews during the rest of the worship service.

The character of your Sunday school programs and the nature of your Sunday morning fellowship comprise just two of many factors taking place outside the sanctuary on Sunday that directly and indirectly influence worship. Even how your faith community lives the *other* six days of the week molds your congregation's unique form of worship. The number of connections and influences can be startling as well as revealing. Your Sunday worship is the sum of all that your congregation does. The following examples from our congregations should get you jump-started in thinking about your own church.

Music in Worship

Are you a "singing" church? Do the worshippers in your sanctuary together lift their voices in praise of God so that you feel embraced and engulfed by the music? If so, that may reflect the sanctuary's acoustics, the pastors' ability to lead the singing by example, or even the amount of music included in the service.

The pastor's relationship with the church's music director is another crucial factor. Associate Pastor David Noble is also the music and choir director at First Presbyterian. Music plays a vital role in almost every facet of church life there. Since he oversees youth programs, music pervades the curriculum. As the leader of an important midweek Bible study (which includes some of the church's most influential core members), David emphasizes key links between the denomination's worship and the scriptures. In an evening music camp for adults and children, he not only provides instruction on playing instruments but also explains the structure and logic of the hymnal. One reason David is effective in these (and other) areas is because of his unusually long-term, close, and trusting relationship with the senior pastor.

One striking difference between our congregations is the rate of turnover for music or choir directors. In one of our churches, the directors changed rapidly, with the position usually filled by an advanced graduate student from a prestigious local school of music. When a nonstudent was hired, partly to provide some continuity, her tenure was brief and marked by incessant controversy. She had been selected for her technical musical credentials, but her own religious background differed markedly from that of the choir and people in the pews. This was reflected in the music she chose and how she led the choir. The effect on worship was obvious. The pastor attempted to deal with the issue behind the scenes. That effort failed, and a major crisis ensued. Another church has had only four organists and three choir directors in over 30 years. The choir directors were all members of the congregation before taking on that responsibility. Indeed, the current choir director, who has served in that position for 28 years, grew up in the church, as did her children. Understandably, visitors are usually impressed by the power of this congregation's singing.

Who are your choir members, instrumentalists, and soloists, and how do they participate in other facets of church life? Answering these questions can help you understand how their music influences your congregation's worship experience. Indeed, who your musicians are can often have a greater impact than the technical quality of their performance. Consider the effect that even the most musically inept children's choir has on proud parents and grandparents. Obviously, that is an extreme example, but it is by no means unique. Much the same can be said when an elderly congregation member (who contributed the instruments to the bell choir in memory of a daughter dead long before her time) sings a solo accompanied by his teen-aged granddaughter. And when a woman going through a rough divorce stands up to sing a solo, the congregation knows it is witnessing much more than a musical performance.

Witness is an appropriate word, since the choir and the people in the pews literally face each other during worship. The choir is among the most visible elements of the congregation and often mirrors the nature of the church's wider life. Here's a simple but revealing exercise: simply look at who is and is not in your choir(s). Aside from the obvious age and gender breakdown, consider what percentage of singers are also core members of your congregation. In one church, for example, many choir members were in the core, and I saw them operate as a cohesive special interest group at a congregational meeting and in discussions about future directions for worship.

A rousing musical performance by a teen choir obviously enjoying itself communicates a great deal to the rest of the church about the state of its youth program. While most churches describe themselves as family congregations, a bell choir that includes three generations of one family and two generations of another publicly affirms that identity.

Because it meets frequently, the choir becomes well known—both in and out of the sanctuary—by those watching them perform on Sundays. Prayer is an integral element of each practice session for one choir, and its members are drawn together by that weekly experience. Some church music groups actively recruit and enthusiastically welcome new members (often regardless of their talent); others make it clear that they are closed to participation by anyone outside their own tightly knit circle. When a musically talented newcomer mentioned to some people at fellowship hour that he was going to join the contemporary music group, the listeners smiled politely but later expressed to each other their well-grounded skepticism about how fully he would be welcomed.

Before moving beyond the musical dimension of worship, it's worth emphasizing one major point about quality: seldom did anyone other than the accompanist approach a professional level of performance. In music, as in many other facets of worship, our congregations are marked by a distinct homegrown, amateur flavor. That is not a criticism. On the contrary, it is one way in which our congregations are truly being countercultural. The Latin root of "amateur" means lover, and our sanctuaries are one of the few public places where many people feel comfortable, secure, and appreciated doing things they adore, even if they are not "professional" at them. These amateurs praise God with the talents they have and are appreciated and enjoyed for that reason.

THE SERMON

In our spiritual life history interviews, many core members in all our churches emphasized how vital the pastor's sermons are to their worship experience. Although we felt that the pastors differed widely in their style and skill as speakers, the people in the pews gave uniformly high marks to their pastors' sermons. Yet core members often had tremendous difficulty identifying the major themes of their pastors' sermons. Thus whether in the pulpit or baptizing a child, the pastor's impact on people's worship experience is primarily the result of who the pastor is beyond the pulpit, more so than what he or she actually says on a given Sunday.

Holy Trinity Lutheran, the one church where core members are clear about the pastor's major sermon themes, is an exception that proves the rule. Pastor Dennis Bux does have a unique speaking style and, week after week, found numerous ways of addressing the same two themes, grace and the Lutheran heritage. But it was the frequency with which he stressed these same themes outside of services that solidly reinforced them in the minds of the people. Dennis attended to these themes in new member classes, men's Saturday morning Bible study, and many other small groups in which he participated.

Initially, we were almost shocked when one congregation gave high grades to their pastor's sermons on our survey. In informal settings, we had heard core members criticize his speaking style. It became clear from the spiritual life history interviews, however, that members found it hard to separate their response to him in the pulpit from their feelings about how he carried out the rest of the job. In particular, the congregation had a deep and abiding affection for a man who evinced his deep commitment to them in so many ways, especially in his willingness to be with people in trouble at any time of day or night.

A Group Undertaking

I've emphasized how some of the most prominent features of your church's worship (e.g., music and sermons) are connected to the congregation's unique community life. However, some less dramatic but vital features of worship are also integrally linked to who you are as a faith community. You can discover this by listing all the people who make your Sunday worship possible. In addition to the pastors, musicians, readers, and worship committee members, include those who serve in the altar guild, bake the communion bread, and assist the pastors during communion. Add to the list the ushers, greeters, and those who prepare the worship folders and keep track of worship attendance. How about those who record the services for shut-ins and drive handicapped members to church? Then consider, why do all these people do it? In some cases, the motivation may be quite ordinary (for example, enjoying working with friends). If you take the time to inquire, however, you will discover that many find this work spiritually meaningful; it's a way to give back to those who have helped them or to show personal devotion.

A Private Experience

Finally, although worship is a very public event, the worshipper's experience can be very private. Don't assume you can read someone's reactions to worship simply through observation. A stone-faced Lutheran man may be as spiritually touched as someone standing up and shouting "Amen!" Don't assume other people respond to worship the way you might. "Assume nothing" became one of our major principles for understanding congregational worship, and it should be one of yours when considering changes in your Sunday services.

The difficulty we had learning about how people respond to worship simply by observing them led to our focus on Bible studies, one of the few places where on occasion folks publicly discuss their private responses to Sunday services. This same difficulty was also a major reason we carried out extensive spiritual life history interviews (which contained

Table 6.2

What Are the Most Important Parts of the Worship Service to You?

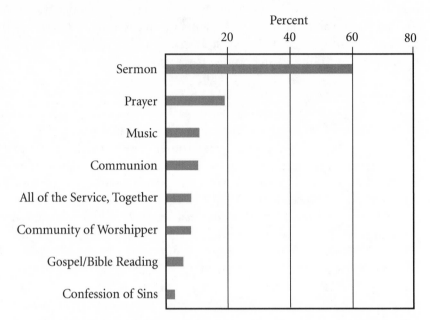

a variety of questions about worship). As table 6.2 demonstrates, we found that while the sermon was generally mentioned as the most important part of the service, people's worship experience was more varied than just a response to the sermon.

The experience of worship can best be described by people themselves. Below is a sample of quotations from spiritual life history interviews in which core members describe their experiences during worship.

> "When we come together in common prayer, that we're really united.... Being together. You know, coming together and sharing the same belief. Being with family."

> "What do I think about? Well, I'm happy to be there, with the people that are there, and I guess I feel really fortunate to be with the people that are there and to have the pastors that we have, and I learn things there. It seems like I'm always learning something."

> "Well, now, the feeling of community communion. I don't mean by that taking the elements of communion, but I feel a sense of worshiping together, whether it's in singing or taking communion or anything else."

> "Well, I really like the sermon, I live for the sermon. I mean, I know that what comes out of that pulpit on Sunday is going to be a big deal. I mean,

I just know it's going to challenge me and that my life and my spiritual life will take a turn every Sunday that I hear that."

"I understand the power of the church, in a community. I think it's one of the last, and it might be the last place where it isn't subject to marketing and commercialism yet. I mean, we don't have the Nike symbol on our Bible yet and we don't have the scroll going across the top, so I think there's an opportunity for freedom of thought within the church."

"I've had several occasions where I've had a strong positive reaction. Where I felt the message and the whole service touch me to the point where I had to act on what was there, and was a wake-up call [to me]."

"It's a time of calmness and openness to thoughts coming and going. It's a meditation really, and I've often thought that it has to do with the long history of feeling that way in that place, from, you know, high school days probably. The way in which the ritual is conducted, even though I may not particularly choose certain parts of it as favorites, but the sum total is one of peace and calm. If one felt they were speaking to God or listening to God, that would certainly be a time when it's possible."

"Well, definitely the fellowship and the community worship is the most important part of it. It's the aspect of getting everybody together and worshiping together, singing together, participating, praying together. Those things are very important. Certainly the message that the pastor, the preacher has that day is important, but that's not really the core thing of coming to church."

"When we have prayer for the people I try to think about those that are mentioned in worship or in prayer that need prayers. Probably at times my mind goes back to the week's activities and what's been going on. Maybe what's coming up the next week. About those sitting around me. About the congregation, who's there and how they're doing, and smiling. And I like to think I think about God and my relationship there."

"I don't know if there is a most important part. The sermon obviously is one opportunity of learning something, and I think our ministers do try to relate to what's going on in the world today as well as doing biblical history. So that's an important part because it's educational. But the music to me is a very important part of expressing the joy that we feel in church. I like being able to look at the stained glass windows that we have now."

"Overall, the service...I mean, it's nothing spectacular. Sometimes I get more out of the service than I do others. Like I've told you before, in all the years I've been coming here I only really felt the Holy Spirit one time."

"Another thing I really do like is the children's moment. I feel a lot of times that the children's moment presents things in a way that is more understandable than the sermon. Well, it does for the children, obviously, but I mean even for the adults. I think sometimes it is a good introduction if nothing else for the sermon, so you know what we're supposed to be learning about today."

"I think that there are times when the sermon really hits you more than others and obviously this is going to make more of an impact on you, and probably for quite a long time. Maybe that's what you needed to hear that morning, or maybe it was what you really didn't want to hear but needed to. Or maybe it was something you just had questioned and it answered questions for you, so I think that's… There have been some that have been very meaningful."

"I like the time with children. I like the hymns. I like the opening sentences a lot of times. The kind of getting ready for worship, the settling. I like being with my family at church, and my friends at church. The surrounding of the connectedness of being there."

"I like the prayers that we have for people."

"I am getting to a point now, in my life, where I can really focus in on the things of God. Now, I used to think about, did I turn the oven off, I wonder what the kids are doing, you know, and just things pulling my mind away. But I am growing to a point now where I can focus in on the message, focus in on the song, and not have my mind drawn, you know, in a number of directions."

"A lot of times during a communion service I'll think about my friends and family that I'm going to see again in heaven. I think about the connectedness of Christians around the world a lot of times when we pray together. That regardless of where people are, that the church is really a huge thing, you know. An ephemeral link between people of all common characteristics."

"Well, my life is so crazy, and that's one of the few times I can sit and just be quiet, so I have to really be careful that my mind doesn't wander. But sometimes I think about my problems, or sometimes I'll just pray about something that's going on. But most of the time I pretty much think about what's going on in the service."

"How good God has blessed me and just keep thanking him for my health. And probably sometimes I think about all those things and not listen to what's going on. I guess I keep praying to myself all the time, too."

"I like the wholeness and the way it moves and flows and has a coherence to it…. Ah the presence of God and how the spirit of God kind of hovers over that congregation drawing people together."

"I think what is most important is what reaches people. Some people are reached with the music, some people are reached with prayer, and some through preaching."

Conclusion

Certainly, I encourage you to change, especially to grow spiritually through your worship. But remember that you have to begin with who you are as a unique congregation, especially if you are proud of who you are, like most of our congregations. And you are more likely to be successful in your change if you begin with your uniqueness and build on your strengths. To do this, you must replace fear and envy as motivations for changing worship (i.e., let's alter our worship to be more like the megachurches so we can lure new members) with a faith-driven desire to have your worship be a beautiful expression of how your church uniquely praises and serves God on Sunday and throughout the week.

7

Evangelism

Is Mainline Evangelism an Oxymoron?

At First Presbyterian's annual officers' retreat, representatives from each of the congregation's standing committees are reporting on their group's activities. I am busily taking notes on a long, bleak discussion of the evangelism committee's efforts when I am startled to hear someone address me, "Isn't there any anthropological research that could help us?" I ignore the question, pretending that—preoccupied with my scribbling—I haven't heard it. I hope the discussion will flow on without anyone noticing that I didn't answer. It does.

I am embarrassed. I have been appealed to as an "expert," and I have no expert advice to offer. I had not intended to study evangelism in this project; the subject isn't included in the original research proposal. Yet the elders and deacons of First Presbyterian are not alone in wanting to know more about the on-the-ground realities of successful evangelism and in hoping our study will provide them with much-needed insight and practical advice. From my very first interviews with church leaders, it had been apparent that they felt inept and frustrated when it came to promoting evangelism.

I am caught in a Catch-22. The project congregations desperately want to know how to evangelize successfully, yet none of them has a program that could be used as a model. Can our study promise the project congregations anything aside from the depressing news that everyone else is in the same boat?

There is another promising alternative. Although organized evangelism efforts are few and seldom successful, people in mainline churches often *talk* about evangelism. They feel strongly about it, especially about the aggressive forms that offend them. I recall a heated argument at a Bible study at Second Baptist between a man who felt that after being a good Samaritan he needed to identify himself as a Christian to the stranger he had assisted and a woman infuriated by that kind of approach.

In my notes from the First Presbyterian retreat, I record that I did break my silence on evangelism later in the meeting. I told First

123

Presbyterian's officers that, at the very least, we would examine why people join churches and would ask congregation members about "unchurched" friends or family. I promised to relay our findings to First Presbyterian.

We did eventually include questions about evangelism in the survey and the spiritual life history interviews. We aimed to provide congregations with extensive and reliable data about what the people in their pews felt about evangelism. If a church is trying to improve its organized evangelism efforts, our findings would let them know what its members are and are not willing to do in that area.

In this chapter, we deal with two fears that frequently hinder, even undermine, evangelism by mainline Protestant congregations. First, there is the fear of guilt by association with stereotypical Bible-thumping evangelizers. Second, there is the evangelism that is motivated by a fear of institutional "death," an approach that eventually reduces evangelism to church growth as measured by number of people in your pews. We will see, as well, that many mainline Protestants already participate in a variety of forms of non-Bible thumping evangelism. We urge congregations to develop evangelism programs that employ a wide range of strategies and to recognize that different types of people are comfortable with different forms of evangelism. We also demonstrate that the reasons mainline Protestants leave and join churches often differ significantly from pervasive commonsense assumptions about these activities. Finally, I suggest that changing your definition of evangelism from church growth to spreading the gospel and making disciples, as well as rethinking who the unchurched really are, can open up new and fruitful fields for evangelizing in your congregation.

Stereotypes and Evangelism

For many people in our churches, the very word "evangelism" conjures up images of Bible-thumping extremists accosting you on the streets or ringing your doorbell. The typical mainline Protestant is uncomfortable witnessing or preaching the gospel to friends, much less to strangers. Mainliners wonder whether they can even mention their religious and spiritual convictions at the workplace without being labeled a fundamentalist by colleagues. The following exchange occurred at a meeting of a women's retreat team at Holy Trinity.

> Alyce[9]: God constantly challenges us, "Do you love me or will you put 'Me' first?" At work I'm trying not to allow my emotions to rule me, but to walk through to Christ.

Betty: I keep hearing, "God never gives you more than you can handle." I can handle a lot.

Carol: Or is it Satan who gives it?

Betty: "Get behind me Satan!" If Satan is behind me, Jesus is in front of me. I've gotten caught saying that at work. I'll get labeled a Bible thumper. I guess that's okay.

Alyce: That's what I've had to learn. Jesus Christ is with me every day to lead me, even if I didn't read the Bible. I learned not to focus on me.

Betty: I need signs and reminders, tapes and candles.

Alyce: I have a little altar at home. I'm afraid to tell people about it.

Betty: I've had to deal with an arrogant Christian young man at work. I complimented him on something he did, and he said, "I have a better co-pilot."

Denise: I'm afraid to talk about faith at work, because I might be labeled a fundamentalist.

Betty: I've put out feelers at work and found like-minded people there. We've discussed faith and, whenever I'm down, one of those [like minded people] seems to drop by. It's not accidental.

This excerpt captures how ambivalent mainline Protestants can be about evangelism, especially in its more stereotypical forms. These women had learned to be comfortable talking about the intimate details of their faith lives with each other and felt that their religious and spiritual convictions should inform all facets of their lives. Yet even mentioning faith at work caused them some trepidation. Betty claims that it would be okay if she were labeled a "Bible thumper" after being caught quoting Jesus' retort to Peter. But at the same time, she finds herself deeply offended by a young man at work who responds to her attempt to compliment him with religious arrogance. Moreover, Betty says she "put out feelers" for fellow believers at work, as though she were part of an underground, deviant group whose members have to contact each other in stealth. Once she did put out feelers, however, she found a powerful support group, which confirms and bolsters her faith.

How could we collect systematic data on such a complicated and emotion-laden subject? How could we discover if women differed from men or different generations from each other in their attitudes towards evangelism? We knew from observation and discussions that there were people in our pews who share, express, and represent their faith—spread the good news—to those within and outside their churches and who do so informally, without any organized program. We included a series of

questions on careers and religion in the spiritual life history interview
that we hoped would shed indirect light on evangelism in the workplace,
while trying to avoid hot-button words like "evangelism" and "fundamentalist" in our queries:

1. Would you give a brief summary of your career?
2. How have your religious beliefs and practices influenced your
   working life or career?
3. How has your working life or career influenced your religious
   beliefs and practices?
4. How would you describe the religious or spiritual atmosphere
   or environment at the jobs that have been most significant in
   your career?
5. Have there ever been any situations in which your religious beliefs have come in conflict with your work?
6. Have co-workers had any significant impact (positive or negative) on your religious or spiritual beliefs and practices?

We were startled to find that very few of our interviewees described their
workplace as a hostile environment for people of faith. In fact, a surprising number reported that they had found comfortable ways to talk about
religion with colleagues or clients at work:

> "I can introduce them to the possibility of Christ if they haven't had it, and
> I'll be honest with you, I'm not an evangelistic type of person. I'm more of
> a joker, but I also am a very compassionate person and so…in my present
> work life, I take seriously that I am a Christian and this is my great opportu-
> nity to get to love people and do the right thing to demonstrate the true
> values, not the worldly crap."

> "A lot of my customers know of my religious beliefs. They respect me for
> that. They know that they're dealing with an honest person. I've earned the
> respect of a lot of people that had no trust in salespeople before."

> "It's really helped me within the work place that the workers know my be-
> liefs. [It] feels good when one of them would come up when there's some-
> thing going on in their lives or something…somebody's sick in their family,
> …[and] I would say to them, 'listen, I'll keep your mom in my prayers, and
> I hope she's doing better.' You know, they kind of look at me and say, 'Hey,
> thanks.' I've had several come up to me and say, 'Hey, in your prayers to-
> night,' you know, like they don't really want to say the word, but 'hey, do you
> think you can remember my sister.'"

> "Other times kids have asked me questions about what I believe or how I
> would handle situations, and I'll respond to them and include…how I was

raised and what I believe as a Christian. I would respond this way and I think that they're really open to that."

"The way I handle myself. I try to set a very positive example. People know I'm a Christian. I don't necessarily...when the opportunity comes up, like, why did you make this decision? Well, because it's the right ethical or moral decision based upon the beliefs that I have as a Christian. This is why I did what I did. You know, those types of things."

"I always told the kids at the very beginning, the first day, we would get to the unit on evolution, and I'm sure most of the teachers did not do this. I said, I am a very religious person. I'm very active in the Presbyterian Church. These things may not interfere with my religious beliefs, I said, if they interfere with yours, I want you to tune out because I would not want to do anything to deteriorate your religious beliefs. And I believe that. I think that there were a lot of parents who felt more comfortable because they had the option—although nobody ever took me up on it—they had the option of not taking that unit. And I had a couple of students who started coming to our church because of this, and [they] were Southern Baptist."

HOW DO PEOPLE REALLY EVANGELIZE?[10]

Mainline fears of evangelizing stem from our concern that we'll wind up looking and acting like the stereotypical Bible-thumper. But our research suggests that such fears are unjustified. There are a surprising number of mainliners who already evangelize in many ways that would be well within the comfort zone of lots of your members. For our survey we wrote down all the ways that we had observed or heard about the people in the pews sharing, expressing, and representing their faith, spreading the good news to believers and nonbelievers, to those within their church and outside it. Our list of evangelism activities was surprisingly long. We included the list on the survey and then asked the respondents to check "any of the following activities you would feel comfortable doing."

When, in a separate section of the survey, we asked people how frequently they evangelized or "shared the gospel with others," 52 percent said once a year or never. But when later asked if they might feel comfortable doing any of the 32 different activities that could be called evangelistic, the survey-takers said yes to an average of *eleven* "evangelizing" actions.

These activities ranged from "offering to pray for someone" and "greeting a visitor to church," which 88 percent of the sample was comfortable doing, to "working as a missionary outside the U.S.," "organizing a prayer group at work," handing out religious leaflets on the street or in the mall," and "criticizing others' beliefs or practice," which less than 10 percent of the sample felt comfortable doing. Many activities involved displaying a religious item (e.g., "wear a cross at work" or "display a religious item in the living room"). Others involved active prayer or testimony (e.g., "offer to pray with someone" or "call new neighbors about your church"). Some activities occurred in the home, some at work, and some in public places.

We found significant differences in comfort level between generations, especially for 23 of the 32 evangelistic activities listed. Older people (over 60) were more likely to be comfortable greeting a new visitor to their church or calling someone who is no longer active in the church. Younger members (under 40) were more comfortable:

- Wearing items (such as t-shirts, bracelets) with a religious message outside of work
- Placing religious items in or on your car
- Displaying a religious statue or other item in your yard
- Displaying a religious picture or other item in your living room
- Visibly wearing a cross or crucifix outside of work
- Visibly wearing a cross or crucifix at work
- Wearing items (such as t-shirts, bracelets) with a religious message at work
- Displaying a religious picture or other item in your workplace
- Having a screensaver with a religious message at work

Clearly, younger people were much more comfortable displaying their beliefs or religious identify in ways that don't require personal interaction, even in public locations and at work.

The differences between men and women are less dramatic. Women were more likely to wear a cross or some other religious item. Men were a little more likely to share their personal faith testimony inside or outside the church. Core members were generally more likely than non-core members to do both active and symbolic (displaying a religious item) evangelism. Table 7.1 lists the 32 evangelistic activities and the percent of people who said they would be comfortable doing them.

A couple of the churches that we studied had organized evangelism committees. Such a committee does well to include both younger and older members and to plan a spectrum of activities that resonate with a variety of people. Activities could range from displaying Christian symbols to initiating personal interactions. Getting people involved in some

Table 7.1

Percentage of People Saying They Were Comfortable with
Different Evangelistic Activities

	Activity	Percent
1	offer to pray for someone	88
2	greet visitor to church	87
3	display religious item in bedroom	64
4	recommend religious publication to friend	63
5	say grace at restaurant	62
6	wear cross outside work	60
7	display religious item in living room	59
8	participate in public worship service	57
9	invite work colleague to church	55
10	wear cross at work	55
11	deliver gift to church visitor	54
12	offer to pray with someone	54
13	share personal faith testimony in church	49
14	wear items with religious message outside work	47
15	share personal faith testimony outside church	43
16	call someone no longer active	41
17	read Bible in public place	40
18	wear items with religious message at work	31
19	after good deed, tell person you are a Christian	29
20	place religious items in car	27
21	display religious item in workplace	23
22	play religious music at work	21
23	have religious screensaver at work	18
24	call new neighbors about church	14
25	work as missionary in U.S.	13
26	display religious item in yard	11
27	work as missionary outside U.S.	8
28	organize prayer group at work	7
29	talk door to door about church	6
30	hand out religious leaflets on street/mall	5
31	carry rosary beads in public	3
32	criticize others' beliefs/practice	1

of the simpler evangelical activities might encourage them to grow comfortable with the more active or challenging activities.

Our eight mainline Protestant churches did not differ greatly from each other in the types of evangelism activities their people felt comfortable doing. However, one congregation was unique. Earlier I mentioned the rather pessimistic discussion of evangelism I recorded at First Presbyterian's Officers' Retreat. Our report to them about evangelism in their congregation was not particularly cheering, but at least it explained why they were having troubles in this area. Out of the six churches in the sample at that time, First Presbyterian's members ranked next to lowest in the frequency with which they reported participating in explicit evangelism ("sharing the gospel with others"). They were also least likely to participate in 20 out the 32 evangelism activities we listed separately in the survey. To some extent this certainly reflected the very gray age structure at First Presbyterian. But at least the 19- to 40-year-olds at First Presbyterian were more likely than the oldest group to participate in 10 of the evangelism activities.

WHY PEOPLE LEAVE OR JOIN A CONGREGATION

I hope you've noticed that only a small number of the evangelism activities included on the survey are inherently linked to the congregation, such as greeting a visitor at church, taking a gift to a recent visitor, or inviting someone from work to church. Evangelism is not necessarily the same as recruiting new members to your congregation. This often overlooked distinction points to yet another dramatic difference between a church and a business.

Along with *It's a Wonderful Life*, the classic *Miracle on 34th Street* is one of our standing favorites each Christmas season. If you're like me, you can't even count the number of times you've seen it. So it's likely you'll remember as well as I do the uproar Kris Kringle initially causes among the executives when, recruited to serve as Macy's Santa Claus, he suggests to a little child's mother that she could get a better deal on a certain toy at Gimbels, Macy's archrival. On the face of it, that's an outrageous idea for a business. And though it may work out as a marketing gimmick for Macy's in the movie, we know in reality that's not how retailers typically operate.

But isn't that how churches should operate? As I've stressed throughout this book, the strength of each congregation is its uniqueness. And, for whatever reason, different people find different types of churches appealing. If the goal of evangelism is to spread the gospel, to make dis-

ciples, that doesn't necessarily mean adding new members to your congregation. To put it another way, evangelism is *not necessarily* the same
thing as church growth—or at least not the growth in the number of
members in your own congregation!

Earlier I used First Presbyterian as an example of a congregation whose
people are unusually reluctant to engage in a wide variety of evangelistic
activities. It seems appropriate to balance that observation, based on average survey results, with a case study of one-on-one evangelism that
resulted in far more than adding another member to the congregation.

When attending First Presbyterian, I occasionally heard disparag-
ing comments about the people in the back rows. Yet one of the most
active members of the church, a deacon, almost inevitably sits in a pew
toward the rear of the sanctuary. This woman had grown up in the Presbyterian Church but as an adult had agreed to worship at her new
husband's church. She never found it spiritually satisfying, and her husband wasn't particularly active in their congregation. Decades later her
husband was suffering from a terminal illness. First Presbyterian was on
the route between her house and the nursing home where her husband
was spending his last days. On an impulse, the woman stopped by the
church one Sunday.

> Well, when [my husband] was ill, I felt God was very close to me and I think
> he was close to me when the car turned into this parking [lot], and I walked
> in. He was close to me when I sat down, and I happened to sit right next to
> [Jane in that back pew]....
>
> And she wouldn't let me get out of that pew without saying who she
> was, and I told her, 'I have to be going. I have to be down to the nursing
> home,'...and she said, 'Come back!'
>
> I was down at the post office and [ran into Jane again], and she said,
> 'Would you like to join a circle?' And I said, 'Well, what do your circles do
> because I belonged to a circle when I was a kid, and we did missions.' She
> said, 'Well, we study the Bible. We do some mission work.' And I thought
> that sounds familiar. She said, 'Different ones do different stuff. Some of
> them go to the art museums. Some of them do plays.' She said, 'Well, which
> one would you like to join?' I said, 'I'd like to join one that studies the Bible.
> There's no point in doing all this other stuff. You can do that with your
> bridge club.' So she said, 'That's the one I belong to.'"

The rest, as they say, is history. The woman continues to prefer the pew
in the back of the sanctuary because that was where she sat the first time
she attended. She also sits there, however, because she is a church shepherd. Sitting in the rear allows her to exit the sanctuary quickly at the

end of services and wait in the narthex to greet the members of her flock. From the vantage point of church growth, the arithmetic of membership rolls, clearly one congregation was a winner and one was a loser. But, from the vantage point of spreading the gospel, aren't they both winners? A woman who most likely would have remained a marginal member of one congregation has found a home in another where she is not only immersed in the good news but also actively sharing it. This story is also a healthy reminder that no matter how much we may want to be in charge, plan, and control things, God is ultimately in charge.

"If You're Not Growing, You're Dying"

"If you're not growing, you're dying." This is one of the gems of corporate wisdom I heard quoted most often at church council meetings, particularly when officers and staff were discussing the future of their congregation. Occasionally someone might mention in passing that growth could include deepening of faith. However, what they really meant by growth soon became obvious: more members. The normally unquestioned underlying assumption is that growth and health are naturally and inevitably associated with each other. Bigger is better or getting bigger is better. I don't recall anyone suggesting that cancer, a tragedy with which all too many congregation members are familiar, is also a form of growth in numbers, an out of control growth of malignant cells. Among the churches we studied and the stories we heard about members' former congregations, there were probably as many examples of institutional failure caused by rapid expansion as from dramatic declines in numbers. And as we saw earlier, size of a congregation does not necessarily indicate its organizational, much less its spiritual, health.

This isn't to say that seeking new members is wrong or that trying to retain the ones you already have is a mistake. I can't stress too strongly, however, that the ultimate point of your congregation is not to build a big institution but to make disciples. Keeping this aim in mind, let's turn to what we learned from the survey about why people leave and join churches.

Why People Leave

There is a lot of movement among mainline congregations and denominations. Over 40 percent of our respondents said they had changed churches as adults for reasons other than moving out of the area. We found some intriguing differences by age group in response to our question about leaving a church. About 41 percent of those under 40 years old reported changing their church membership for reasons other than moving, while the corresponding figure for those between ages 40 and 60 was 50 percent. Of those over 60, 33 percent had changed churches under those circumstances. These are significant findings! Your church may recruit new members from among the previously unchurched or from people who moved into the area, but a significant number of new members may have simply switched from one church in the area to another.

Why are these people changing churches? We asked this question of the 41 percent of respondents who said that they had changed churches. Out of 31 choices, respondents cited the following with most frequency (chosen by over 15 percent of those who changed churches):

- To be in a spouse's or other family member's church (36%)
- The leaders of the church were out of touch with the needs and beliefs of ordinary members (29%)
- Disagreement with the pastor (25%)
- Change in pastoral leadership (21%)
- The form of worship (20%)
- People not welcoming (18%)
- Children's programs (17%)
- Fellowship (15%)

The most important reason for changing churches was to be with one's spouse or family. Church membership is obviously a family experience for many, one that can bring families together—or divide them if spouses and other family members cannot comfortably worship in the same congregation. The men were slightly more likely to choose this reason than the women. The next three reasons for changing churches pertain to the church leadership. Not liking the leadership team—or feeling conflict with the pastor, staff, and lay church leaders—serves as an important incentive for many church-changers. The form of worship, or the worship service itself, was the fifth reason people gave for leaving a church. Thus although people find the worship service important, they do not rank it as high as conflicts with the leadership or the desire for family togetherness. As might be expected, finding people unwelcoming and not liking the fellowship also constituted frequent reasons for changing churches. Women found the social aspect of membership a little more important than men did.

Interestingly, the youngest age group—from 18 to 39—gave more reasons for leaving, and some of these reasons differed from those favored by respondents as a whole. As you can see from the list below (all the options chosen by more than 15 percent of the 19- to 39-year-olds who changed churches), the role of lay people and women in the leadership and worship, the diversity of the congregation, approaches to the Bible, and the absence of friends in the congregation were all important to this group. And social issues and social interaction are strikingly important to young people.

- to be in spouse's church (43%)
- leadership out of touch (34%)
- people not welcoming (27%)
- fellowship (26%)
- form of worship (24%)
- role of lay people in leadership (23%)
- role of women in leadership (20%)
- approach to the Bible (19%)
- role of women in worship (19%)
- change in pastoral leadership (17%)
- level of diversity (17%)
- disagreement with pastor (16%)
- lack of friends (16%)

Core and non-core members were equally likely to change churches; however, their reasons were different in significant ways. Core members were more likely to change churches because of children's programs (23%) or a lack of opportunities for spiritual growth (16%), while non-core members were more apt to be concerned with the form of worship (21%) or with the perception that the pastor was not effective when needed (16%). Of particular interest is the finding that non-core members were significantly more likely to change churches because of changes in pastoral leadership (35%) than were core members (11%). Perhaps because they feel part of the decision-making process for choosing a new pastor, core members are less likely to leave because a pastor leaves. Or the core members may be more loyal to the congregation itself than to the current pastoral leadership.

Because so many leaders of our congregations are focused on the need for change, I need to observe that *pace* of change is not a factor that led many people to leave a church. Only 10 percent of the survey respondents indicated that they had left a congregation because change was taking place too slowly. And only 3 percent checked "change taking place too fast" as a reason to switch churches.

Why People Join

What did people look for when they searched for a new church? We provided a list of 22 possible explanations for joining a new church. We asked the 40 percent of those who said that they had voluntarily changed churches as adults to check all that applied. Here are their most frequently chosen reasons:

- Felt welcomed (78%)
- The pastor (70%)
- Liked the people you met in the church (69%)
- Liked the form of worship (62%)
- Liked the music played in worship (41%)
- A lot of programs for children (such as Christian Education) (40%)

You can see that people agreed more on why they chose a new church than on why they left their old one. The most important reasons included feeling welcomed and liking the people they met. The pastor was the second most important reason for joining. The form of worship, the music, and children's programs also served as major reasons for deciding to join a church. There were no major differences between men and women, core and non-core, and age groups on these items, although those over 60 were less concerned with programs for children and those under 40 were more concerned with liking the pastor. Some differences did arise, however, within the less frequently chosen reasons for joining a church. Core members, women, and the under-40 age group were all more concerned with opportunities for spiritual growth. The core was also concerned with opportunities for growth in knowledge about faith. The under-40 group was more concerned about how lay people could be active in the leadership of their new church.

How Can Your Church Spread
the Gospel and Make Disciples?

What can you conclude from all this? Obviously, patterns and trends appear in the reasons why people leave and join churches, and you should be aware of them. However, there are no simple and powerful patterns, and there are certainly no magic formulas or programs to be bought and applied that will automatically lure large numbers of a certain type of people to your pews or keep them from leaving.

Whether you are dealing with leadership or worship styles of a specific congregation, you should be aware by now that you are dealing with unique facets of your church, which are the complex results of many forces and historical factors. Is this a counsel of despair? No. It's another reminder that your congregation has a unique identity as a faith community, and each of the people you are trying to attract has his or her own distinctive set of religious and spiritual needs.

Although evangelism may have some things in common with mass marketing, it is also dramatically and vitally different, even when it attempts to build or maintain your church's membership rolls. Evangelism is ultimately about something of unsurpassed value: the spiritual health and potential salvation of one unique individual at a time. This process always needs grace and forms of wisdom that may not necessarily be of this world.

In other words, evangelism is a matter for prayer as well as for planning, analysis, and implementation by church leadership. Above all, it calls for discernment: what has God called your congregation to be as a faith community, and what can your church uniquely offer to your members' and potential members' spiritual needs and cravings? Answering these questions may not necessarily lead your church in the same directions that human ambition and pride would seek for it.

WHO ARE THE UNCHURCHED?

Especially in the early stages of our research, when I interviewed denomination officials and discussed with church councils the possibility of including their congregation in the project, they were likely to ask me, "What about the unchurched? Are you going to be able to help us with information about the unchurched?" Initially, I felt dismayed by the question. It fell far outside the boundaries of my research. Was I supposed to add a sample of the unchurched to the project? Eventually, I decided on a more practical and productive approach to finding out about the unchurched: redefine what the term means. Generally, it refers to those who don't belong to a congregation. The unchurched are often discussed in an abstract, impersonal way, as though they were people "out there" whom the church will have to spend great amounts of energy to discover and contact.

But is that a spiritually significant definition? Does it provide a practical approach to churching the unchurched? As our study progressed and we learned more about the congregations, we realized that each church had one potentially invaluable and accessible source of information on the unchurched, especially the type of people likely to join that congregation: its own worshiping community. For that reason, in the survey we asked, "As an adult (since you were 18), have you ever had a significant period of time when you were unchurched or inactive in church? That is, did you not belong to a church or regularly attend a church for over one year?" The responses overwhelmingly confirmed my hunch. Over 50 percent of the people in the pews responded yes to that question, and it was a common answer for each age group (61% of those from 19 to 39, 64% for those from 40 to 59, and 40% for those 60 years of age or older).

As noted earlier, most congregations claim approximately twice as many official members as there are active members of the worshiping community. For some, the lack of involvement might simply be temporary. But are many on the rolls anything more than nominally churched? Even taking into account demographic factors such as women's longer life expectancy, the gender imbalance of our churches remains considerable. There are plenty of men who don't belong to their wives' churches or are only nominally involved. Because I seldom if ever saw any energetic and successful programs for evangelizing these types of unchurched, I have no specific advice to offer. But I do believe that if congregations put significant amounts of energy and thought into an evangelism that focuses close to home or *at home*, the results are more likely to succeed than if they vaguely targeted a large, unknown, abstract demographic group. I also believe that these efforts can be spiritually rewarding for evangelizers as well as the evangelized. For many active members of the churches, a loved one's indifference or hostility to their faith constitutes a private source of pain and sorrow.

WHO EVANGELIZES THE EVANGELISTS?

In focusing on evangelism close to home, my concern is with less active members of your congregation or nonparticipating spouses of active members. This can be an emotionally loaded activity. Let me also suggest that a potentially even more sensitive but still fruitful arena for evangelization is among *active members* of your congregation.

In the chapter on organization, I emphasized that as a religious and spiritual community your church needs to be very clear about what it does and does not believe. Furthermore, your congregation should consciously embody its religious beliefs and principles in daily organizational practices. This is rarely the case in mainline Protestant congregations, because in practice an important mainline value—mutual tolerance—

becomes mutual ignorance. Members coexist, although differing widely in their religious beliefs and values, by taking the approach that Jodie Davie (1995:25) has characterized as "don't ask, don't tell." Or, in terms of the church's organizational life, they suspend their religious beliefs when making decisions and instead rely primarily on their professional experiences and expertise.

In the context of evangelization, I want to return to these issues by providing some concrete guidelines and examples of how mutual tolerance can be maintained in a congregation that is extremely clear about what it communally believes: where people *do* ask and *do* tell.

Above all, I believe it is overwhelmingly important for your church to decide prayerfully what religious issues are vital and essential to congregational identity and to the spiritual health of its members. These are the issues you consider to be the very heart of your faith community's understanding of the good news. They should comprise the foundation of all your evangelism efforts whether within or outside your church.

There are other beliefs or practices, of course, that you might find important but less central to your church's core mission. This is necessarily a question of priorities, of choices. You may decide as a congregation to agree to disagree on these somewhat secondary issues. For example, your congregation may discern that the heart of its Christian mission is to nurture the needy and the weak, to feed the hungry, clothe the naked, and care for the ill. In your mind this is the real essence of the gospel message. You hope and expect that your members will share that commitment or through involvement in the church will come to share it. At the same time, you might also decide that taking a stand on abortion or ordination of gays would so divide and weaken your congregation that it would seriously hamper the church's ability to pursue its *primary* mission, to be a church of servants.

A liturgical example here might take the form of a Lutheran congregation's decision about communion approaches. Although officially our project churches varied widely on the meaning of communion, they shared at least one common denominator: anger and resentment at not being allowed to take communion when visiting a Catholic church. Among Lutherans in our sample, whose liturgies most closely resembled Catholicism, this resentment of churches practicing closed communion was heightened by Missouri and Wisconsin Synod Lutheran churches' routine refusal to open communion to members of other branches in the Lutheran church family (i.e., the ELCA).

Yet officially the ELCA churches in our study interpreted the meaning and significance of communion quite differently than did the other denominations surveyed in our project. According to the ELCA, Jesus is really present in the elements during the communion. Whatever the theological subtleties behind this understanding (consubstantiation vs. transubstantiation), communion for ELCA Lutherans was officially supposed to be much more than a symbolic remembrance or reenactment of an historical event. So it is not surprising that the Lutherans in our sample were the most likely to agree or strongly agree with the statement in our survey, "When I take communion, I feel that Jesus' actual body enters into me."

However, not all Lutherans in our study agreed or strongly agreed with that statement, just as a minority of Baptists emerged to support or strongly support it. Clearly there are people in the pews at our Lutheran churches who don't know—or don't agree with—the official Lutheran position. Thus, questions for a Lutheran congregation would be: How important is doctrine to your church? Is belief in the real presence crucial to what you consider the unique way that your congregation understands itself to be Lutheran? Is it a question of central spiritual significance that should not be compromised, or should it be benignly neglected?

At Bethlehem Lutheran, as part of the welcome at the service's beginning the pastor announces that anyone who believes "Christ is truly present in this sacrament" is welcome to take communion. The same statement is included in the worship folder. Yet 39 percent of the people in Bethlehem's pews had no opinion, disagreed, or strongly disagreed with the statement in the survey that affirmed belief in the real presence.

Should Bethlehem, as a church, be actively evangelizing its membership (not to mention its visitors who might be considering membership) about communion? Let me be clear; I am *not* recommending that Bethlehem or any other ELCA church exclude all who don't believe in the real presence. A whole range of better options is available.

First, you may decide that the meaning or significance of communion is not an issue of crucial importance to your church, at least in comparison to doctrines of Christ alone, grace alone, or scripture alone. If emphasizing, much less insisting on, a specific interpretation of communion might mean losing members and potential members otherwise open to your message, then you might give lip service to the official position of the ELCA but nothing more.

Even if you decide that a particular understanding of communion is absolutely essential to the identity and spiritual health of your Lutheran congregation, you need not make it a litmus test by which to explicitly exclude people from participation in the sacrament. Instead, you might decide that your pastor should preach nonjudgmentally and regularly on the subject. Adult forums could take various aspects of Lutheran communion as a topic; communion could become a central facet of the new members' curriculum; programs could be developed to provide homebound or hospitalized members with the sacrament on a regular basis.

In that way, at least your members and potential members will know what your congregation specifically believes about communion. They may individually decide that they disagree and look for another congregation that approaches communion as they do. Or they might disagree but decide that, compared to other questions of faith and belief, this is an issue about which they do not feel strongly enough to leave the church. Or they may come to understand, appreciate, and even agree with the congregation's view. It is their free choice, and at least they will know that from your congregation's perspective it is an important choice to make.

CONCLUSION:
BE SURE YOU WANT WHAT YOU'RE ASKING FOR—
YOU MIGHT GET IT!

Throughout this chapter, I've assumed that your church is seriously committed to evangelism. I've raised a whole series of questions for you to consider. There is one last question to pose: how *serious* is your commitment to evangelism? Sharing the good news with others can bring joy, but it can also bring pain and trial for both the evangelizer and the evangelized.

Earlier in the chapter I quoted from an exchange during a meeting of a women's retreat team at Holy Trinity. That retreat program, Christ Renews His Parish (CRHP), had a powerful spiritual impact on many of its participants. Lives were changed as individuals found themselves on fire with a zeal for their faith. As the excerpt illustrated, one question that CRHP participants struggled with was how to share their faith with others, particularly in the workplace.

This issue frequently came up in the men's retreat teams, as well. One man was particularly inspired by a variety of experiences at church to push the evangelistic envelope at his job, where he held a highly paid management position. In a spiritual life history interview, he described himself as struggling to arrive at a comfort level with "how far I can push things without pushing people away." His screensaver at work had a Christian message. When a storm inflicted tremendous damage on Holy Trinity's sister church, a predominantly black congregation in Detroit, he sent an e-mail around to solicit help. "You know, we're [people from Holy Trinity] going, you can meet me at this church, and I need chainsaws." He talked with work colleagues "about getting Bible stuff off the Internet, and it was an open area with a bunch of other people just kind of listening. I'm sure that they were kind of like aghast that we were talking about that." At a company retreat, as part of an exercise, he had been asked to take a piece of nature and describe himself.

> There was a cluster of three trees that were on the grounds of the hotel. Huge, like a foot and a half diameter. And two of them were still there, and one was cut down at the base and that's where I sat and wrote my piece, and I said basically the two tall trees were God and family; and the one cut off was career and that I was cutting career off...so that sunlight would hit the other two and grow, but that I think my career needed to be cut down so that it could be pruned and flourish as well. And, you know, instead of always working more hours, working kind of smarter type of approach as well. And I kind of wonder whether or not that was kind of the message that the owner didn't really want to hear. And, well, anyways, we got a new [chief of his division], and I lost bunches of perks that I had.

At a CRHP meeting a few months later, he announced that he had just been told in a seven-year review that he was being replaced, and the next day he no longer had a job. The news had surprised him; he had assumed that the worst of his company's restructuring had passed. He did not accuse the company of religious prejudice. But he did describe a conversation he recently had with a corporate headhunter:

> I shared with him putting God first. I don't want to work more than 50 hours a week. His answer was that "when people get paid what you do, they [the company] want them [the employers] put first and 80 plus hours. They want someone with 75 hours per week." I walked away feeling down. It took a day to sort it out. That's okay. I keep praying to put my life priorities right.

Though his family was struggling, he and his wife both felt that "if we hadn't gone through CRHP, it would have been a lot different in stress and communication and sharing with the kids." And his wife and his CRHP team, as well as other members of the congregation, continued to be tremendously supportive during his period of unemployment.

This man tried not to view the firing as a tragedy. Rather, he felt that "God's got bigger plans for me." He even briefly considered going to seminary. He spent much of his involuntary free time on church activities. Eventually, the crisis was resolved when he took another executive position.

This story had a happy ending, but it clearly demonstrates that, in Bonhoeffer's words, there are "costs of discipleship." If your church decides to take its evangelism efforts seriously, you also need to be ready to take the risks and accept the responsibilities that may grow out of your evangelism.

8

Nurturing

What Is Your Church's Nurturing Style?

How do you as a faith community minister to the ill, injured, dying, hungry, lonely, sorrowful, infirm, and aged; in short, how do you care for those who are hurting in body and spirit? I briefly raised this issue in chapter 1. I wanted to remind you early on that it is when your congregation ministers with compassion and love to the suffering, inside and outside your pews, that you are most truly counterculturally Christian. Before turning to the concluding chapter, I ask you to ponder in more depth that same issue: what is your congregation's nurturing style?

My motivations for raising this question are biblical as well as personal. Throughout the gospels, we are enjoined to care for those in need (physically and spiritually). Jesus tells us that whether we will be judged righteous or accursed will depend upon whether we fed the hungry and the thirsty, welcomed the stranger and clothed the naked, cared for the ill and visited the imprisoned (Matt. 25:31-36). As Jesus informs the righteous, "Truly, I tell you, just as you did it to one of the least of these who are members of my family, you did it to me." (Matt. 25:40). In the book of Acts and the New Testament epistles, members of Christian communities are praised for how they care for each other spiritually and materially. You can easily come up with your own favorite examples of this theme.

As for my personal motivations, I did not grow up in a churched family. Yet at the lowest points in my adult life, when most stressed, anxious, downcast, or bewildered, I turned to religion. Precisely why remains a mystery to me, though I know that I never viewed religion as a form of escapism. Rather, faced by adversity, it was as though I instinctively recognized my need to grow spiritually or else be overwhelmed.

For many years, however, my quest was a solitary one. I read about religion or spirituality. Perhaps because I hadn't grown up in a faith community, I was wary of "organized religion." Only well into middle age did I take the plunge. Sensing the limitations of religion outside of community, I was baptized, confirmed, and became a member of a church, a faith community. Like virtually anyone else who has been active in a congregation or parish, I have seen the seamier side of church life: the hypocrisy, self-righteousness, and pettiness. At the same time, however, I've also experienced the variety of ways in which congregations succeed at nurturing their members, including me.

What is nurturing? When I first thought of the title for this chapter, I hadn't checked the word's dictionary meaning. Nurturing. The word just felt right. I had in mind how churches deal with what are ultimately matters of the heart and the soul, dimensions of life that may deeply engage the mind but also go far beyond the intellect.

For me, nurturing is what we need and sometimes seek when we hurt, hunger, desperately question, and face the challenge of growing— rather than wilting—in the face of heartache and tragedy. And as I have come to realize as I age, nurturing is *also* what we need when all seems to be going well, when we feel smug and satisfied and thus need the challenge of growing spiritually rather than just acquiring more things, getting more comfortable, or enjoying greater power and prestige.

The Oxford English Dictionary's definition of nurturing, while more clinical, encompasses most of the dimensions I've just described: "To feed or nourish; to support and bring up to maturity; to rear;" "To foster, cherish;" and "To bring up, train, educate."

Earlier in our discussion of worship, I suggested that the unique way a congregation worships on Sunday powerfully expresses much of what goes on in that church's life outside the sanctuary and during the other six days of the week. The nurturing style of each congregation is just as distinctive. But it is less easily identified since it does not express itself quite as clearly in one particular time and place. Nurturing style is an accumulation of what occurs across a congregation's diverse activities, from worshiping to two members eating breakfast together at a local restaurant, to members of a woman's circle bringing a meal to a grieving family.

Your nurturing style may not be why newcomers are initially attracted to your church. But it may well be why your members stay and become deeply committed to your congregation—or remain only marginally attached. Most important, it may be why your members grow or fail to grow as Christians. And the potential for failing to grow is great in a society that celebrates the cult of happiness and health. We fear getting too close to those who suffer and hurt, as though their afflictions might rub off on us and we might become "losers" by association. Yet by word and action Christ taught us that we are closest to him when we nurture those in pain and need. In the pages that follow, we explore how our mainline congregations have responded to that spiritual challenge, each in its own unique way.

This chapter tries to show, in short, that your faith community's identity and mission are in great measure defined by its nurturing style. It is as a nurturing congregation that you are most counterculturally Christian. You are both being disciples and making disciples by your example.

THE SPIRITUAL IMPORTANCE OF NURTURING

Whether as a researcher or a church member, witnessing how congregations nurture their members has often moved and inspired me. Anyone, believer or not, can be touched by the material help a congregation may offer its members. As a Christian researcher, however, I found myself particularly affected, most tempted to cross the boundary line between observer and participant, during events like Bible studies. Questions of faith were explicitly voiced or articulated on those occasions, especially when participants brought deep personal concerns to the table.

After all, I too puzzle over, struggle with, and ponder how to relate faith to daily life. And well into my 50s, how to nurture and how to be nurtured are issues closely intertwined with my religious life. I have had to deal with the debilitating illnesses and subsequent deaths of both parents. Like an ever-increasing number of friends and colleagues of my generation, I have had to face the mounting evidence of my own frailty and mortality. My thoughts go well beyond the practical concerns of nurturing (e.g., expenses and medicines) to a quest to understand and respond to illness, aging, death, and tragedy in the context of my religious convictions and practices.

I take this quest—which I have in common with many people in the pews—to be realistic and not illusory or delusional. Throughout this research and the writing of this book I try, as an anthropologist, to relate (and urge you to relate) what goes on in our congregations to other secular forces, including economic and political developments and other variables like education, gender, and generation. I certainly don't assume, however, (and don't expect you to assume) that those are the only forces at work. I collected vast quantities of qualitative and quantitative empirical data on our congregations and have spent years analyzing them rigorously. But I have never seen myself as just "solving" some intellectual or practical puzzles.

Congregations, particularly as they nurture their members, are also mysteries deserving of wonder. I believe that while sharing in the lives of project congregations, I have seen God's grace and the Holy Spirit actively at work. When a congregation sings *Veni sanctus spiritus* ("Come Holy Spirit"), the haunting hymn from Taize, or when, at the end of a meeting, a group holds hands while reciting in unison the Lord's Prayer, I believe those voices are not merely drifting into a void.

I sometimes wonder about researchers without any faith or belief in the religious or spiritual traditions they're studying. Are they like tone-deaf people trying to describe music? A tone-deaf person could productively study music by analyzing sound as it is transformed into lines on an oscilloscope. The tone deaf researcher observing music on the oscilloscope may discover significant patterns and regularities that might not be apparent to a mere listener. However, that researcher would also miss whole dimensions of what the listeners are experiencing in the music. He or she would most likely be oblivious to what entrances and delights the listeners, what lifts the listeners to sublime heights or plunges them into abysmal depths. I have never felt compelled to choose between a quest to understand intellectually and a quest to appreciate through the eyes and heart of faith. In this research I have tried to do both, and each quest has, I believe, enriched the other.

A QUANTITATIVE LOOK AT NURTURING IN CONGREGATIONS

Let's start by examining nurturing with our "oscilloscope," looking at what our survey statistics suggest. How often do the worshiping communities of our churches participate in nurturing kinds of church activities? We asked people to estimate how often they participate in 33 widely varied church activities. We categorized four as nurturing: (1) "Visiting nursing homes, hospitals, shut-ins or other people facing difficulties;" (2) "Writing cards or notes to people who are ill, shut in or having difficult times;" (3) "Prayer chain or small group prayer in response to prayer requests;" (4) "Taking a meal to people who are housebound." We combined these four activities into a nurturing "index," a rough measure of how often church members participate in at least one of these activities. We also developed indexes for church work, socializing, small group, adult education, and music activities.

THE NURTURING INDEX AND THE PEOPLE IN THE PEWS

We found that over 46 percent of the people in the pews participate in a nurturing activity more than once a year (table 8.1). On the other hand, of the five indexes, nurturing has the second lowest frequency of participation; only involvement in musical groups comes in lower. There is a wide gap between nurturing and the more frequent activities. For instance, attendance at adult education is over 10 percent higher, while taking part in social or small groups, fellowship between services, and doing church work are approximately 30 percent higher.

Before looking more closely at what the nurturing index tells us, we need to remember that it does not represent all possible nurturing activities. Nurturing also comprises an important part of educational, social, and worship activities in a congregation. Think, for example, of when an individual asks for prayers for an ill family member at the start of a church council meeting or when women at a circle gathering walk over to hug someone who has been going through a rough time with her elderly parents.

A closer examination of our nurturing index results reveals that nurturing patterns are not at all simple. We'll explore these patterns with the expectation that observing the complexity in other churches can help

Table 8.1

Types of Activities that Congregation Members Participate in

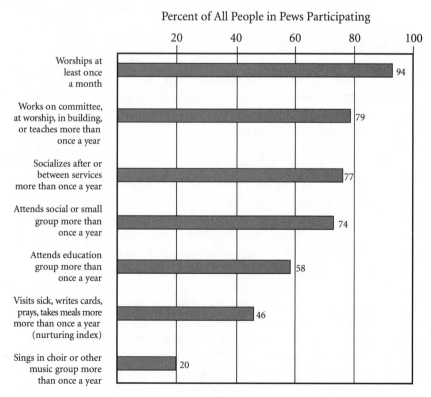

Percent of All People in Pews Participating

you recognize the complexity you need to address in your own church. But let's start with some fairly clear-cut findings about general patterns among core and non-core, younger, middle-aged, older, male and female, low-income and high-income members.

Older members are most likely to have the time and inclination to be involved in nurturing index activities. Sixty-three percent of those 60 years of age or older participate in nurturing activities more than once a year. This is one area of congregational life where a real generation gap does exist. There is a mere 3 percent difference between the youngest (18- to 39-year-olds) and middle-age groups (40- to 59-year-olds) in nurturing participation levels; approximately 40 percent of each group reports engaging in nurturing activities more than once a year. When we examine those involved in nurturing activities more than once a month, the older people remain considerably more involved, and the relative gap between them and the two younger groups increases. Members of the oldest group are two times more likely than younger members to be involved in nurturing more than once a month.

The findings also indicate gender and core/non-core differences in nurturing. Women and core members participate more often in these activities. This is not surprising. But you might be interested to learn that people in the highest household income bracket ($100,000 or more) are less involved in nurturing than those with fewer financial resources (table 8.2). This is true among retirees (the over-60 group), as well as among those more likely to be professionally active (the two groups under 60 years of age). It is possible that the wealthier provide more financial support to their congregations, and those monetary resources certainly can be vital to nurturing activities. However, the rich don't give as much of their time to nurturing others.

There are thus considerable differences by age, gender, core and non-core members, and household income in frequency of nurturing activities. But in none of the cases are those differences absolute, or even close to absolute. In all instances, there are plenty of people within the categories of those less likely to nurture who do, in fact, do so.

In popular culture, particularly self-help books, there is a tendency to make extreme absolute statements about various populations. These statements have the virtue of being simple, dramatic, and memorable. And all too often I heard those types of observations repeated in church groups, especially when it came to gender. Unfortunately, like any caricature or stereotype they can often be quite inaccurate. Many men may be from Mars, but some are from Venus; and many women may be from Venus, but some are from Mars. Not recognizing this fact can do great

Table 8.2

Members Who Nurture Others, by Age and Income

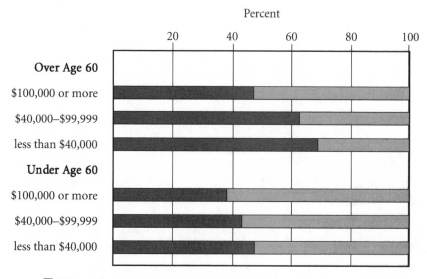

Percent

■ Visits sick, writes cards, prays, takes meals more than once a year
□ Does not

disservice to the many exceptions to the rules. When dealing with nurturing, it's important to know that some populations may be more amenable to certain approaches. It is equally vital, however, not to ignore or write off the others in your planning.

NURTURING STYLES OF CONGREGATIONS

What type of nurturing occurs when a particular mix of people comes together to form a unique faith community? And what changes occur when that mix of individuals interacts with institutional factors: denomination, size of the congregation, percentage of long-time members, pastor's nurturing style, and the nature and structure of the congregation's core?

What happens? The simple answer is that nurturing patterns become incredibly complex. There is no substitute for discovering your own congregation's uniqueness (particularly by comparing it with realistic information about other churches) before you plunge into a prepackaged program to improve this central element of your mission. Prepackaged programs are usually built on some underlying (probably unconscious or unexamined) assumptions about the nature of a congregation. But there are no generic congregations. Chances are high that the multifaceted character of your congregation will not match the program's assumptions. It's somewhat like installing a new program on your computer. No matter how wonderful the program's potential, it will only work on your computer if it is compatible with your system.

NURTURING ACTIVITIES BY CONGREGATION

Do congregations differ significantly in how frequently their members nurture each other? Yes, and the range of variation is startlingly wide, whether we look at nurturing for more than once a year (where one congregation had 72 percent and another had 36 percent participation) or for more than once a month (where the same congregations had 43 and 14 percent participation.)

What explains these dramatic differences? Tables 8.3 and 8.4 provide details of the variations.

The two Baptist churches have the highest nurturing index percentages at more than once a year, and more than once a month. In the chapter on denomination, we saw that despite radical differences in ethnic background, education level, size, history, and location, Bethel Baptist and Second Baptist share surprising similarities with regard to many issues of faith, belief, and practice. This looks to be another case where denomination may really matter, with a particular commitment to nurturing forming part of a denomination's ethos.

How about size as a factor influencing nurturing? After all, in a small congregation members are most likely to know each other, and the types of activities we've included under the nurturing index presumably would be most apt to occur. Bethel Baptist, with its worshiping community of only 71, has the highest frequency of participation in nurturing index activities. And St. Timothy Presbyterian, which also ranks high on nurturing, is the second smallest worshiping community, though its membership differs radically from Bethel's in education and income levels. By contrast, Holy Trinity Lutheran, the church with far and away the largest worshiping community, has the lowest percentage of people in the pews participating in nurturing activities. Perhaps size is related to participation in nurturing among project congregations.

But how about Second Baptist? Second Baptist's worshiping community of 266 is the third largest congregation in the project, almost four times bigger than Bethel Baptist and nearly twice the size of St. Timothy. Nevertheless, the people in the pews at Second Baptist are the

Table 8.3
Members Who Perform Nurturing Activities More Than Once a Year

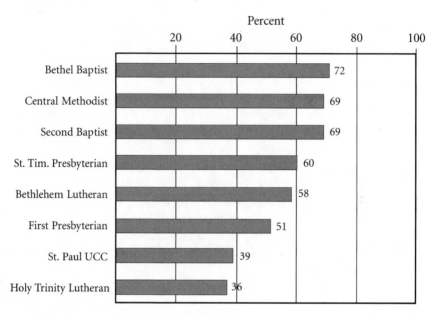

Table 8.4
Members Who Perform Nurturing Activities More Than Once a Month

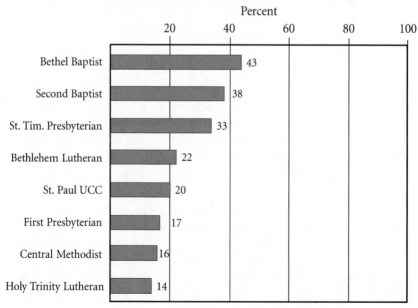

second most likely to participate in nurturing activities. Might factors
other than denomination explain this apparent anomaly? There are several other possibilities. Since Second Baptist is our only black congregation, the most obvious one is "race." Due to the nature of our sample,
however, it's impossible to test that possibility systematically.

Second Baptist also distinguishes itself in at least two other ways
that invite more rigorous examination. Age has a powerful impact on
nurturing activities, and Second Baptist is the most elderly of our congregations. Holy Trinity Lutheran, with its very low levels of nurturing,
is the youngest congregation in our sample, with few people above 60
years of age.

Second Baptist may be an exception that helps to explain a basic rule
of understanding congregations: seldom, if ever, does one factor (in this
case size), no matter how significant, completely or adequately explain
as complicated a phenomenon as nurturing in as complicated an organization as a congregation. In consequence, analyses and programs for
change that focus almost exclusively on one dimension of your church
frequently fail and frustrate.

Does the character of a congregation's core influence its nurturing
style? Intuitively it would seem that a core that includes a large proportion of the congregation's worshiping community would result in a high
level of nurturing for that congregation, and, conversely, a proportion-
ately smaller core would lower the level of nurturing. I spent much time
trying to find a simple pattern relating core size to the nurturing index.
Rather than bore you by reviewing all those numbers, let me simply assure you that there isn't any.

FEELING NURTURED BY THE CONGREGATION

What if we look at the relationship between your church's core and nurturing from a different angle? Let's examine how often people feel nurtured *by* their congregation, rather than how often they nurture others.
Viewed this way, the nature of a church's core and the character of its
pastor do play an important role, one that may help you understand
your own church.

We were able to learn about the recipients' perspectives on nurturing from a series of survey questions on help *received* during a life crisis.
We asked survey respondents to "Recall a major illness or accident or
other life crisis recently experienced by you or a family member. Did
religion or spirituality play any role in how you or your family responded
to it?" We then asked those who responded "yes" to describe the type of

crisis and to put a check next to any of a series of 18 religious or spiritual activities or experiences that they felt "were important in dealing with the crisis."

Approximately 85 percent of those surveyed recorded that they could recall a recent life crisis, and a hefty 92 percent of those reported that religion or spirituality had, indeed, played a role in how they or their family responded to it. The most frequently mentioned life crises were illness or accident (44%) and death (40%). Surprisingly, mental illness or drugs, family or marital crises, and financial crises were each reported by less than 5 percent of the respondents.

Just over 90 percent of those who indicated that religion or spirituality had played a role in the crisis reported that their support had included individual practices or experiences: their own prayers, reading from the Bible, their own feelings of peace, or hearing the voice of God inside themselves. In addition, exactly 80 percent reported that support had come from members of their congregation, usually in the form of congregational prayers, visits, counseling, cards, calls, or material support. Pastoral visits or counseling (including counseling by a church professional other than a pastor) were mentioned by 62 percent of those responding. Obviously, most people in the pews rely on a combination of their own inner resources and support from church members and staff to help them deal with life crises.

Looking a little closer at the individual religious or spiritual experiences that helped support people during life crises, we might find it striking that reading the Bible did *not* play a very prominent role. People most frequently drew support from their own prayers (80%) and feelings of peace (67%). Only 40 percent listed "reading the Bible" as a source of support during the life crisis, four percentage points below those who were helped by hearing "the voice of God within."

That reading the Bible played a comparatively minor role in the way people in the pews dealt with life crises—especially compared to prayer— was underscored by responses to a related survey question. We asked anyone who had recently experienced a life crisis to indicate if they had used any of 17 religious and secular sources of information (regardless of whether or not the sources were helpful or harmful). At 76 percent, prayer stood as the most frequently listed spiritual source of information, just as it had been the most frequently listed source of support. About 50 percent of the respondents mentioned their pastors, other church staff members, or small group meetings (like circles and Bible studies). Only 37 percent mentioned the Bible (although over 50 percent of the Baptists did). This certainly fits in with our findings about the relative importance of prayer as opposed to the Bible in mainline congregations.

If we look by church at what people report when asked whether congregational support (in the form of prayers, visits, cards, etc.) or pastoral visits or counseling helped them during a recent life crisis (tables 8.5 and 8.6), a somewhat different order appears than in our findings for how frequently people participated in nurturing others.

Bethel Baptist retains its top position as a highly nurturing congregation. On the other hand, St. Paul UCC, Holy Trinity Lutheran, and First Presbyterian ranked relatively low in terms of percentage of people nurturing *other* members (see table 8.4). But the people in the pews at these very same churches are among the most likely to report *receiving* support during a recent life crisis.

St. Paul UCC, First Presbyterian, and Holy Trinity Lutheran also rank near the top of the list of those who felt support from pastor visits or counseling. Note, as well, that here Bethel Baptist drops to one of the lower positions.

What could these rankings indicate? I can make a good guess based on our experiences in these congregations. It may not be common among

Table 8.5
People Reporting Support from Congregation Members during a Recent Life Crisis

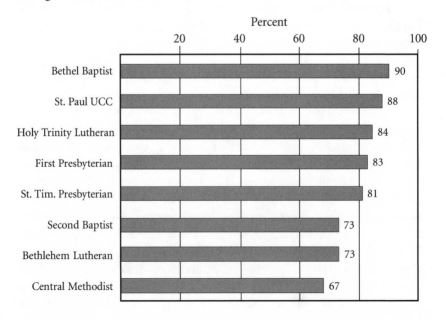

Table 8.6

People Reporting Support from Pastor Visits or Counseling during a Recent Life Crisis

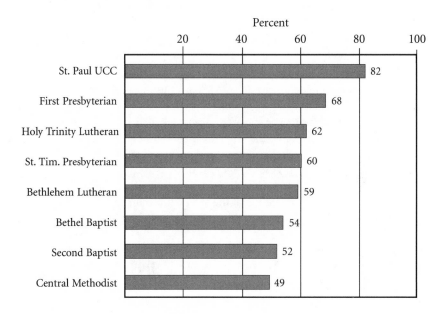

the people in the pews at St. Paul, Holy Trinity, and First Presbyterian to be active nurturers. A small number of people there, however, make a point of participating in those activities when something serious happens to other members.

I am confident that the pastors' style and dedication to nurturing (the priority he or she puts on that facet of ministry) have a powerful effect on their congregations. That certainly would be the case at St. Paul UCC. Pastor Geoff Drutchas has a deep commitment to nurturing his church community, and the people of St. Paul strongly appreciated his dedication to them. In fact, his associate pastor even reported that she didn't "get to work that much with [life crises], since Geoff is more likely to get the problems."

This is how some core members described Geoff's role in their life crises:

> "The next thing I remember is Geoff was there. It's just like, I don't know, if an angel went to get him...I just remember him being there, and from that day on, I mean, he was always here."

"I confided a lot in Rev. Geoff, and he, through his prayers I guess or whatever, things worked out and worked out for the best, and [my wife] and I have resolved our differences."

"Geoff was the only one that knew. I didn't tell anyone else about it."

Curiously, Geoff himself was also among the most realistic and modest of the pastors when discussing his role as nurturer.

Lots of issues don't come to me.... A lot of things in this congregation are private, and...the family network is very real. You're told "everybody is related to each other here, so watch what you say." This is of some concern. Some churches are alter[nate] families, and people bring [problems], hash them out, and then come back and deal with the family. Here that doesn't happen. You come to church, and your family is here. Some areas that do come up...When ill, dying, then people feel safe enough. Some of the areas I don't get approached about—divorce, which I suspect is a major crisis spiritually.

Spiritual life history interviews, though drawn from a limited sample, also suggest that pastors don't get approached very often on family, marital, or work issues. Only a little over 10 percent of our interviewees reported receiving support from a pastor in dealing with an adult life crisis of that sort. This low figure also may reflect some pastors' self-perception that they're not really trained to deal with such crises, and so their role is to provide these members with referrals to other trained professionals.

This does not mean that people feel they have to go it alone, relying only on their own faith and prayers for spiritual support when faced with family, marital, financial, or work problems. Over 40 percent of those with this type of crisis mention receiving support from fellow church members. The importance of church member support is underlined by another startling finding: fewer than 10 percent reported receiving such support from their own family.

What have these results of our study told us about nurturing? I think it's fair to say that when it comes to nurturing, people in the pews are as much "active ministers" as their ordained leaders. For members going through hard times, their congregation may even become a more supportive family than their real relatives. The discussion above has introduced some of the numerous factors that can influence your congregation's nurturing style. In order to fully appreciate the complexity of nurturing styles (including your own church's), we need, however, to look beyond the quantitative data considered so far.

We now turn to an in-depth comparative case study of nurturing in two congregations. It provides a detailed view of what nurturing styles look and feel like on the ground. Although their nurturing styles differ radically, these congregations are based on the same spiritual foundation. Their members minister to each other in a spirit of Christian humility. They do not shy away from acknowledging their own flaws and failings as they reach out to others in need. Above all, the nurturing styles of both congregations are solidly based in a countercultural bottom line, a recognition that we are all sinners dependent on God's mercy and grace.

Nurturing Congregations: A Ground-level View

Bethel Baptist and Holy Trinity Lutheran represent the extremes of nurturing as determined by the measures we described in the previous section. While these congregations part ways with each other in virtually every arena, in both churches I sensed the Holy Spirit intensely at work and felt the glow of spiritual fire. At the end of this section, I suggest some major lessons about nurturing styles that you can draw from the experiences of these two churches.

Nurturing at Bethel Baptist

Rev. Geoff Drutchas once told me that "lots of things are private at St. Paul." But Bethel, which is located just a few miles away, seems to take the opposite approach. As at St. Paul, there are significant family ties among Bethel members. Even the pastor has married into the congregation. Yet many Bethel members seem deeply attached to their congregation precisely because they feel safe sharing their personal and family concerns there.

A Bible Study

At some churches, months passed before we became privy to the personal and family turmoil often seething beneath the apparently staid congregational surface. At Bethel, however, merely listening to the prayer requests in a Sunday Bible study would alert a visitor to the difficult times many members experience.

There are the usual major and minor illnesses, and, as in several other congregations, people regularly pass around get-well cards to be signed by Bible class members. However, Bible studies at Bethel are also likely to include frank and personal discussions of the stress of living on the financial edge and the struggle to raise children. Here is an example from my field notes.

Helen announces that she can only stay at Bible study for half an hour. She has to work one of her part-time jobs this Sunday morning.[11] Helen does have time, however, to report that she's asking for a modification of her child support payments. She woke up one morning and asked herself, "Why was I working two jobs, when my ex-husband had enough money to be taking my son to a hockey tournament in Vancouver?" Helen also hopes that her car will keep working until she's financially solvent enough to purchase another, and is thankful for surviving a series of financial crises. She then returns to what she's really upset about: her son.

He's loud and obnoxious. He won't listen to her. Recently they went shopping, and he was touching everything and then acting like she was going to hit him. She imitates her son shrinking away from her as though he were afraid. Helen had a real fear, though: people in the store might call the police, thinking she actually hit her son. That's a charge she vehemently denies and appeals to a friend in the class to confirm her innocence.

Instead, Sam, a stocky, middle-aged construction worker, interrupts Helen: he'd wait until he got the boy out into the car, and *then* he'd hit him. Was Sam joking? It's not clear, to me at least.

Helen is not to be diverted: she told her son that he was acting like his father. She divorced his dad for acting that way. If that's the way her son acts, it's not surprising that he complains about having no friends.

Barb, the Bible study teacher, takes it all in quietly. Pastor Dahlen describes Barb as "a pillar of the church, a real link from the past to the future." She grew up in Bethel and started teaching adult Sunday school when only 17. "She may not be aware of it," says Pastor Dahlen, "but she has the respect of virtually everyone."

Barb exudes authority and is clearly at ease in front of a group. She worked as a teacher and counselor in the Detroit Public Schools for 25 years, though she had only gone to college after raising five children. She began teaching in the "racially" tense period following the riots in the city, having decided to go where she felt the Lord wanted her to be.

Barb's professional expertise in counseling is in evidence as she tries to help Helen deal with her anger towards her son. Barb suggests that her son may be responding to Helen's lack of time for him. Helen strongly denies this possibility. Barb takes another tack, urging Helen "to separate [her son's] behavior from him as a person." While Helen also ignores that piece of advice, she tells the group just how much she appreciates its support. She has to go to work in a few minutes, but wants them to know: "I had to come in order to get through the next week."

For the day's Bible lesson, Barb turns to Romans 7:15-24: "I do not understand my own actions. For I do not do what I want, but I do the very thing I hate.... Who will rescue me from this body of death?" Sam responds as though Paul had just personally posed the question to him: "I then ask God through Jesus." When Barb asks the group, "Do you ever feel mixed up?" Sam again answers for himself, "All the time."

Sam is not ashamed to admit publicly his past failures while praising the saving grace of the Holy Spirit in his life. In contrast to the unspoken rules of decorum in other mainline churches, Sam's blunt openness is acceptable, not even exceptional, at Bethel. It's no secret that some of the congregation's mainstays have occasionally slipped from the straight and narrow way.

Sam recently asked to be rebaptized at Bethel. It is the church's policy to ask prospective members with a Christian history to discuss their background with the deacons. Sam was typically forthright:

> I have been away from the Lord and come back, thank God. The love of God has brought me back to church. I belong to God's church. This church. I associate with the members and praise the Lord in this congregation.... In my past life, I've failed. But I've been washed in the blood of the Lamb. I get emotions some time, because I can feel the Spirit. My calling is to spread that Spirit. I'm human. I have a tendency to make mistakes.

One of the deacons responded, "You're in good company." And everyone, including Sam, knew that the deacon was not just paying lip service to that sentiment. For that deacon is not ashamed to admit that his alcoholism almost destroyed his own family.

Sam's admission that he feels "mixed up all the time" allows Barb to redirect attention back to Helen's problems. "I think of Helen, with so much to do," she says, and proceeds to list all the tasks Helen needs to accomplish in order to care for her child and herself. "She can't do it all by herself." When Helen admits to the group that she does find it hard to ask for help, Barb sympathizes: "It's humbling. That's why we're here as a Christian body." Sam chimes in. "That's why I come to...Bible study. To get through the week," to which Barb adds, "That's why I go to choir practice, where we always have prayer requests."

And everyone in the group knows that Barb has indeed needed others' prayers. Like Helen, Barb became a single mother after her first husband died in a train accident, leaving her with four young kids. She learned from her first husband's tragic death that "each day was a gift." Barb loves scripture, and her favorite verse is Romans 8:28: "We know that all things work together for good for those who love God, who are called according to his purpose." Barb claims "that's what has got me through my problems." And there have been many in addition to her first husband's death.

Fifteen years ago Barb was diagnosed with colon cancer and given six months to live. "I dealt with that pretty calmly.... I relaxed. The doctor thinks I recovered because of my positive attitude." Just five years ago, physicians gave Barb a five percent chance of survival when she had a severe allergic reaction to a medicine and suffered kidney failure. But Barb is not afraid of dying, and again she miraculously survived.

As Pastor Dahlen observes, Barb has always come through these trials "with an upbeat faith and testimony." In a Sunday school class led by another member, the teacher asked about people who may have planted the seeds of faith in their lives, who helped to form their faith. "Barb has had a big effect on me," volunteered one woman. The rest of the class chimed in: "On a lot of us!"

A Community of Believers

Barb is not unique at Bethel. The Sunday school class readily named plenty of Bethel people who had influenced their faith and that of their children, including some folks sitting in the class with them. The teacher emphasized the importance of Bethel as a community of believers: "I can look around and see people who helped me.... No matter where, it's a struggle. We're part of a community and don't know how we affect people."

From the first time I attended worship at Bethel, I felt the presence of a close-knit and intimate faith community: "The whole church is alive with people of every age, circulating and loudly greeting each other. The church feels more like a large family living room than a solemn place of worship." Yet Bethel is also extraordinarily welcoming to outsiders and newcomers, including our research team. As researcher Dr. Mike McCallion recorded in his field notes from his first Sunday visit to Bethel:

> As I came into the church, three people immediately came up to me and welcomed me to their church. They asked me if this was my first time to the church and where I was from. They knew that I was new to the church. So it was a very warm and comfortable feeling as I entered the church. Then I sat down in the last pew, which was very comfortable, and said "hello" to the woman in the pew in front of

me. She asked me several questions, and we ended up having a rather lengthy conversation. As we were talking, Harry from the Men's Breakfast came by and said "hello" and kept walking. Then two other people from the parish introduced themselves to me and said "welcome." And, finally, the woman in charge of welcoming guests asked me if it would be all right if she introduced me at the beginning of the service. I said "sure," and she took down my name and practiced pronouncing it a couple of times.

Like almost all of the project churches, Bethel is better at welcoming people once they're in the doors than at getting newcomers to come through the church portals the first time. "They are not good at inviting," according to Pastor Roger Dahlen, "but once here they take visitors very seriously." He is not alone in recognizing this shortcoming. While at Bethel, we heard much discussion of expanding evangelism efforts, particularly in the local neighborhood. Historically, Bethel has not enjoyed close ties to its immediate surroundings in Southgate.

When first founded in 1917, the congregation was located in another Downriver community, Wyandotte. In 1954, the congregation agreed to the denomination's request that they relocate and become a mission church in the present location. "They stopped being a neighborhood church and became a driving church," according to Roger. "It was a bold step of obedience and faith in God, and they had to pay a price for it, but I admire that about this community, a bold and faithful move. It is really something."

The Bethel welcome was especially warm for those in need of nurturing, like Helen. The first thing Barb said about Bethel in our initial interview was "We collect hurting people.... We're more a church of servants. Our goal is to serve people." She described how Bethel had nurtured a man who became a deacon and much respected member of the church, a person mentioned by the Sunday school class as a source of spiritual inspiration: "Al walked to church five miles. We taught him how to drive."

I attended Al's last deaconate meeting, after he had served in that position for three years. This quiet, determined man, who needed Bethel so much at the beginning, is now vitally important to the congregation in many ways. But Bethel still subtly nurtures him. The pastor reminds the chair of the deacons that it's time to say goodbye to Al. The chair responds, "I was getting to that.... I wanted to say something about my buddy. First, let me read some of the responsibilities of the deaconate." The list includes scheduling ushers and filling the immersion baptismal pool, which are Al's special tasks. "My question is," the chair continues, "the person who takes care of the ushers, is it necessary that an active deacon is responsible for it or is the deaconate responsible to get someone?"

The pastor assures the chair that "the deaconate is responsible. It doesn't have to be an active or former deacon who actually performs those duties." The chair continues his not very subtle maneuvering, "Mr. Al, having served with you for three years, I appreciate all your hard, silent work.... But, believe me, you're still my baptism pool man. No one cleans and fills a baptism pool like you. There's not a drop of water on the floor when you fill it."

Al interrupts the chair to describe some of the technical difficulties of keeping the floor dry when filling the baptismal pool. The pastor then decides to be more direct and prompts the chair, "You might want to ask if Al would continue along with other things." After explaining that he had just felt it was time for a break after three years, Al agrees to continue filling the baptismal pool, as well as some other responsibilities.

At first glance, the deacons' discussion centers on a pretty mundane issue: ensuring that one of their numerous organizational responsibilities, filling the baptismal pool, will be efficiently fulfilled despite a change in the committee's membership. Yet, learning about Al and the Bethel baptismal pool was an "ah ha" moment for me. Although the chair took a light-hearted approach, he and everyone else in the room knew that they were dealing with what was, for Al, a profoundly sacred issue. Al might not be able to articulate in eloquent words his deepest spiritual convictions, but the loving care with which he undertook a potentially messy chore spoke volumes to the congregation's members about what remained a profoundly sacred issue to many of them as well.

For Bethel is, after all, a Baptist church. Baptism is central to Bethel people's denominational identity. Recall how Sam felt compelled to be rebaptized when officially joining Bethel, as had the chair of the deacons who had originally been baptized in a different tradition. To witness the deacons' discussion with Al about the baptismal pool was to see a living confirmation of Paul's wise admonition to the Corinthians: "Now there are varieties of gifts, but the same Spirit; and there are varieties of services, but the same Lord; and there are varieties of activities, but it is the same God who activates all of them in everyone" (1 Cor. 12:4-7).

The Role of the Pastor

Pastor Dahlen takes no credit for the welcoming and nurturing nature of the congregation, a view confirmed by our survey. The survey validated our fieldwork-based impression that Bethel is one of the most nurturing churches, but it also revealed that the pastor's role in nurturing remained comparatively minor. Roger sees himself, instead, "as a preacher and worship leader primarily. I focus on worship more, and I try to help people to do that better, worship better." He also, somewhat guiltily, admits to thoroughly enjoying administration: "I could just sit at this desk all day and organize things."

Roger, too, has experienced the power of Bethel's nurturing style:

> I know people here, when there is a crisis, realize the importance of the community of faith. This church will surround people and support them. Over the years, I have seen people who have been helped. When it actually happened to me, when last December my mother died and I found myself at the receiving end, it was breathtaking.

If the congregation takes the major responsibility for nurturing its members, it may be due to its small size. Historically, Bethel's pastors have not remained in this tiny church long enough to become immersed in the community. "I have the longest tenure of any pastor," Roger explained. "One was here for 13 years, and…the rest of the pastors were [at Bethel only] 3 and 4 years."

Nurturing, a Double-edged Sword

An essential component of Bethel's style of nurturing is to welcome people just as they are and then surround them with a loving and caring faith community. At the same time, this style also points to one of the congregation's fundamental weaknesses: "We don't want to hurt feelings. We want people to be happy, and that's not the real world," was how Barb phrased it. Her comment came after she had described the time-consuming, circuitous way in which Bethel's deacons handled a minor liturgical crisis that occurred when one of its pastors wanted to show up at services wearing a robe he had received as a gift:

> No pastor at Bethel wears robes. It was not a good idea. [The pastor was already a "very formal" person and]…didn't need any more barriers. No one ever wore a robe…the meeting [of the deacons]…lasted 3 hours. We all knew that he [the pastor] shouldn't do it, but no one wanted to hurt his feelings. They knew someone's feelings would be hurt, but they didn't want a robe.

Barb's own ambivalence about what she saw as a congregational weakness (as well as strength) was clear when I asked her a different question, "Who are the key people in the church spiritually, in worship?" She described the first person who came to her mind as "the sweetest person. He never wants to hurt people. He influenced me. He epitomized love." Bethel also avoids "hurting people" by sidestepping issues that might split the congregation. I asked Pastor Dahlen, "What are some recent issues you're facing right now?" Roger found it necessary first to explain another distinctive characteristic of Bethel.

> We have not been issue-driven like with others on the issue of
> abortion, sex, or politics. These things are not brought up here. They
> have agreed to disagree. So, like pro-life, some are involved, but they
> don't bring that issue with them here, and they do not ask me to
> support them. It is really driven by love, and we grow in faith and
> encourage that very much. It is a simple vision.

In theory, it's a simple vision. In practice, what happens when an individual joins Bethel and, consciously or unconsciously, breaks this unspoken ethos? What happens when a newcomer rejects the idea of agreeing to disagree and chooses to be confrontational or at least vocal on a potentially divisive issue? How does Bethel's leadership respond? Does it avoid hurting the newcomer's feelings (accept the newcomer just as she is) and allow the newcomer to hurt others in the congregation?

We glimpsed how much Bethel struggles with such questions towards the end of our research there. In a variety of small groups, a newcomer began voicing strong opinions on the divisive issues that Bethel tries to avoid (e.g., abortion, gay and lesbian rights). Moreover, he expressed those views in a tone oozing with contempt for anyone holding an opposing opinion. His entire demeanor seemed diametrically opposed to Bethel's vision of being "driven by love." It's not surprising that Bethel lay leaders at first did not respond directly or decisively to this individual. Comments made to our researchers made it clear that the younger lay leaders were deeply disturbed by his behavior but baffled by how to deal with it. Perhaps, in part, it was their relative inexperience as church leaders that made this newcomer such a thorny problem for them.

Resolving Conflict

I had seen some of these emerging church leaders struggle with other decisions in which complex and sensitive personal and religious issues were inextricably entwined. One involved a long and anxious discussion by the church deacons over how to handle the request of several of the church's children to be baptized at a much younger age than was customary at Bethel. Did these kids really know what the decision to be baptized means and why you do it? How would turning down a child's request for baptism affect him or her, as well as the families? How would the rest of the church react if some or all of these kids were turned down—or were baptized? The chair of the deacons openly admitted how much these questions perplexed him:

> There's no written gospel that says what age it can take place.
> However, some people tell their kids they should wait until a certain age before they will discuss it with them. I've been asked, "Doesn't Bethel have the age in its constitution?" I always answer that "It's not the type of question for the by-laws." Usually, the question of baptism has been easy. This is a tough one.

He had hoped that the kids' parents would let the deacons off the hook by telling their children that they were too young. The parents hadn't, and so the decision was left to the deacons.

The chair of the deacons had thought about the problem all day. In a different context, Pastor Dahlen had commented that this emerging leader "really thinks things through. We had a conversation after a meeting in the parking lot on the nomination committee [for members of boards]. The next day he called and said he was up to 2 o'clock a.m. thinking it over."

Just before the first candidate for baptism was to come into the meeting room, the chair once more expressed his uneasiness. "I'm nervous. It's new to me. I go back to the Bible, where the Lord said, 'Bring me the children.' But I don't know if he wants them yet." The deacons eventually resolved this issue by considering each child individually. Two of the children were to be baptized, one because the deacons believed he was ready and the other only after they were certain that he understood the commitment he was making. The deacons spoke with the third boy and asked him to wait until he was older.

I have continually emphasized the spiritual danger of unconsciously importing inappropriate ideas from the professional world of work into the life of your faith community. Notice, however, that in the two examples from Bethel the lay leaders did not turn to management techniques or interpersonal communication skills to solve their dilemmas. They instead relied on biblical principles. In dealing with a disruptive member of the congregation the challenge was viewed as spiritual—how to be a Christian faith community of loving, nurturing servants in a world where people in need are not necessarily loveable. Dr. Angela Martin, the researcher who spent the most time with Bethel, suggested that, rather than using a business model in dealing with a disruptive person, Bethel chose to take seriously its commitment to being a spiritual family. In a family, you tolerate your relatives despite the disturbance and dysfunction some of them may foster.

In both cases, the leaders did not take a bureaucratic approach to their quandaries. They did not cleverly contrive rules and regulations that would give the superficial appearance of being objective and impersonal. Rather, they perceived the challenge to be the appropriate application of spiritual principles to the unique character and situation of each individual.

I think we can credit the leaders' backgrounds for this difficult but more spiritually meaningful approach. Very few of them were white-collar professionals. In fact, when Angela Martin made a presentation to Bethel on our survey findings and reported that two individuals in the church had a household income of over $100,000, the audience was shocked and became preoccupied with figuring out who in the world they could be.

Part of Bethel's strength as a nurturing community may be precisely that its leaders do not import lots of management ideas from the corporate or business world to the congregation's life, but approach running a church from a more spiritual and faithful perspective. There are many successful ways for a church to nurture its members. For example, Bethlehem Lutheran's highly successful health ministry and neighborhood outreach programs have been developed with the guidance and support of the congregation's nurses, physicians, and social workers. On occasion, however, Bethlehem has had to remind itself that what works for a nurse, physician, social worker, and childcare professional in a hospital, state agency, or daycare center is not necessarily appropriate in a faith community, especially one run almost exclusively by volunteers. Churches with many highly skilled and educated professionals must seriously ponder *how* they should appropriately draw upon those forms of knowledge and power.

Although I have stressed that Bethel provides some serious lessons about nurturing for your church, I suspect that some of you could dismiss them as irrelevant to your church's needs. After all, Bethel is the smallest church in our sample, and its economic and professional profile is much less middle-class. For that reason, I chose Holy Trinity Lutheran as a second case study on nurturing style. Holy Trinity will provide some new lessons about how congregations nurture. But it will also confirm some of the major points that emerged from our research at Bethel.

Nurturing at Holy Trinity Lutheran

Bethel and Holy Trinity differ from each other in virtually every facet of congregational character. Holy Trinity has the biggest worshiping community in the sample and a relatively large paid staff. Located in an up-scale middle-class suburb, its members are highly educated and typically employed in professional occupations, many as engineers or managers in the auto industry. Holy Trinity has an unusually small number of older members. Although it occasionally experiments with contemporary services, worship at Holy Trinity generally reflects a Lutheran, high liturgical tradition.

Holy Trinity's nurturing style also stands in striking contrast to Bethel's. Bethel's pattern is, with the exception of the role of the pastor, quite straightforward and consistent. Whether measured in terms of the percentage of people involved in nurturing or the percentage of them who have received help from fellow members during a recent life crisis, Bethel ranks at the top of our sample. The pattern of Holy Trinity's nurturing style is more complicated. In comparison with the rest of the project churches, the members of Holy Trinity's worshiping community are least likely to participate in nurturing activities. Yet a relatively high percentage of the worshiping community report receiving help from a congregation member or from a pastor during a recent life crisis.

How does this fit with what I experienced when attending Holy Trinity's Sunday worship? I've described the project experience at Bethel. Once more, Holy Trinity provides a vivid contrast.

Sunday Morning at Holy Trinity

"Comfort the afflicted and afflict the comfortable" is how some pastors describe their goal as preachers. At Sunday morning worship, few churches would have appeared more comfortable and less in need of comforting than Holy Trinity Lutheran. As the youngest congregation, bursting at the seams with children, you seldom saw elderly people shuffling painfully down the sanctuary aisle. Few walkers and wheelchairs were in evidence. The large sanctuary was elegant, with a wall of beautiful stained glass windows behind the altar. Banners and vestments were all in exquisite taste, as though Martha Stewart had been the liturgical consultant. Fellowship after services appeared restrained, with those who remained behind to socialize sticking close to their small circle of friends. Holy Trinity was so large that I sometimes wondered how folks distinguished between a first-time visitor and a long-time member. I attended worship at Holy Trinity almost every week for a year, and each Sunday many faces seemed unfamiliar.

Yet as I sat in the back of the sanctuary and looked around, I could see people whose outwardly comfortable, prosperous, and successful appearances were at odds with the hurts, traumas, scars, and agonies that they had actually suffered. I recognized a woman who had only begun to deal with the long-suppressed memory of a rape, a man who had grown up in an orphanage, a woman whose first marriage had ended when she finally could take no more physical abuse from her spouse, a man whose adultery had almost destroyed his marriage, a doting father who had to live with guilt for helping a girlfriend have an abortion years before, a dedicated mother who gave her first child, born out of wedlock, up for adoption.

Probably every church, even the most "respectable," has members who have suffered through similar traumatic life experiences. During our spiritual life history interviews, we witnessed tearful recollections and wept in sympathy with our interviewees. We had learned from our survey that pastors seldom hear about many of the non-health-related life crises that members experience. Certainly such crises were rarely discussed openly, even in small group activities. When First Presbyterian experimented with a special healing service, for example, few attended it. Pastor David Noble afterwards commented that it was sad so few had participated. David mused that when he looked out at the congregation during a sermon on Sunday, he could see the faces of many people who he knew were suffering and in need of healing.

So how did I come to know something about the pain behind the prosperous, smiling faces in the Holy Trinity sanctuary on Sunday? I had heard some people's stories during the spiritual life history interviews. But I learned more during my time with participants of spiritual retreat teams, groups of men and women involved in an ongoing program called Christ Renews His Parish (CRHP). Somehow, almost miraculously, Holy Trinity had developed a subculture of people who nurtured each other in a way that fostered sometimes startling leaps in their levels of spiritual engagement, commitment, and growth. I can't know for sure, but I strongly suspect that when a high percentage of the Holy Trinity worshiping community reported having received assistance from other congregation members during a recent life crisis, that help had often come from those in CRHP.

Christ Renews His Parish (CRHP)

When I first came to Holy Trinity, I asked some staff members to provide me with a list of spiritual leaders in the congregation. At that time, the list included a number of the CRHP people. If, two years earlier, I had asked for such a list, this list probably would have been a lot shorter. Had I asked again at the end of my stay, many more would have been added. The CRHP participants had turned Holy Trinity into what a number of people saw as a cutting-edge congregation. How had this happened?

First, let me briefly summarize Christ Renews His Parish. A retreat program developed by a Catholic pastor, Rev. John O. Jacoby, CRHP originally provided partial fulfillment of the requirements for his Master of Divinity degree. The program's process was eventually described in a detailed and comprehensive handbook and made available to those outside the divinity school arena (Jacoby and Edwards, 1980). As adapted by Holy Trinity, members of a "giving team" spend a year meeting approximately once a month to spiritually nurture each other and to prepare a weekend-long retreat. At this retreat, in turn, they would spiritually nurture a new set of members, the "receiving team." In its invitation letter to potential participants, one giving team described the retreat as "an opportunity for you to devote a weekend exploring your Christian journey with other men of Holy Trinity. It is a time for singing, communing, praying, listening and scripture study. It is a time of spiritual renewal and growth." Soon after the weekend retreat, the "receiving team" would hold an "Evening of Discipleship." Each member of the receiving team would individually discern if he or she felt called to continue the retreat cycle. Those who chose to do so became the next giving team under the leadership of a spiritual director from the previous giving team.

The retreat encompassed a variety of activities: skits based on Bible passages, the celebration of Eucharist, individual reflection, and a time for each member of the receiving team to write about his or her present spiritual journey and then discuss it with a partner. CRHP's spiritual heart and underlying structure consisted of a series of "witnesses" by giving team members on particular topics and questions. As the CRHP guidebook indicates, these included Christian Awareness, Christian Community, A Father's Loving Care, New Life in Christ, and Spirituality.

An individual initially presented his or her witness to the rest of the giving team at regular meetings during the year preceding the retreat.

Before a witness, other members of the retreat team gathered around the speaker to lay their hands on him or her; afterwards, they shared their responses to the witness.

During these witnesses, members of the giving team often revealed extraordinarily intimate (and sometimes traumatic) details about their lives. As one woman commented, "Christ Renews His Parish shows everyone is wounded." Feelings frequently ran high during and after a witness, with tears and hugs common. Just rereading my notes from the CRHP meetings and retreats, I can feel again the emotional heat they generated. Nothing could have been farther removed from Holy Trinity's usual public face.

Rereading the notes also reminds me of how uncomfortable I often felt as an observer at those meetings. After attending my first meeting of a women's giving team, I wrote:

> This is the closest I have come [in all my years of field work] to
> feeling like a "fly on the wall," or more accurately like a non-person.
> Until the very end of this sometimes very intimate event, people
> act[ed] as though I was not there. Oddly, this makes me more
> uncomfortable than usual about taking notes, since I feel like a
> voyeur.

I did not feel as much a voyeur in the men's group meetings, which I attended regularly. I did feel, however, that I was watching something that required my active participation, not detached observation. I paid attention to the complex group dynamics at work in the meetings, which I will analyze below. But I also keenly felt that the Holy Spirit was at work in those groups in ways that went beyond anything I could analyze from a social scientific perspective. Eventually, I stepped over the normal line for researchers and become a fully engaged participant in CRHP. After attending a retreat as a member of a receiving team, I joined a giving team. Long after my official research at Holy Trinity had ended, I continued to participate in meetings and eventually presented witnesses at a retreat. Obviously, these very personal experiences inform much of what I write about CRHP at Holy Trinity. But in my writing I try, as much as possible, to respect the confidentiality of my giving team by not using specific examples and illustrations from our meetings.

The shared intimacy of the witnesses was a major factor in the development of intensely nurturing relationships among the members of a giving team. Equally important was the sharing of personal highs and lows that often dominated the first part of giving team meetings. At one men's group meeting, the airing of individual highs and lows—most of which had transpired since their last meeting—took up half of a four hour meeting. Highs were volunteered, but usually the focus was on lows. After listening to them at one meeting, I wrote, "These men are hyper-involved in their kids' lives." When they were not working, they seemed to spend much of their time taking their children from one organized activity to another and helping their children on projects for school. What also struck me was that these men seldom bragged about their kids' accomplishments, but mostly talked about their problems (e.g., their learning disorders or difficulties with school authorities).

In addition to difficulties with children, problems at work and relationships with spouses were prominent themes. In fact, one new CRHP member mentioned to my colleague Mike McCallion (who helped with research at Holy Trinity) that he "came away with one thing really. All of the men there shared, and really they didn't share their accomplishments of status or their achievement but talked and shared about their relationships and that their relationships mattered most. It was really moving."

Men and Nurturing

I was startled to discover that such mutually nurturing discussions were taking place in a group setting and in a spiritually oriented men's group at church. A gender imbalance exists in all of our project churches, with over 60 percent of the people in the pews being women. That gender imbalance is not necessarily reflected among the church officers where men continue to be overrepresented. However, men's groups, particularly spiritually or biblically oriented men's groups, were rare in the project churches.

There are very few male equivalents to the women's groups (e.g., circles) and women's retreats that provide important nurturing for female participants. Even at a church like Bethlehem Lutheran, which had a rich tradition of women's circles and women's retreats, it was considered a major breakthrough when a Saturday morning men's Bible study (which generally attracted fewer than 8 or 10 members, including the two pastors) began to meet twice a month. More typical was Bethlehem's recent attempt to run a men's retreat; it failed from lack of interest. Many of Bethlehem's men are spiritually sensitive and nurturing. Few, however, have chosen to nurture each other in organized, ongoing groups or events where newcomers are welcome and, especially, where the Bible and biblically based spirituality frame the context for mutual nurturing.

It is the consistently high degree to which their activities were rooted in or based on the Bible and Christian spiritual traditions that made the CRHP groups (male and female) so extraordinary. Everyone knows that highly intimate discussions can take place among friends and within families. But the hallmark of intimacy and nurturing among CRHP members was the framing of discussions in terms of Christian beliefs, hopes, and faith. Similarly, even the most personal concerns often found expression through prayer, witnessing, ritual, and mutual blessing.

Nurturing and Spiritual Growth

Discussions at CRHP meetings frequently included comments on how participation in CRHP had provided the discipline members needed to focus on the really important concerns of life. For example, at a giving team meeting, one participant related the beatitudes to a recent sermon by Pastor Bux that had raised the question, "Just what do you think you have or need? What's important?" The participant expressed the belief that the beatitudes are built on the central statement, "Let your light shine." He then observed that he was getting to a "comfort level" with that command. "If I put my faith in God, he allows me to do it."

A fellow member responded, "For me there's a pattern of myself. When I'm coming here for Bible study or church, I'm feeling, 'Oh brother, I don't feel like doing it.' I'm trying to push back [at that feeling], so I get out the door. Once I'm there, I'm glad. The process of getting here is the most difficult." Others provided their own examples of the temptations they constantly fought: "There were times when I was sitting there looking at my CRHP witness in pieces, bits and pieces. I've been working on it, and I should be doing the Bible study. But it's really such an effort to do, while you know you should. But watching TV and flipping between three basketball games [is so much easier]." At the same time, however— and he pretends to be pushing a channel changer—"my thumb doesn't need a workout."

The whole congregation received earnest invitations to CRHP retreats, but only a relatively small proportion of members participated. After all, it was well known that the retreat required you to be spiritually and personally open to new and sometimes very emotional experiences. Furthermore, the retreat required a whole weekend away from home, and joining a giving team entailed a yearlong commitment. Anyone who attended a CRHP retreat had to be impressed not just by the fervent religious atmosphere but also by the sheer amount of effort that went into weekend preparations. Since CRHP was strictly a lay-led activity, it was also clear that virtually all that time and effort came from the giving team members themselves, not from the church pastoral or office staffs.

Anyone who attended the retreat meeting could join the giving team. Once you had committed yourself, group dynamics made it incredibly hard to withdraw or to shirk responsibilities. A giving team became a tight-knit and exclusive unit, though it was also seen as part of a larger yet no less exclusive group consisting of all those who had been through the CRHP process at Holy Trinity in the past.

Virtually all other activities in our project churches were open to anyone, and people were actively encouraged to drop in even if they were not official members of the group (even church council meetings). Bible studies and circles might have guests or members who only sporadically attended. Church groups were almost always "transparent." However, by its very private and personal nature, the giving team's meetings were opaque, and each group remained somewhat of a mystery to those in the congregation who had never participated in CRHP.

There is another crucial aspect of group dynamics of CRHP that I've mentioned but haven't yet commented on: the exclusively male and female teams. This separation by gender probably fostered the "secret society" feeling of the groups. Paradoxically, however, it seemed to strengthen bonds between spouses when both went through the CRHP process in separate groups. In witnesses and in the sharing of highs and lows, relationships with spouses were frequent topics. Sharing insights into both the high points and low points of their marriages seemed to relieve people's anxiety over whether they were the only ones in the church whose family life was not perfect. When spouses were simultaneously involved in CRHP, they often shared intense discussions on serious spiritual and religious issues. Although they were going through the process separately, knowing that they were both growing and moving in similar directions seemed to help their relationship.

I've purposely presented you with a number of details (though certainly not the whole story) on the dynamics of CRHP at Holy Trinity. It should be abundantly clear by now that a huge gap exists between how a program for congregational change appears in a book, pamphlet, videotape, or a workshop and how it actually operates (or fails to do so) in your unique congregation. In the next section, I want to use the case study of CRHP to address a question of great importance to your church. What sorts of factors do you need to consider when deciding whether or not to adopt a program for change in your church? In this particular case, what lessons can your church learn about nurturing from Christ

Renews His Parish at Holy Trinity? If you do decide to adopt CRHP or a similar program, what sorts of adjustments and adaptations might you need to make in order for it to be successful in your church?

Why Christ Renews His Parish Worked at Holy Trinity

Though I found CRHP at Holy Trinity to be an effective and inspiring program for spiritual growth, I am not necessarily recommending that your congregation adopt it. As mentioned throughout this book, each congregation is unique. Certainly, the successes of CRHP at Holy Trinity (as well as some significant problems it eventually created) were due in great measure to the particular moment in that congregation's history, as well as to the personalities, talents, and stage-of-life of key participants.

CRHP at Holy Trinity was not initiated by a pastor but by a woman named Joyce, a relatively new member of the congregation. Before moving to Detroit with her husband, she had been the spiritual director of a CRHP giving team in her church in Cincinnati. After moving to Detroit, Joyce decided to continue as spiritual director in Ohio, driving to Cincinnati when necessary. She asked the then senior pastor of Holy Trinity if she could start CRHP there, with several women from the congregation joining the Ohio retreat as part of the receiving team. Pastor Seltz agreed, although according to him he made it clear that he could not provide much support. During my research at Holy Trinity, Joyce completed a professional degree at an ecumenical seminary and served as a paid pastoral associate for the congregation.

One reason for the success of CRHP, in other words, is that a thoroughly committed individual introduced the program and had extensive personal involvement with it at another congregation. In fact, Joyce was in the midst of her third cycle through CRHP when she arrived at Holy Trinity. She also had extensive experience as a volunteer and paid professional in organizations dedicated to nurturing. Her husband's high-paid executive position also gave her the freedom to dedicate much of her time to church-related work.

The version of CRHP that Joyce brought to Holy Trinity emphasized lay leadership. It arrived at a particularly opportune moment in Holy Trinity's history. The church was in the midst of a transition to a new senior pastor, Dennis Bux, who was fervently dedicated to empowering the laity. CRHP at Holy Trinity produced what might be considered a small but self-confident spiritual movement with ambitious plans for the church. These people were also articulate spokespersons for their faith and served as an *ad hoc* evangelism committee for the congregation. I suspect that many pastors might have felt threatened by such a group; Pastor Bux did not. Although Pastor Bux did not try to control CRHP and did not play a major role in its activities, he was a powerful spiritual influence. One of the most striking facets of CRHP meetings was how often Pastor Bux's lively and provocative sermons regularly came up in the giving teams' discussions.

There were a number of other historical factors that probably explain some of the success of CRHP at Holy Trinity. Holy Trinity had a tradition of both women's and men's annual retreats. In addition, there was a small but intense monthly men's Bible study that met at a local restaurant, although its membership overlapped only partly with the CRHP teams. Finally, the church had a number of Bible studies that met in people's homes.

As a Lutheran congregation with a relatively "high" liturgical tradition, Holy Trinity felt comfortable with a program that originated in a Roman Catholic parish and still retained elements of the Catholic ethos. For example, CRHP at Holy Trinity emphasized communion (including a Eucharist Witness), physical symbols (like crosses and candles), and blessings. In fact, several times CRHP was held in a Catholic retreat center.

In the Catholic Church, confession is now termed the Sacrament of Reconciliation. Holy Trinity's CRHP retreats included a Reconciliation Witness followed by a Reconciliation Period, "a time for personal reflection and taking stock of personal life." A spiritual director or pastor or both made themselves available for one-on-one sessions during this period. As Pastor Bux reminded folks, the *Lutheran Occasional Services Book* also includes a rite of confession.

I noted earlier that one of the striking characteristics of the two Lutheran churches in the project was their high proportion of ex-Catholics, particularly among the younger members. This was especially true of Holy Trinity, and that Catholic background was a commonly expressed theme at CRHP. One of the giving teams included a potter who was creating communion cups for the retreat. She felt compelled to ask her fellow members, "Do we need them blessed? I'm pulling from my Catholic background. They would have some rite." Recollections of childhood experiences in the Catholic Church were prominent in several of the witnesses I heard.

As practiced at Holy Trinity, CRHP also exuded a pervasive and distinctly upper-middle class, professional ethos. This upper-middle class bias was evident in a letter of invitation to the CRHP retreat. In its very first line, the letter appealed to what the inviters assumed would be a shared professional experience for many: "Have you ever gone to a seminar or training session that has given you a new perspective? Did you feel refreshed after that experience? Did you ask yourself, 'Why don't I do this more often?'"

The character of witnesses clearly reflected this social class ethos. CRHP witnesses at Holy Trinity were almost invariably based on long, skillfully crafted written essays. Although the intimate content of witnesses would have been totally inappropriate in the work place, the format and structure of witnesses clearly came from CRHP members' extensive experience speaking in front of professional audiences. By the time of the retreat, these witnesses had become polished performances, and a giving team member without a professional background might well have found them intimidating.

Despite its many positive features, the men's retreat had at least one dynamic that left me ambivalent. A number of the younger men in the giving team (at the time, I was on the receiving team) were deeply involved in their children's lives, often in very nurturing roles. They were predisposed to accept males as sensitive, open, and vulnerable, at least in their relationships with spouses and families. What fascinated and sometimes disturbed me, however, was how this openness and sensitivity could become linked, at least at CRHP, to a more traditional workplace value—competitiveness.

Let me explain what I mean here. A key term at the retreat was "comfort zone." Early in the weekend a giving team member told the group, "It's important for people to stay within their comfort zones," even though one purpose of the retreat was for receiving members to learn how to widen that zone. When they were witnessing, however, the giving team members seemed to go beyond modeling openness and, instead, began to "show off" just how intimate they could be, how far they could push their comfort zones. Drawing on metaphors that occurred to me at the time, though not explicitly used by participants, I recorded in my field notes, "The retreat provided an extended opportunity to observe a male version of vulnerability: comfort zones become territories to be conquered, and it takes a tough man to be vulnerable."

The competitiveness that the giving team brought to their CRHP experience may reflect as much their interest in sports as their professional backgrounds. When the men of that giving team got together to jointly bless the individual about to give a witness, it was like a prayer huddle. The giving team members not serving as table leaders sat together at a kind of dais. In my notes I describe the dais as being "like the bench, where the players on the sidelines cheer on their teammates on the field (i.e., those providing a witness or making an introduction). In fact, the giving team occasionally held up placards to the witness, like 'He loves you.'"

This competitive dynamic did not develop in my own giving team, where several members were considerably older than the men who led the retreat we attended. A few of us were closer to the end of our careers than to the beginning, and our children were already adults. I also must emphasize that, while I was somewhat put off by the competitiveness of the other giving team, it worked well as a group dynamic with that particular set of men, for whom I have enormous personal respect. They were spiritually vibrant and growing. I was proud to have been associated with them and am grateful that they let me share so intimately in their lives.

CONCLUSION

Throughout this discussion of CRHP at Holy Trinity, my aim has not been to argue that the program ran perfectly. Rather, I have tried to demonstrate that even in a large church, one not very nurturing as a whole, small and vital groups can develop a nurturing environment that fosters spiritual growth. These groups, in turn, may eventually have an effect on the rest of congregation.

Let me conclude this chapter by summarizing several major points that have been raised in these two case studies and in our larger discussion of nurturing:

- Older members are far more likely to be sources of nurturing than the younger ones. But you may already have a number of younger members in your pews who can together become a powerful source of strength, support, and inspiration for your church.
- The need for nurturing can be as great in a younger, middle-class congregation as in a more elderly church or one where a fair number of members may find themselves financially at the edge. One key to successful nurturing in a "visibly prosperous" church is to develop means by which members feel comfortable and secure in dropping their masks of middle-class success.
- Men's spirituality is not an oxymoron. The males in your church may well be a very rich field for spiritual growth.
- Successful nurturing programs can be deeply rooted in Bible-based spirituality, and discipline is not necessarily a dirty word in the context of religious life.

- To attract participants you don't always have to emphasize how little they will have to do. In fact, the opposite approach can be highly effective.
- Whatever program you choose to build your church's nurturing style, you will need to put a great deal of thought and effort into adapting it to the unique history and present character of your congregation. Current nurturing style, social class, age structure, denomination, pastoral style, and the particular talents of the individuals committed to leading the program are among many factors you will need to take into account.

Every program or nurturing style has trade-offs. At Bethel, we saw that their open and loving community ethos could lead to problems in certain circumstances. At Holy Trinity, the development of a powerful spiritual movement within the parish had a number of negative repercussions on the congregation. Some individuals felt a bit inadequate or defensive when dealing with CRHP members. The radically different approaches to spiritual commitment between the CRHP members and the rest of the congregation could and did lead to serious conflicts. The former felt that Holy Trinity needed to develop some new programs more quickly than the rest of the congregation was ready to move—especially when the new programs required additional funds.

In this chapter, I've illustrated a variety of ways in which congregations nurture their members, described the many factors and forces that significantly influence a church's approach to nurturing, and suggested ways that you can go about discovering your own faith community's unique nurturing style. There are no quick fixes when it comes to improving how your congregation nurtures its members. I hope, however, that I've shown how a faith community's identity and mission are in great measure defined by its nurturing style. It is when your congregation ministers with compassion and love to the suffering, inside and outside your pews, that you are most counterculturally Christian. If your congregation approaches nurturing on the basis of faith and knowledge, you can find powerful ways to support and enrich this wonderful gift.

9

Conclusion

Moving Beyond Fear: Embracing Faith and Knowledge

One question recurred to me as I thought about writing the conclusion to this book: what did I want you to discover through reading the previous chapters? I have provided lots of statistical data and numerous case studies from our eight congregations, but I hope you've done more than just learn about those churches. For in writing this book, I have had two overriding goals. The first is theological: I want to remind you that living in fear and anxiety prevents us from embracing the life that God calls us to live. The best way to embrace our unique place in this world, as individual Christians and as faith communities, is to name our fears, ask where they come from, and then—in faith and in knowledge of the issues—to move beyond fear and be willing to risk living counterculturally. The second, more practical goal is inextricably linked to the first: I want to help you develop productive and realistic ways to think about your own congregation and the unique challenges it faces.

In the rest of the chapter, I provide a summary of the central concepts and approaches presented in this book as I strove to reach both of these goals. I also raise some key questions for you and your congregation to ask yourselves.

1. Be Not Afraid!

Yes, these are not necessarily the best of times for many mainline congregations. But if you evaluate a faith community's health by spiritual and religious measures and not by the standards of contemporary popular culture, there are many vibrant mainline Protestant churches. Yours may be one of them. These faith communities have cores and worshiping communities deeply committed to their congregations' key activities. Moreover, the lay and ordained leadership of those congregations are rarely complacent; rather, these leaders are constantly considering new programs. Unfortunately, all too often the programs for change implemented by the leadership in those churches are unsuccessful because they

179

are motivated by misplaced anxieties based on fundamentally wrong diagnoses of the congregations' problems (such as fears about generation gaps, which probably do not exist in their pews, or concerns that if their church is not growing in membership or number of programs, it's dying).

Some questions for you and your church
- What does your congregation fear?
- How do its fears compare with those I've described?
- Which anxieties are shared with our churches?
- Which reflect your church's unique history?
- How has your church responded to those fears and anxieties?
- In the light of our findings and analyses, should you reevaluate and revise your fears, anxieties, and the programs they may have prompted?
- Have your fears and programs been based in fact?
- Above all, have they been rooted in secular popular culture or Christian faith?

2(a). Your Congregation Is Wonderfully Unique.

Discovering who you are as a congregation and what makes you unique as a church is fundamental to planning your faith community's future course. Your congregation is so complex as an organization that any one factor, like size, is unlikely to have a determining impact on your church's character. Your congregation has its own styles of worshiping, nurturing, evangelizing, and relating to its denominational heritage. Any particular element of your church life (e.g., your worship style) should not be evaluated in isolation. It must be understood as significantly reflecting (directly and indirectly) many facets of the historical and contemporary life of your faith community. If you don't understand and recognize those connections, you are likely to be disappointed by your attempts to improve your church.

2(b). You can discover your congregation's uniqueness by realistically comparing it with other mainline Protestant churches.

Just because nondenominational megachurches may attract many new members, don't assume that denominational identity is unimportant for your present members and the people likely to join your congregation. A major source of pessimism about the future of mainline congregations is a sense of inadequacy based on inappropriate or unrealistic comparisons. It also can lead to an unproductive church version of "keeping up with the Joneses."

Some questions for you and your church
- What does make your congregation unique?
- If you compared your church with the ones we've described (qualitatively and quantitatively), what would be its unique profile in terms of demographics, patterns of activities, beliefs, attitudes towards your denomination, styles of worship, evangelism, and nurturing?
- How do your styles of worship and nurturing reflect the way your faith community operates seven days a week?
- Could you pick and choose from the types of questions we used in our survey (see appendix B) to create and then administer a relatively short questionnaire that moves beyond impressions or myths to uncover the facts about your congregation's profile on important issues?

3. In implementing changes, congregational leaders are often preoccupied with attracting new, especially younger, members.

Christ commanded us to "go and make disciples!" Making disciples is not necessarily the same as recruiting new members for your church. The size and demographic profile of a church's membership rolls (e.g., its percentage of young members) are not necessarily accurate indicators of a congregation's spiritual health.

Some questions for you and your church
- What about your congregation's unique identity keeps your current members (including your younger people) coming back to your pews each Sunday and actively engaging in activities throughout the rest of the week?
- Who are the younger people in your pews (both in terms of their involvement in your congregation and their beliefs and faith)?
- How do the younger, middle-aged, and older people in your pews interact with each other?
- Above all, for your congregation, what does it mean to be a disciple of Christ?

4. The vital importance of gray power to a congregation is far too often overlooked.

The people in the pews 60 years and over are typically a congregation's greatest resource for nurturing its members and others outside the church. They can model what it means to be faithful servants for the rest of the congregation.

Some questions for you and your church
- Who are the older people in your church?
- How do they participate in congregational life?
- How do they serve the congregation?
- How do the elderly in your pews contribute to your congregation's unique identity?
- What are the spiritual and practical needs of your older members?
- How does your congregation strive to meet those needs?

5(a). Congregations are fundamentally different from businesses and other organizations.

(1) Each church routinely deals with the major joys and sorrows of life, from birth to death. Mainline churches are most truly countercultural in their approach to death and illness. After all, your church's bottom line is not some form of short-term success but its members' eternal salvation and the spreading of the good news. (2) Congregations are typically multi-generational and kinship based. (3) Congregations are truly full-service organizations. (4) Congregations require both professionals and volunteers to flourish.

5(b). Your members' lived Christianity includes the types of knowledge, beliefs, practices, experiences, and feelings that they bring to their religious lives.

Many of your church members probably work in managerial or professional occupations. It's not surprising that they draw heavily upon those experiences when participating in congregational activities. As churches differ fundamentally from most secular institutions in their ultimate goals and forms of organization, your congregation must carefully and consciously decide when those professional and managerial approaches are and are not appropriate.

5(c). Religious or spiritual principles, sources, and visions rarely play a major role in congregations' decision making processes.

Participation in your church's organizational life seldom offers your members significant opportunities for spiritual growth. Otherwise active and committed members can be reluctant to participate in church committee meetings and other organizational activities when they are merely inefficient versions of what members do during their day jobs.

Some questions for you and your church
- What makes your congregation different from a business in how it runs its daily life?
- How does your church respond to the special nature of a congregation as an organization of the people of God?
- Does it nurture and nourish that special identity, or does it constantly attempt to make your church more like the other institutions in which your members spend the rest of their lives?
- If you tape-recorded a variety of meetings at your church and checked to see how those groups make decisions and discuss issues, what would probably be the results?
- Would you expect that spiritual and biblical principles and reflections play a major role?
- What's stopping you from carrying out that simple exercise? (Note: Your church's group dynamics are probably so engrained that, even when people are aware of being taped, members will usually quickly fall into their normal patterns of behavior.)
- Based on how your church makes decisions and discusses major issues, how would you describe its "theology" and view of discipleship?

6. Congregations often aim to be inclusive, but it is an inclusivity based on the principle of "don't ask, don't tell."

As a result, the line between mutual tolerance and mutual ignorance is quite thin. Your congregation should prayerfully decide on those religious beliefs and principles that are central to your congregation's identity and to the spiritual health of its members. Your church should explicitly incorporate those religious principles into your faith community's daily life. Your congregation cannot have an effective evangelism program if there is no explicit consensus on what the good news means to your faith community. This does not mean that your church needs a litmus test for "correct faith and belief." However, your members and potential members should at least know what your congregation considers vitally important, and then they can freely and consciously choose their own responses to those principles.

Some questions for you and your church:
- Could you pick and choose from the sorts of questions we used in our survey to create and then administer a relatively short questionnaire on religious beliefs and principles, which would go beyond impressions and find out the facts about your congregation's unique "theological" profile?
- Could you decide on the biblical principles that would guide how your church, as a faith community, could choose (a) the specific religious beliefs and principles most central to your congregation's identity and the spiritual health of its members and (b) how those beliefs and principles can be incorporated into your church's daily life?

7. Mainline Protestants are often ambivalent about evangelism.

They are especially afraid of being labeled fundamentalists if they attempt to share their faith with others. There are many different forms of evangelism, and your church should provide a wide variety of opportunities since different types of people are comfortable with different approaches. Remember that there may be a great need for evangelizing people already connected directly and indirectly to your congregation.

Some questions for you and your church:
- If you look at the list of types of evangelism activities in the chapter on evangelism, how many of your members already engage in a number of them?
- Do you build your congregation's evangelism program on the interests and talents of your members or on a stereotypical view of what evangelism should be?
- Is the fruitful field for evangelism primarily or even exclusively outside your church's walls?
- How many of your "official" members are "churched" in name only?

8. Each member is unique.

There are statistically significant differences between men and women, core and non-core members, young and older members in their religious beliefs and activities. Such differences are often quite small in magnitude, however, and rarely, if ever, are they absolute. Within each group of men and women, old and young, persists a wide range of beliefs and values.

Some questions for you and your church:
- How often do the programs your church adopts rely too heavily on stereotypical views of a particular category of people—views that are likely to limit the potential for spiritual growth in individuals who don't match those views?
- How much do you really know about the complicated spiritual life histories of your members?
- Would administering a brief version of our spiritual life history interview (see appendix C) to a carefully selected sample of your core members help you understand the foundations of their faith and beliefs?

9. Being a pastor in a mainline congregation is a complex and often stressful job.

Programs for change in your church need to take into account the myriad challenges routinely faced by your pastor. A pastor's unique style of leadership reflects a combination of abilities, skills, inclinations, passions, interests, strengths, and weaknesses deeply rooted in his or her own personal and professional history. Just as you should build upon your church's unique strengths, so you should take advantage of your pastor's unique gifts and talents.

Some questions for you and your church:
- If you evaluated your pastor on the qualities and characteristics we used in chapter 5, what would his or her unique profile look like?
- Do the programs your congregation adopts build on that unique set of traits?
- Look at the series of questions we asked our pastors during the study (see our pastor interview form in appendix D). How many of your core members would have a good sense of how your pastor would respond to those questions? If they don't, shouldn't they?

To paraphrase Mark Twain, reports of the death of mainline Protestant congregations have been greatly exaggerated. While conducting the research for this book, I never felt that I was preparing to write obituaries or epitaphs for the project congregations we studied. Rather, I felt extraordinarily blessed by the opportunity to live within vibrant faith communities and to witness how deeply committed so many of the people in the pews were to assuring the future of their churches.

As I emphasized in the introduction, none of the project churches is extraordinary in the sense of unusual. Like your own congregation, however, each is unique, and each has been—and continues to be—an extraordinary blessing for many members. Yes, like the project churches, you and your church will obviously need to change over time. But if there has been one truly consistent message throughout this book, it is that as mainline Protestant congregations deal with contemporary and future challenges, they need to begin by truly understanding who they have been and who they are now *as faith communities.* Above all, when they interpret and evaluate their past and present, and when they plan their future, the standards they use should be deeply and unequivocally rooted in each congregation's Christian faith and practice.

Appendix A

Discovering and Analyzing Your Core

I'M CONVINCED THAT IT IS VITAL FOR THE LEADERSHIP OF A CHURCH TO UNDER-
stand the nature of that congregation's core. If you agree, you'll want to
discover who is in your church's core. How do you go about that task?

In all but the smallest church, it is hard for any one person to know
all that is going on in the congregation. For that reason, I suggest that the
group that is given the responsibility of preparing the core list should
consist of three to five individuals who together have firsthand knowledge of all of the major areas of congregational life. Make sure that the
group includes women and men and that its membership is not restricted
to one age group.

We relied almost exclusively on members of the pastoral staff to help
us in developing our core lists. You may well prefer to include others in
the group preparing the list. For example, if your pastor is relatively new,
you probably should also tap into the invaluable local knowledge of long-
time members of the congregation. Your new pastor is likely to find his
or her own understanding of congregational dynamics growing expo-
nentially if he or she lets these lay people take the lead in the process (by
listening to them discuss who does and does not belong in the core).

HOW SHOULD YOUR GROUP GO ABOUT
CONSTRUCTING ITS CORE LIST?

Once you have a group in place, provide each member with a copy of the
pages of this book where I describe the nature of the core and its importance to a congregation (see pp. 27-34). Ask the committee members to
read through that material and then to individually write out a list of all
the congregation members he or she considers part of the church's core
on the basis of the following criteria:

> If a significant change were to be proposed for the church, would the
> individual play a role for or against and would the person have any

significant impact? In making this decision, we're not asking you to evaluate whether an individual is a good or bad core person.

Whenever possible, committee members should include a best guess at that person's age or profession next to each name on the list. Although some churches do try to keep records of their members' ages, there are always gaps in even the best systems.

It is important that members not consult with each other or with any other people in the congregation when constructing their original lists. In fact, it is vital that they treat the whole process as confidential. Otherwise, it is easy to see how this process could be misperceived as a popularity contest and end up with hurt feelings.

Keep in mind that eventually your final core list, like ours, should not identify individuals by name but, instead, be presented in terms of such variables as size of core, distribution of ages, gender, professions, and years in the church of the individuals in the core.

Committee members should come to the meeting with their initial lists of core names. However, the first order of business should be for each person simply to report on the number of individuals on his or her list. It is almost inevitable that there will be some variation in the length of lists. These simple differences should lead to a discussion of how each person actually went about constructing his or her list.

Although everyone had the same basic criteria to work with, they are broad enough to allow a variety of interpretations in practice. Talking through your differences will help the group come to an agreement about a more complete set of criteria that are best adapted to the unique characteristics of your church.

After that discussion, we suggest that people be given a few minutes to review their lists and edit them in light of the group's more complete set of criteria. These edited lists should then be the basis of your group's comparison of lists of names and its compilation of a composite core list.

Remember: Don't let your group get tangled up in long arguments over whether one or another particular individual should or should not be on the list. The overall structure of the core is what counts, and that is unlikely to be affected significantly by a few names being added or subtracted.

After the discussion of the core lists is over, we strongly suggest that the preliminary lists be destroyed. Names should be eliminated from the composite list as soon as there is complete demographic data on individuals (e.g., age, profession, years in church).

How Do You Analyze Your Core?

Now that you've systematically developed your core list, it's time to systematically analyze it.

For example, what percent of your core are:

- Men? Women?
- 19 to 39 years old? 40 to 59 years old? 60 or older?
- Members of your congregation for one 1 to 9 years; 10 to 19 years; 20 to 30 years?
- Managers or professionals?
- Life-long members of your church's denomination?
- College graduates?
- Single, Married, Divorced, or Widowed?

Although you can compute all these figures by hand, it is faster and easier to put them into a simple spreadsheet like Excel. The spreadsheet will instantly calculate percentages and allow you to sort and resort your core list.

For example, you can re-sort your list by years in congregation to see if the core members who are recent members (i.e., 1 to 9 years) are also younger people (i.e., 19 to 39 years old).

What Does This Mean for Your Congregation and Its Future?

Once you have analyzed your core list, you need to consider the implications for your congregation of what you have found. Those implications obviously depend upon your church's particular context, its concerns and worries, its resources and goals. But there are some questions you almost certainly want to ask about your core:

- What percentage of your worshiping community is in the core?
- If you compared the basic demographics of your core with those of your worshipping community (e.g., its percentages of men as opposed to women; older as opposed to younger members; very long-time members as opposed to more recent members), how representative is your core?
- If there are any key demographic groups missing or underrepresented in your core, why is that the case?

That last question is important. Remember that your congregation is unique, and that uniqueness reflects its distinct history as well as its current dynamics. You must take the time to understand why your congregation's core developed its present profile and how that profile has influenced the life of your faith community (including how your church has responded to programs for change). Otherwise, you won't know whether you need to find ways to alter the core (in its size or composition). And if you do decide that it is important to alter the size or composition of your core, this background knowledge will help you develop successful strategies for changing this vital element of your faith community's future.

Appendix B

A Sample of Survey Questions

BIOGRAPHICAL INFORMATION

1. Year you were born: _____

2. You are: [ ] Male [ ] Female

3. Current Marital Status: (check one)
   [ ] Never Married   [ ] Divorced   [ ] Widowed
   [ ] Married   [ ] Separated   [ ] Living with Partner

4. How many children do you have? _____

5. Check your *highest level* of education:
   [ ] Less than 8th grade (grammar school)
   [ ] Through 8th grade (grammar school)
   [ ] Some high school
   [ ] High school graduate
   [ ] Some college
   [ ] Technical school
   [ ] Completed college
   [ ] Some graduate school
   [ ] Completed graduate school

6. Check your household's income range:
   [ ] $19,999 or less
   [ ] $20,000 to $39,999
   [ ] $40,000 to $59,999
   [ ] $60,000 to $79,999
   [ ] $80,000 to $99,999
   [ ] $100,000 or more

7. What do you do for a living? (Or what did you do before retirement?): _____

RELIGIOUS BACKGROUND

8. How long have you been at your present church? _____

9. Have you ever been a member of (or regularly attended) a church
   of another denomination or a non-denominational church?
   [ ] YES   [ ] NO

   If you answered YES, which denominations or non-denominational churches? (check as many as apply to you)
   a. [ ] Baptist
   b. [ ] Catholic
   c. [ ] Episcopal
   d. [ ] Lutheran
   e. [ ] Methodist
   f. [ ] Presbyterian
   g. [ ] United Church of Christ (UCC)
   h. [ ] Other(s), please list:

   _____

   _____

10. Has your spouse ever been a member of (or regularly attended) a
    church of another denomination or a non-denominational
    church?   [ ] YES   [ ] NO

    If you answered YES, which denominations or non-denomina-
    tional churches? (check as many as apply to you)
    a. [ ] Baptist
    b. [ ] Catholic
    c. [ ] Episcopal
    d. [ ] Lutheran
    e. [ ] Methodist
    f. [ ] Presbyterian
    g. [ ] United Church of Christ (UCC)
    h. [ ] Other(s), please list:

    _____

    _____

11. On the scale below, indicate by circling a number how important it is for you to be in your present denomination as opposed to another.

Not at all *Very*

1   2   3   4   5   6   7   8   9   10

DENOMINATION

12. For you, what are the three most important features of your denomination?

a. _____

b. _____

c. _____

CHURCH ATTENDANCE AND PARTICIPATION

13. Estimate how many *hours a week* you are normally in church activities other than worship services:
[ ] none   [ ] 1 to 2   [ ] 3 to 4   [ ] more than 4

14. Estimate how many *times a week* you are in the church building other than for worship services:
[ ] none   [ ] 1 to 2   [ ] 3 to 4   [ ] more than 4

15. Are you *now* a church officer (for example, elder, deacon, board member)?
[ ] YES   [ ] NO

16. Have you *ever* been an elected officer at your current church?
[ ] YES   [ ] NO

Owners of this book may access the entire survey on the Alban Institute's Web site. Please visit http://www.alban.org/BookDetails.asp?ID=1850 *to download the full survey. This tool is free for those who have purchased the book. Readers will need the book with them to access the survey.*

Appendix C

A Brief Spiritual Life History Interview

After some comments about why the person was asked to take part in this interview, the interviewer begins with:

We're interested in finding out about your core religious or spiritual beliefs and practices and how you have come to hold them. For many people that's a long and complex story, so it may help if you would think back on various stages in your life and describe your religious or spiritual life during each of those periods. Let's start with your childhood; say up to when you finished high school.

1. Growing Up
   1.1. Family Background
      1.1.1. Would you tell me about your family background, the type of work your parents did, the places where you lived as a child, whether you had any brothers and sisters?
      1.1.2. What were your parents' and grandparents' religious backgrounds?
      1.1.3. Were there any church or religious groups or activities you participated in? How often? Did you participate in any church-related trips or retreats that had a significant impact on your perspectives?
      1.1.4. How would you describe the nature of the churches with which you or your family had significant involvement?
      1.1.5. Were there any major changes in your family's church affiliation or spiritual orientation while you were growing up?
      1.1.6. Were there any people at the churches, pastors or nonclergy, who had a particularly strong effect—positive or negative—on you or your family?

1.2   Home and Family
    1.2.1.   What were the core religious beliefs and practices that your parents tried to teach you?
    1.2.2.   What place did the Bible have in your life and the life of your family?

1.3.   Beliefs
    1.3.1.   Were there any differences or disagreements within your family on religious or spiritual issues?
    1.3.2.   Did anyone ever challenge or attack your religious beliefs while you were growing up? When? What happened?

1.4.   Life Crises
    1.4.1.   Do you remember any major life crises (e.g., illness, death, unemployment, family quarrels, romantic difficulties) faced by you and/or your family while you were growing up? Did religion or spirituality play any role in how you and your family responded to them? If you or your family belonged to a church at the time, did it play any role?

1.5.   Others
    1.5.1.   Were there any books or movies or radio or television shows that significantly affected (changed or reinforced) your religious or spiritual beliefs or practices while you were growing up?
    1.5.2.   What were the religious or spiritual groups other than your own that you were most aware of at that time? What did you think about them?
    1.5.3.   Did you have any experiences at school, inside or outside the classroom or with friends, which strongly affected, negatively or positively, your religious beliefs or perspectives?

1.6.   Direct Experiences of God or Evil
    1.6.1.   While you were growing up, did you ever feel you heard God or a messenger of God speak to you or that God was communicating directly with you in some way?
    1.6.2.   While you were growing up, did any people you knew well tell you that they heard God speak to them or that God had communicated in some way with them?

We'd like to move now to your life after high school—adulthood, including education, marriage and family life or other significant relationships, and work.

2. Adulthood
   2.1. Post-High School Education
      2.1.1. Did you go to college or other higher education after high school?
             IF "NO" SKIP TO SECTION 2.2 BELOW
             IF "YES," CONTINUE
      2.1.2. Where? Why there? What was your major?
      2.1.3. How would you describe the religious or spiritual atmosphere or environment at the college?
      2.1.4. During this period, did you have any experiences involving religion or spiritual issues that particularly stick in your mind?
   2.2. Marriage / Children (if relevant) or Significant Others
      2.2.1. Are you or have you ever been married?
             IF "YES" – GO TO NUMBER 2.2.2 BELOW
             IF "NO" – ASK ABOUT SIGNIFICANT OTHERS
      2.2.2. If the individual has been divorced or separated: Did religious or spiritual issues play any role in your divorce or separation?
      2.2.3. Has marriage had any significant impact on your religious or spiritual perspectives? Your spouse's?
      2.2.4. Did your spouse come from a different faith tradition? Do your spouse's core or central religious beliefs and practices differ from yours? In what ways do they differ? Are there situations in which those differences have had important repercussions? How do you deal with those differences?
      2.2.5. Do you have any children?
             IF "NO" – SKIP TO 2.3
             IF "YES" – CONTINUE: How many? What ages?
      2.2.6. Has being a father or mother had any significant impact on your religious or spiritual perspectives?
      2.2.7. What were (are) the core religious beliefs and practices that you tried (try) to teach your children?
      2.2.8. Do your children's religious or spiritual beliefs, perspectives or practices (including membership and participation in a church) differ from your own? How? How do you deal with that difference?
   2.3. Work
      2.3.1. Would you give a brief summary of your career?
      2.3.2. How have your religious beliefs and practices influenced

your working life or career? How has your working life or career influenced your religious beliefs and practices?

2.3.3.   How would you describe the religious or spiritual atmosphere or environment at the jobs that have been most significant in your career? Have there ever been any situations in which your religious beliefs have come in conflict with your work?

2.3.4.   Have co-workers had any significant impact (positive or negative) on your religious or spiritual beliefs and practices?

Having looked at your adult years in the specific terms of education, marriage and family life, and work, I'd now like to ask you to look back over your adult years in general and answer these questions about your experiences up to the recent past. At the end of the interview, I'll ask more specifically about your current situation.

2.4.   Church

2.4.1.   Did you attend church? How regularly? Were there any church or religious groups or activities you participated in regularly?

2.4.2.   How would you describe the nature of the churches with which you had significant involvement during this period?

2.4.3.   Were there any major changes in your church affiliation or spiritual orientation during this period? Were there any periods when you were more or less actively involved in church-related or spiritual activities? What caused the differences?

2.4.4.   Were there any people at the churches, either pastors or non-clergy, who had a particularly strong effect—positive or negative—on you?

2.4.5.   Did you go on any church-related trips or retreats that had a significant impact on your perspectives?

2.5.   Prayer, Bible, and Beliefs

2.5.1.   What place did prayer have in your life?

2.5.2.   What place did the Bible have in your life?

2.5.3.   How would you describe your core or central religious beliefs and practices during this period of your life?

2.5.4.   Has your understanding of God changed during your adult years? How?

2.6. Conflict and Change

    2.6.1. Did you, or members of your family, or close friends experience significant changes in their relationship with God or religion during your adulthood?

    2.6.2. Were there any differences or disagreements within your family on religious or spiritual issues?

2.7. Life Crises

    2.7.1. Do you remember any major life crises (e.g., illness, death, unemployment, family quarrels, romantic difficulties) faced by you and/or your family during your adulthood? Did religion or spirituality play any role in how you and your family responded to them? If you or your family belonged to a church at the time, did it play any role?

2.8. Others

    2.8.1. Were there any books or movies or radio or television shows that significantly affected (changed or reinforced) your religious or spiritual beliefs or practices during adulthood?

    2.8.2. With whom did you discuss religion or spiritual issues or from whom did you seek support and advice?

    2.8.3. How would you describe your closest friends' religious or spiritual activities in adulthood? What did you think about them? What did your friends think about your religious or spiritual activities during that period?

    2.8.4. What religious or spiritual groups other than your own were you most aware of? What did you think about them?

    2.8.5. Did you have any experiences in classes or courses since high school that strongly affected (negatively or positively) your religious beliefs or perspectives?

    2.8.6. Did you have any friends or relatives with whom you disagreed on religious issues? What issues? How were the disagreements handled?

2.9. Direct Experiences of God or Evil

    2.9.1. During adulthood, did you ever feel you heard God or a messenger of God speak to you or that God was communicating directly with you in some way?

    2.9.2. Did any people you knew well tell you that that they heard God or a messenger of God speak to them or that God had directly communicated in some way with them?

2.9.3.   Did you ever feel there was a real form of evil having a direct influence on you or your world? How do you visualize or conceptualize this form of evil?

I'd like to turn now to your current situation and ask you some questions about your current beliefs and your church affiliations and activities.

3. Contemporary Experiences
   3.1. Church Affiliations
      3.1.1.   In the last few years, have you belonged to or regularly attended churches other than this one?
               IF "YES" – Continue to QUESTION 3.1.2
               IF "NO" – GO TO QUESTION 3.1.3
      3.1.2.   Which ones? How long were you a member of or did you regularly attend each of those? Why did you leave each of those churches?
      3.1.3.   How long have you been at [insert church name]?
      3.1.4.   What originally brought you to this church? Why did you decide to join this church?
   3.2.   Denomination
      3.2.1.   What do you describe as the major or distinctive characteristics of your denomination? What do you see as the major or distinctive characteristics of worship in your denomination?
      3.2.2.   On a scale from 1 to 10 (with 1 as "not important at all" and 10 as "very important") how important is it to you to be a member of a church of your denomination (rather than of another denomination)?
   3.3 Current Church Involvement
      3.3.1.   How would you describe [insert name of church] and its members?
      3.3.2.   What do you see as the church's greatest strengths? Weaknesses?
      3.3.3.   What do you see as the major challenges this church faces over the next five years?
      3.3.4.   What church activities or religious or spiritual organizations do you currently participate in? In the past, have you participated in other activities or organizations?
      3.3.5.   Are there any new groups or activities that you would like to see this church establish?

3.3.6. How does your level of involvement in this church compare with your levels of involvement in other churches during your adulthood? What caused the differences?

3.4. Pastor [If there is an associate or assistant pastor, these questions can also be asked about him or her.]

    3.4.1. In what areas is your pastor most effective in meeting the needs of the church?

    3.4.2. In what areas is your pastor least effective in meeting the needs of the church?

    3.4.3. In what areas is your pastor most effective in meeting your needs or the needs of your family?

    3.4.4. In what areas is your pastor least effective in meeting your needs or the needs of your family?

3.5. Congregation

    3.5.1. Are there any issues of religious belief, practice, or worship on which you are in disagreement with your denomination? Your pastor? Members of your congregation? How do you deal with those issues?

3.6. Others ("Unchurched")

    3.6.1. Have you any close friends or relatives who don't attend church? Have you ever discussed with them why they don't attend church?

3.7. Bible and Other Sources

    3.7.1. How often do you read the Bible? In what situations do you read it?

    3.7.2. What do you usually read in the Bible?

    3.7.3. What is your view of the nature and significance of the Bible?

Finally, I'd like you to look back over your lifetime experience with churches or religion and reflect on some major issues.

4. In Retrospect

    4.1. Over your lifetime, if you have regularly attended or been a member of several churches, do any of the churches stand out in your mind either negatively or positively? Why?

    4.2. It is not unusual for any congregation to have issues that generate controversy or conflict. Are there church-related internal conflicts that stand out in your mind for how well or poorly they were handled? What were the conflicts about? What happened?

4.3. Have you or someone close to you ever felt healed as a result of prayer, a healing ritual, divine intervention, or a miracle?

4.4. During the course of a lifetime, people often have low and high points. What do you consider the low point of your life? Did religion or spirituality play a role in dealing with that low point?

4.5. What do you consider the high point of your life? Did religion or spirituality play a role in dealing with that high point?

Appendix D

Some Pastor Interview Questions

A. BACKGROUND INFORMATION

1. First, please tell me a little about your background and how you arrived here, in this position?

   [Generally, pastors provide extensive and elaborate answers to this question without any need for further probes by the interviewer. In those rare situations where that is not the case, the pastor should be probed about his or her family background, education, and professional history (e.g., previous positions or interest in another profession). Another possible probe is "What have been the major influences on you?"]

   [Insert the following question at the appropriate spot.]

1a. A number of pastors have commented that the seminary experience left them with a core or sanded down set of beliefs. Was that your experience? If so, with what core or sanded down set of beliefs were you left?

B. BEING A PASTOR

2. What do you see as the role of a pastor in the life of a congregation?
3. How would you describe your present job?
4. What are its major challenges?
5. Its most rewarding features?
6. Its most frustrating features?
7. What have been your major accomplishments?
8. Your major failures?

9. In what directions do you hope to move the congregation? In your experience, what's the best way of introducing change into a congregation? What are usually the major challenges faced in introducing such changes?

10. Five years from now, what would you like to see the congregation look like?

11. Dealing with people in life crisis situations and/or with spiritual crises and questions must be an important element of your work. What are the most frequent spiritual issues or quandaries that your congregation brings to you?

12. What are the most difficult questions and situations for you to handle?

13. What do you find to be the most frequent and important sources of beliefs and values that people bring to bear upon these spiritual issues and questions? Have they changed over the time of your ministry? In your different pastoral callings?

14. Clearly preaching is a major part of your work. Do you believe that there are any central and recurring themes in your sermons?

15. How would you describe the way you typically go about preparing a sermon?

C. THE CONGREGATION

16. What are the most significant or distinctive characteristics of your congregation?

    [Sometimes, the pastor answers the following questions in the course of responding to the above question. However, if he or she does not, ask them explicitly.]

17. What are the most significant or distinctive characteristics of the way in which your congregation worships and lives as a community?

18. What are the major influences on the religious or spiritual lives of the members of your congregation?

19. What are the most important segments of the congregation, both in terms of organizations and in terms of more informal dynamics?

20. At present, are there any ideas or practices or policies involving worship, belief, or faith that you or other staff members are attempting to encourage or implement but are finding there is significant opposition or that it's difficult to gain widespread support from the membership? What are the primary obstacles?

D. THE DENOMINATION

21. What are the distinctive features of your denomination and its membership?
22. What are the biggest challenges your denomination faces today?
23. How important is the denomination or denominational issues to you?

Notes

1. Mainline Protestant denominations are those that have been "associated with the Federal Council of Churches and its successor, the National Council of Churches," and whose leadership has been "theologically inclusive and tolerant" (Marsden 1994: footnote 1 pp. 8-9).

2. Long before we administered and analyzed our survey with its questions on religious background, we were struck by the role of ex-Catholics in the leadership of several of our Protestant churches. Once we had noticed this trend and collected systematic data, its importance certainly made sense. Take, for example, a congregation like Holy Trinity. This was the church with the youngest population. Its Lutheran liturgy was quite similar to the post-Vatican II Catholic forms of worship in the U.S. In fact, at Holy Trinity, 41 percent of the denomination switchers in the pews were ex-Catholics. However, ex-Catholics also played crucial roles in congregations with older memberships and less formal liturgies. At Bethel Baptist one of the most dynamic and respected of the younger male church leaders was an ex-Catholic whose parents had been active leaders in their parish when he was growing up. The issue was even more fascinating because this young man had married into Bethel, his wife's family being long-time core members at the church. And now, his wife had converted to Catholicism—while keeping up her close connections to Bethel.

3. Some worship changes with a profound impact on our congregations may well have been linked to the sensibilities of the increasing number of ex-Catholics in those churches. These included moves to more frequent communion and Catholic-like forms of communion (intinction—dipping a wafer in a wine chalice at a Presbyterian church) and of devotion (prayer vigils at Baptist and Lutheran congregations). These worship changes may also reflect the fact that, in the post-Vatican II era, even the older members of mainline Protestant

congregations were far more likely than their parents or grandparents to have daughters or sons-in-law who were either ex- or practicing Catholics. Protestants today are much more likely to have firsthand and positive experiences with Catholic worship and particularly with its reformed liturgies that are not nearly as "foreign" to Protestants as were the pre-Vatican II versions. In addition, there is now much interaction between the mainline Protestant and Catholic liturgical professionals; however, in the cases we observed, the move to a higher liturgical approach seemed to be truly grass-roots based and not inspired by pastors or lay leaders attending a conference or reading an article.

4. For a full discussion of the significance of this phenomenon, see Chapter 8: Nurture: What Is Your Church's Nurturing Style?

5. There are, at least, two important and legitimate reasons to insist on the use of the elaborate scholarly apparatus in academic publications. The first is to assure that an author does not claim originality for theoretical insights that derive from others' works. The second is to be sure that one author does not make use of another's words without proper acknowledgement (i.e., to prevent plagiarism).

   I don't claim any great theoretical originality for this book. I have simply applied some widely used contemporary concepts and ideas from the social sciences (particularly anthropology and sociology). For the reasons mentioned above, I have also avoided direct quotation or paraphrases from others' books or articles. The vast majority of quotations and close paraphrases in *Be Not Afraid!*, instead, are from the people in the pews. To protect their privacy, I usually attribute quotations to specific individuals only when it would be virtually impossible to actually provide confidentiality (e.g., when the context makes it clear that I am quoting from the pastor of a particular congregation).

   It also seems important to note that I refer by first name only to those pastors with whom I had opportunity to develop a close working relationship during the research project.

6. Other project researchers prepared several of the portraits. Dr. Randal Hepner wrote the portraits of Central United Methodist Church of Detroit and Second Baptist Church of Detroit. The portraits of Bethel Baptist of Southgate, St. Paul United Church of Christ in Taylor, and St. Timothy Presbyterian Church of Livonia are the work of Dr. Angela Martin.

7. In our sample, we include congregations that vary significantly in terms of potentially important factors, e.g., size, social class, type of

pastoral leadership, and denomination. However, all of our congregations are in Michigan. With the exception of Bethlehem Lutheran, the churches are located in the very diverse Detroit metropolitan area. Bethlehem is in Lansing, Michigan, within a 15-minute drive of the Michigan State University campus.

8. The idea for the Slice of Life messages originated with one of Pastor Bux's mentors from seminary, Dr. Robert Bertram. According to Pastor Bux, Dr. Bertram had developed this approach "out of his experience with base Christian communities in Latin America." Dr. Bertram had been afraid to try out this approach in a parish in the United States. Dennis, characteristically, was not.

9. All names in this passage are pseudonyms.

10. The following three sections draw heavily upon the work of Dr. Angela Martin, who prepared material on evangelism for a demonstration project Web site.

11. Except for Barb, all the names of Bethel members used in these passages are pseudonyms.

References

Bibby, Reginald W. "On Boundaries, Gates, and Circulating Saints: A Longitudinal Look at Loyalty and Loss." *Religious Research* 41:149-164, 1999.

Davie, Jodie Shapiro. *Women in the Presence: Constructing Community and Seeking Spirituality in Mainline Protestantism.* Philadelphia: University of Pennsylvania Press, 1995.

Glassner, Barry. *The Culture of Fear: Why Americans Are Afraid of the Wrong Things.* New York: Basic Books, 1999.

Greeley, Andrew M. *The Catholic Myth: The Behavior and Beliefs of American Catholics.* New York: Charles Scribner's Sons, 1990.

Jacoby, John O., and Robert P. Edwards. *Christ Renews His Parish: A Parochial Spiritual Renewal Process.* Cleveland: Christian Life Services, 1980 (Third edition).

Maltin, Leonard, ed. *Leonard Maltin's 2002 Movie and Video Guide.* New York: Signet Books, 2001.

Marsden, George M. *The Soul of the American University: From Protestant Establishment to Established Nonbelief.* New York: Oxford University Press, 1994.

Metzger, Bruce M. *Breaking the Code: Understanding the Book of Revelation.* Nashville: Abingdon Press, 1993.

Roberts, Fredric. "Lived Research on Lived Religion." *Theology and Lived Christianity. The Annual Publication of the College Theology Society,* Vol. 45, David M. Hammond, ed., pp. 38-71. Mystic, Conn.: Thirty-Third Publications, 2000.

Warner, R. Stephen. "The Place of the Congregation in the Contemporary American Religious Configuration." *American Congregations, Vol. 2: New Perspectives in the Study of Congregations.* James P. Wind and James W. Lewis, eds., pp. 54-99. Chicago: University of Chicago Press, 1994.